"This book is overflowing with fresh, power[...]
are both accessible and crucial for develo[...]
topics discussed in the book are precisely th[...]
but Inman provides his own unique take on many of them. As a result, *What Is Reality?* should be required reading in classes in philosophy, philosophy of religion, apologetics, theology, and worldview. And it is just what thoughtful lay folk need to study to deepen their ability in apologetics. I very highly recommend this book. Read and tell others about it."

J. P. Moreland, distinguished professor of philosophy at Talbot School of Theology, Biola University

"The close relationship between metaphysics and theology has been recognized from the very beginnings of both Greek philosophy and Christian theology, yet it came to be neglected in the contemporary discussion until recently. Ross Inman's *What Is Reality?* is an important and lucid contribution to the revival of rigorous, metaphysically informed theology."

Edward Feser, professor of philosophy at Pasadena City College

"People often ask me for a solid but gentle introduction to contemporary metaphysics that is written from a Christian perspective. Up until now, I have been unable to recommend anything, but Ross Inman's new book fits the bill perfectly. The opening chapters do a great job of defining metaphysics and disposing of the standard scientistic objections to it, and the succeeding chapters introduce the readers to the very best metaphysical options available, drawing from both ancient and modern sources."

Rob Koons, professor of philosophy at the University of Texas at Austin

"I love this book. It's clear, accessible, and covers everything an introduction to metaphysics should cover, all with sensitivity to ways metaphysics connects to the Christian worldview. Inman is the perfect person for a project like this, and it shows."

Tim Pickavance, professor of philosophy at the Talbot School of Theology at Biola University and scholar in residence at Redeemer Presbyterian Church in Orange County, California

"An inspiring achievement! Ross Inman ably demonstrates the vital role of metaphysics in clear thinking about God and all things in relation to God. Conversant with the best in contemporary analytic metaphysics, rooted in historical Christianity, and surprisingly practical, Inman's *What is Reality?* offers a rare and delightful blend of philosophical rigor and spiritual nourishment. This book is Christian philosophy at its best."

Paul M. Gould, associate professor of philosophy of religion and director of the master of arts in philosophy of religion program at Palm Beach Atlantic University

"A fantastic work! Professor Inman's book is a brilliant exploration of fundamental concepts that shape our understanding of reality. With exceptional clarity and an engaging style, this work is indispensable for philosophy students who aspire to engage the best work in metaphysics. I highly recommend this guide to anyone interested in developing a robust vision of reality."

Joshua Rasmussen, associate professor of philosophy at Azusa Pacific University and author of *Who Are You Really?*

QUESTIONS
IN CHRISTIAN
PHILOSOPHY

WHAT IS
REALITY?

—

AN
INTRODUCTION
TO METAPHYSICS

—

ROSS D. INMAN

ivp
Academic
An imprint of InterVarsity Press
Downers Grove, Illinois

InterVarsity Press
P.O. Box 1400 | Downers Grove, IL 60515-1426
ivpress.com | email@ivpress.com

©2024 by Ross David Inman

InterVarsity Press® is the publishing division of InterVarsity Christian Fellowship/USA®. For more information, visit intervarsity.org.

Scripture quotations, unless otherwise noted, are from The Holy Bible, English Standard Version, copyright © 2001 by Crossway Bibles, a division of Good News Publishers. Used by permission. All rights reserved.

The publisher cannot verify the accuracy or functionality of website URLs used in this book beyond the date of publication.

Cover design: David Fassett
Interior design: Daniel van Loon
Image: © Tatyana Olina / iStock / Getty Images Plus

ISBN 978-1-5140-0680-1 (print) | ISBN 978-1-5140-0681-8 (digital)

Library of Congress Cataloging-in-Publication Data
Names: Inman, Ross D., author.
Title: What is reality? : an introduction to metaphysics / Ross D. Inman.
Description: Downers Grove, Il : IVP Academic, [2024] | Series: Questions
  in Christian philosophy | Includes bibliographical references and index.
Identifiers: LCCN 2024012533 (print) | LCCN 2024012534 (ebook) | ISBN
  9781514006801 (print) | ISBN 9781514006818 (digital)
Subjects: LCSH: Metaphysics. | Philosophy of mind. | Reality. | BISAC:
  PHILOSOPHY / Metaphysics | PHILOSOPHY / Religious
Classification: LCC BD331 .I43 2024 (print) | LCC BD331 (ebook) | DDC
  110–dc23/eng/20240412
LC record available at https://lccn.loc.gov/2024012533
LC ebook record available at https://lccn.loc.gov/2024012534

33 32 31 30 29 28 27 26 25 24 | 13 12 11 10 9 8 7 6 5 4 3 2 1

For Jay,

who first modeled for me how to "get metaphysical" in

the power of the Holy Spirit

CONTENTS

LIST OF FIGURES

LIST OF "GETTING THEOLOGICAL" CALLOUTS

QUESTIONS IN CHRISTIAN PHILOSOPHY

JAMES K. DEW JR.
AND
W. PAUL FRANKS

C. S. Lewis once remarked, "Good philosophy must exist, if for no other reason, because bad philosophy must be answered."[1] About that he is surely right. Unfortunately, many today are in the same position as those Americans Alexis de Tocqueville described in 1835: "They possess, without ever having taken the trouble to define its rules, a certain philosophic method which is common to all of them."[2] That is, many people today have embraced, often without even realizing it, an approach to knowing reality that undermines their ever coming to truly understand it. They draw inferences about everyday life, theorize about major events and developments in the world, and do all of this while blindly utilizing philosophical categories and tools. In other words, they've embraced a "philosophic method" that generates "bad philosophy." The cure is not to reject philosophical discourse altogether but to embrace good philosophy.

Thankfully there is more to good philosophy than simply answering bad philosophy. It also enables one to entertain questions that are central to one's

---

[1]C. S. Lewis, "Learning in War-Time," in *The Weight of Glory* (New York: HarperCollins, [1949] 2001), 58.

[2]Alexis de Tocqueville, *Democracy in America: Historical-Critical Edition of De la démocratie en Amérique*, vol. 3, ed. Eduardo Nolla, trans. James T. Schleifer (Indianapolis: Liberty Fund, 2010), 699.

worldview—questions related to the nature of truth, the nature of goodness, and the nature of beauty. However, finding examples of those doing philosophy well can be difficult. Yet, given the importance of questions we are interested in, doing philosophy well is critical.

For this reason, a contemporary introductory series to the major questions in philosophy is incredibly valuable. IVP Academic's Questions in Christian Philosophy series seeks to meet that need. It provides introductory volumes on the various branches of philosophy for students with little or no background in the discipline. Our authors have written their volumes with their students in mind. They don't presume prior philosophical training but instead provide careful definitions of terms and illustrate key concepts in ways that make philosophy tangible and useful for those who need it most. After all, it is not just professional philosophers who seek answers to philosophical questions—anyone attempting to love God with their mind will find themselves asking questions about the world God has created and seeking answers to them.

The authors have also approached their volumes in a way that takes seriously the claim that all truth, goodness, and beauty is found in God. That is, in undertaking Questions in *Christian* Philosophy, the authors are not merely engaging in these philosophical pursuits and then adding Jesus to the mix when they're done. Instead, they are pursuing these questions out of a love and devotion to Jesus that not only guides the questions asked but also motivates attempts to answer them.

It is our hope that each volume in this series will not only help readers become acquainted with various approaches to important topics but will also encourage people in their devotion to our Lord.

PREFACE

There are many outstanding books out there designed to introduce you to contemporary analytic metaphysics, why yet another? A good question! Here's one thing that sets this book apart from the others: It aims to introduce you to key concepts in contemporary analytic metaphysics from the standpoint of Christian theism. Let me unpack this statement, piece by piece.

First, the book is an introduction to contemporary analytic metaphysics in particular, which is the dominant mode of metaphysical inquiry in most English-speaking colleges and universities today. So, the book doesn't attempt to directly interact with historical figures or how certain topics developed in the history of metaphysics in the Western philosophical tradition (although we will certainly meet some historical figures along the way!). Of course, this is not to say that the history of metaphysics is unimportant, or that the analytic mode of doing metaphysics is the only respectable mode worth pursuing; far from it! Rather, the limitation in scope is, alas, a feature of my own intellectual limitations; my competence to write an introductory book like this is limited to contemporary analytic metaphysics.

Second, the book is geared toward those with little philosophical background and toward those who strive to learn more about analytic metaphysics in a distinctively Christian key. It is written and designed for motivated and engaged students who are distinctively Christian. I have tried very hard to offer some concrete steps on how to go deeper in your study of metaphysics. Toward this aim, I have included "Going Deeper" sections at the end of each chapter and a "Next Steps?" at the end of the book. At the end of each chapter in the "Going Deeper" section, I have included a list of central concepts and terms ("Key Concepts") that are keyed to the helpful and accessible resource titled *Metaphysics: The Key Concepts*, edited by Helen Beebee, Nikk Effingham, and Philip Goff.[1] I have also included a list of noteworthy subject-specific readings in metaphysics for further exploration, from both a historical and contemporary perspective.

I have also written the book in a distinctively Christian key when it comes to both content and method. Regarding content, there are topics and questions treated that are uniquely important for Christian metaphysicians (a fancy name for a philosopher who reflects deeply on the nature and structure of reality). Along the way, you will find various "Getting Theological" callouts that aim to apply the specific concepts in metaphysics to an area of theology or philosophical theology. My aim here is to put on display the long-standing and enduring relevance of metaphysical reflection for Christian theology. I simply can't put it better than Gisbertus Voetius, the metaphysically astute Dutch Reformed theologian (1589–1676), when he said, "A theologian can miss metaphysics and logic no less than a carpenter a hammer and a soldier weapons."[2] I hope to show you why.

As for method, I seek to model for you, the reader, a posture in how to approach the study of contemporary analytic metaphysics as a Christian—in particular, how one's distinctively Christian theological beliefs can and should shape one's metaphysical inquiry. My hope for you (as it is for my students) is that you would not only learn something about the contemporary lay of the metaphysical landscape, but that you would also catch a posture concerning what it means to be a Christian metaphysician and how to take seriously one's theological convictions when doing metaphysics. For the Christian, metaphysics is about wading into the wonder and depths of created being, ultimately for the sake of being enthralled by the depths of God's own uncreated being, the wonder of it all.

---

[1]Helen Beebee, Nikk Effingham, and Philip Goff, eds., *Metaphysics: The Key Concepts* (New York: Routledge, 2011).
[2]Quoted in Herman Selderhuis, ed., *A Companion to Reformed Orthodoxy* (Leiden: Brill, 2013), 33.

ACKNOWLEDGMENTS

Measuring the influence of one's teachers and friends on one's own moral and intellectual formation is not always exact. Nevertheless, there are a few individuals that come to mind who embody an approach to metaphysics that has shaped my own in clear and unmistakable ways. More than anyone else, J. P. Moreland has modeled for me in his Spirit-led life, teaching, and his academic work what an exemplary Christian metaphysician looks like. J. P. was the first to model for me how to take metaphysics seriously as a Christian and to strive for philosophical excellence as an act of piety unto the Lord. Over the course of nearly twenty years, I've learned from J. P. far more than I can convey in words about philosophy and the Spirit-led Christian life. Indeed, it's often difficult to know where I end and where he begins.

My personal and professional relationships with Jonathan "E. J." Lowe (1950–2014), Anna Marmodoro, and Peter Simons (my doctoral supervisor) have further clarified and fortified my conviction that serious ontology should continue to play a fundamental role in contemporary analytic metaphysics. Moreover, Jonathan Lowe's gentle, sincere, and nonconfrontational philosophical posture modeled a different way for those seeking refuge from the often cutthroat one-upmanship that sadly marks many professional philosophical circles.

I owe a debt of personal and professional gratitude to Christian metaphysicians Fred Blackburn, Jeffrey Brower, William Lane Craig, Robert Garcia, Paul Gould, Robert Koons, Timothy Pickavance, Alex Pruss, Michael Rea, and Eleonore Stump. Each is a superb metaphysician from whom I have learned and continue to learn a great deal; more importantly, each is an outstanding human being and exemplary follower of the Way. I want to thank each of them for their friendship, support, encouragement, and philosophical influence over the years.

I want to note my appreciation for my college and seminary students, past and present, with whom I've had the joy and privilege of exploring the contours of metaphysics for nearly a decade. Your simple and not-so-simple questions and comments have helped make me a better teacher and a better metaphysician.

I also want to thank both Southeastern Seminary and the Eidos Christian Center for providing generous research grants in support of this work.

Last, I am grateful to the friends and colleagues who read portions of the book and offered helpful feedback, including Paul Gould, J. P. Moreland, Timothy Pickavance, and J. T. Turner. I'd also like to thank Chris Lee, my graduate teaching assistant at Southeastern Seminary, for reading the entire draft and for his invaluable help with some of the figures and charts. Any remaining metaphysical blunders in the book are my own.

1

WHAT IS METAPHYSICS?

In this first chapter I want to introduce you to several prominent characterizations of metaphysics, both past and present. What exactly *is* metaphysics? What are the distinctive aims of metaphysical inquiry that set it apart from other areas of inquiry like the natural sciences and theology?

After we get an initial handle on metaphysics in this chapter, we'll turn in chapter two to explore whether genuine metaphysical discoveries are indeed possible. I'll guide you through several well-worn historical and contemporary criticisms of metaphysics and argue that no matter how hard you might try, metaphysical inquiry is unavoidable and conceptually necessary. Wherever you run, metaphysics will find you. If so, we'd better learn how to do metaphysics well as distinctively Christian philosophers (chap. 3). So, let's get to it already!

WHAT *IS* METAPHYSICS, EXACTLY?

As my first metaphysics professor and friend J. P. Moreland likes to say, metaphysics currently has a bad public relations problem. Before we attempt to unpack what metaphysics is and how it has been understood by several influential historical and contemporary practitioners, let's briefly reflect on a common misconception of metaphysics as a systematic area of philosophical study.

Every budding philosopher studying metaphysics has the firsthand experience of that look of sheer puzzlement or terror when they mention to their immediate family (or better, their in-laws) at the Thanksgiving table that they are enrolled in a metaphysics course. "You're studying *what*?! How can a Christian institution offer a class on the paranormal?" Alternatively, one might try taking a leisurely stroll through the metaphysics section at a brick-and-mortar bookstore (if you can find one!) and see what I mean when I say that metaphysics has a bad public relations problem. In fact, it's a custom of mine to head straight to the metaphysics section whenever I visit a new or used bookstore; I just can't contain my curiosity as to what awaits me. Without fail, my eye quickly lands on book titles (real titles, I might add!) such as *Metaphysics of Astrology: Why Astrology Works*; *The Top Ten Things Dead People Want to Tell You*; *Crystal Skull Consciousness*; and so on (I could go on, really). I recall an instance several years ago when I was delightfully hunkered down, surrounded by stacks of old dusty tomes at of one of my all-time favorite used bookstores in my hometown of San Diego, California. As I was browsing the titles in the philosophy section, back turned toward the door, I heard a woman enter the store and ask the clerk for the "metaphysics section." As a philosopher, of course, my ears perked up and I immediately thought: *Absolutely splendid! Another aspiring metaphysician looking to go deeper in the quest to understand the fundamental nature of reality. I wonder if she's majoring in philosophy at San Diego State University. Perhaps I'll go over and start up a conversation about metaphysics . . .* But my elation soon came to a screeching halt. As the clerk ushered the woman to the metaphysics section, he asked, "What exactly are you looking for?" "Spell books," the woman replied, "I'm looking to learn how to cast spells," she said. As you can imagine, my elation quickly dissipated.

What, then, *is* metaphysics if not the study of the paranormal and the art of casting spells? Before we get to some of the more formal characterizations of the subject given by ancient and contemporary practitioners of the discipline, let's remind ourselves of the fact that wonder has traditionally been the lifeblood of philosophy from beginning to end.[1] And metaphysics, one of the main branches of philosophy in the Western tradition, is no different. In fact, I'd go so far as to say that wonder, astonishment, and awe are perhaps most intense and pointed when it concerns matters of existence and ultimate reality. Wonder suffuses the study of metaphysics from beginning to end. In the opening lines of his *Metaphysics*, Aristotle famously remarks, "All men by nature desire to know." At our core, we have a deep hunger to understand reality—for knowledge of *what* kinds of entities exist, *how* these entities exist, and *why* these entities exist.

It is largely historical happenstance that we use the word "metaphysics" today to pick out the types of inquiry and questions that you'll typically find

---

[1]See chaps. 1 and 2 of my *Christian Philosophy as a Way of Life: An Invitation to Wonder* (Grand Rapids, MI: Baker Academic, 2023).

in introductory metaphysics courses and textbooks like this one. The word originally derives from the title of one of Aristotle's works *Ta meta ta physika*, which literally means "after the physical ones." As the story goes, about a decade after Aristotle's death, his lecture notes were compiled and edited into treatises, one being what we now call Aristotle's *Physics*. The editor decided to call the lecture notes immediately after *Physics* in Aristotle's corpus *Metaphysics* (*meta-* being the Greek prefix meaning "after"). And there you have it.

More seriously, the careful reader will notice that the very question "What *is* metaphysics?" itself appears to be a metaphysical question on its face, a question about the nature, boundaries, and proper modes of inquiry of a particular subject matter. Historically, metaphysics has been one of the main branches of philosophy in the Western tradition, and there have been a few prominent characterizations of the discipline down through the ages.

Yet I think it is important to clarify at the outset, lest I set you up for disappointment, what we are *not* seeking when we ask the question "What *is* metaphysics?" in this context. Many philosophers, myself included, are less than optimistic about the prospects of finding a complete, airtight definition of metaphysics. While we can provide a loose but helpful characterization of metaphysics—its distinctive aims, goals, and methods—identifying a clear-cut, universally satisfying definition of the discipline of metaphysics turns out to be extremely challenging.

What exactly do I mean by a precise, airtight "definition" in this context? When I speak of a "definition" your mind may immediately think of a dictionary or verbal definition, the kind you'd find in a trusted dictionary (as in the definition of the word "abdicate" as "to fail to fulfill one's duty or responsibility"). While dictionary definitions are important, they are historically not the sorts of definitions philosophers are after. Rather, philosophers aim primarily at defining things, *what things are* at their core—in other words, their essential natures. Socrates's unrelenting quest to discover the nature of piety, temperance, justice, courage, virtue, and beauty was a quest to grasp what each of these things is at its essential, defining core.

Aristotle himself, along with many metaphysicians who followed suit, referred to this sort of definition as a "real definition."[2] In fact, the great medieval

---

[2] Aristotle says, "Clearly, then, definition is the formula of the essence." See Aristotle, *Metaphysics* 7.5 (1031a12), in *The Complete Works of Aristotle*, ed. Jonathan Barnes (Princeton, NJ: Princeton University Press, 1991), 2:1628.

Christian theologian Thomas Aquinas (1225–1274) said that "it is clear that the essence of a thing is what its definition signifies."[3] So, to illustrate, a common real definition of a human being, one that is predominant in the Western philosophical tradition, is that human beings are rational animals; both rationality and animality are *definitive* of human beings and distinguish them from every other kind of being.

Let me make an honest admission to you: It's actually quite challenging to come up with a complete, clear-cut real definition for most matters of substance—whether beauty, goodness, or justice (just read Plato's dialogues and you'll see what I mean!)—let alone entire conceptual disciplines like theology, philosophy, science, and in this case, metaphysics.

One reason metaphysics is so hard to define in this complete, clear-cut sense is that any proposed real definition will likely (a) favor one particular, heavyweight metaphysical view over another (and thus be highly controversial), (b) leave out an important aspect of traditional metaphysical inquiry or unconsciously cross over into foreign disciplinary territory (and thus not be complete or clear-cut, respectively), or (c) be so large and unruly that it will be profoundly unhelpful as a useful working definition (what philosophers call a conjunctive definition: metaphysics is a and b and c and d and e and f and ...).[4]

So, what we are after in this chapter is better described as a loose characterization of the aims and methods of metaphysical inquiry that help set it apart from other forms of conceptual inquiry, nothing more. With this important qualification in mind, let's look at some of the most influential characterizations of metaphysics, past and present.

METAPHYSICS AS THE SCIENCE OF BEING QUA BEING

One traditional way of characterizing metaphysical inquiry, going all the way back to Aristotle himself, is the idea that metaphysics is the study of "being qua being" (i.e., being as such), as Aristotle put it. In fact, let's hear from Aristotle himself on the nature of metaphysics as the science of being qua being:

---

[3] Thomas Aquinas, *On Being and Essence* 1.11, in Joseph Bobik, *Aquinas on Being and Essence* (Notre Dame, IN: University of Notre Dame Press, 1970), 45.

[4] To illustrate (a), if one thinks that metaphysics is best understood as the study of ultimate reality, this of course presupposes that there is an aspect of being that is *ultimate* or *fundamental* in the first place.

> It is the work of one science to examine being qua being, and the attributes which belong to it qua being, and the same science will examine not only substances but also their attributes, both those above named and what is prior and posterior, genus and species, whole and part, and the others of this sort.[5]

Try not to be thrown off by Aristotle's use of "science" here. By "science" Aristotle roughly means "an organized and articulable body of knowledge."[6] But what exactly does Aristotle mean when he says that there is a single body of knowledge that examines being qua being or being as such? Aristotle and many subsequent philosophers in the Aristotelian tradition, were of the opinion that "being" (and similar terms like "existence") had different senses or meanings relative to the kind of thing in question. Another way of saying this is that, for Aristotle, "being" is not univocal (i.e., of the same sense or meaning). While we can predicate "being" or "existence" of both a kite and a dog, for instance, the kite and the dog are not said to "exist" in precisely the same sense for Aristotle. For Aristotle, since a dog and a kite belong to very different categories of being, they cannot be said to "exist" in precisely the same way. For those squarely in this Aristotelian camp, a key task of metaphysics is discovering what it is *to be* in each sense of the word.

At the heart of Aristotle's conception of metaphysics as the science of being qua being is the notion of an ontological category. You might roughly think of ontological categories as reality's objective classifications or groupings; the deepest joints that carve up reality (we will explore the ontological categories in much more depth in chap. 5).[7] For Aristotle, there were ten categories of being—*Substance, Habit, Position, Time, Place, Passion, Action, Relation, Quality, Quantity*—with *Substance* being the most primary and fundamental category insofar as substances exist in their own right; for Aristotle, if substances "did not exist, nothing else could exist."[8] You can think of the category of *Substance* as the root or foundation of all the other ontological categories, for Aristotle.

According to this rich and long-standing Aristotelian view, metaphysics aims to discover not only the different kinds of *beings* (tigers, poodles,

---

[5]Aristotle, *Metaphysics* 4.2 (1005a14-17) in *The Complete Works of Aristotle*, 2:1587.
[6]Christopher Shields, *Aristotle* (New York: Routledge, 2007), 237.
[7]The metaphor of carving reality at its joints goes back to Plato. See *Phaedrus* 265d-266a, in *Plato: Complete Works* (Indianapolis: Hackett, 1997), 542.
[8]Aristotle, *Categories* 2b5-7, in *The Complete Works of Aristotle*, ed. Jonathan Barnes (Princeton, NJ: Princeton University Press, 1984), 1:4.

numbers, people, etc.) that exist but also different kinds of *being*. Did you catch that very subtle distinction? So, we might predicate the quality of *being healthy* to a thing, say a lion, when we say, "The lion is healthy." But, for Aristotle, the quality of *being healthy* and the lion itself do not exist in the same way since they belong to the distinct ontological categories of *Quality* and *Substance*, respectively. Since qualities (like *being healthy*) characterize substances (like a lion) and not the other way around, qualities do not exist in themselves and are thus not primary. They ultimately depend on substances (which are the modified things that don't themselves modify anything).

Since metaphysics is the science of being qua being, in particular, it differs from other areas of inquiry, like biology, physics, or even theology. Biology, for example, specifically aims to study a limited category of existing things, namely living beings, primarily by way of empirical observation; biology is the natural science of being qua living, we might say. Moreover, theology, as the science of God and all things in relation to God, can be thought of as an organized and articulable body of knowledge that works from principles supplied not from empirical observation (as in biology) or the natural light of reason (as in arithmetic), but from the more radiant and enduring light of divine testimony in Holy Scripture, first and foremost.[9]

Metaphysics as the science of being qua being, on the other hand, aims to investigate the many senses of "being" along with the most general categories of being as a whole, including how these different senses of "being" relate to one another. As such, metaphysics is uniquely different from other sciences (e.g., physics and biology) by virtue of its generality/universality: Metaphysics stands under and is arguably conceptually necessary for every other science that is limited to a particular domain of reality (what is physical and exists in space and time, what is living, what has a chemical structure, etc.). And as we will see in the next chapter, metaphysical inquiry is both indispensable and unavoidable at some level.

METAPHYSICS AND WHAT THERE IS: A QUINEAN APPROACH

While the above Aristotelian conception of the nature and aim of metaphysics is very old and is perhaps the most common way that metaphysics has been understood throughout the history of Western philosophy, a very

[9]See, for example, Thomas Aquinas, *Summa Theologiae* Ia, q. 1. a. 2, in *Summa Theologiae*, trans. Fr. Laurence Shapcote, OP (Lander, WY: Aquinas Institute, 2012).

different conception of metaphysics now dominates the contemporary metaphysical landscape.

One contemporary way of characterizing the discipline of metaphysics, a way that has been very influential among analytic philosophers of the latter half of the twentieth century, stems from the work of Willard Van Orman Quine (1908–2000), whose influence on the contemporary metaphysical landscape is hard to overstate. Quine was a professor at Harvard University from 1936 to 1978 and worked primarily in philosophy of logic. He is one of the most influential analytic philosophers of the second half of the twentieth century. Without question, David Lewis (1941–2001), Quine's most famous student, has had the most significant influence on how metaphysics is conceived of and practiced today.

Quine is often credited with reclaiming the discipline of metaphysics from its demise at the hands of the logical positivists, an influential group of European philosophers who thought metaphysical claims were strictly nonsensical (you'll meet the positivists up close in the next chapter). Be that as it may, Quine was a sharp critic of traditional metaphysics as it had been practiced throughout much of the history of Western philosophy. The irony here is sharp; the very person who is largely credited with restoring metaphysics to its rightful place in contemporary philosophy was himself a sharp critic of a traditional, Aristotelian approach to metaphysics.

Quine's influential critique of metaphysics as traditionally practiced, along with his alternative logical-formal approach, is clearly unpacked in his seminal 1948 paper "On What There Is."[10] For Quine, the primary aim of metaphysics (or "ontology," as he puts it) is to say what exists or ask, "What is there?" Thus, existence questions such as, "Do numbers exist?" "Do holes exist?" "Does time exist?" and "Do fictional characters like Pegasus exist?" are the target of metaphysical inquiry. The metaphysician is to provide a list, an "ontological assay" as some philosophers put it, of beings that exist. This compiled ontological list need not specify any particular ordered or structured relationship between the items on the list.

To help illustrate the Quinean approach to metaphysics, it may help to compare two very different types of grocery lists. When I go to the store, my grocery list includes a simple itemized list of grocery items in no specific

---

[10]W. V. Quine, "On What There Is," *Review of Metaphysics* 2 (1948): 21-38. This essay is reprinted as chap. 1 of *Metaphysics: An Anthology*, 2nd ed., eds. Jaegwon Kim, Daniel Z. Korman, and Ernest Sosa (Malden, MA: Wiley-Blackwell, 2012).

order: eggs, spinach, apples, flour, almond butter, ice cream, and (when I was in college) Top Ramen. My wife's grocery list, on the other hand, is highly structured and organized; each item is neatly sorted into a particular category, and each category is properly arranged with respect to one another. Wait, oh yes, there's more! My wife even has each category correlated with the various regions of the grocery store to make the trip smoother and more efficient (which helps with three young children along for the ride!). For Quine and those contemporary philosophers who follow in his wake, the metaphysical task is to simply itemize what *is*, in no particular order—just like my grocery list.

Quine's particular approach to metaphysics is very closely wedded to a particular method for doing metaphysics, namely, the use of a formal-logical framework to clarify and simplify what it is we are committed to as existing in reality (what we are "ontologically committed" to, as philosophers put it) when we claim that our best scientific theories of the world are true. At the risk of being overly technical here, I need to say a bit more here about the Quinean task of answering existence questions, if for no other reason than the monumental influence such a method has had on the practice of contemporary metaphysics.

Let's ease in here as slowly as possible. Consider the mathematical truth: 2+3=5. The statement is a simple statement of arithmetic and is clearly true. Now ask: What must the world be like in order for this statement to be true; what must we be ontologically committed to in order to affirm this simple mathematical truth? On the surface, the fact that the statement is true would also seem to require reality to be a certain way, in particular, to include things like numbers. If the numbers 2, 3, and 5 must exist in order for the above arithmetic statement to be true, then you are, according to Quine, ontologically committed to the existence of numbers. Let's put this a bit more precisely in terms of a three-step Quinean approach to answering existence questions (which, again, is the primary task of metaphysics):

1. Determine which statements are true in our best, scientific theories of the world.

2. Organize, clarify, and simplify these statements by symbolizing them in a particular formal-logical framework (first-order predicate logic, for Quine).

3. Voila! You are ontologically committed to all and only those entities needed to stand in as the values of the bound variables in order to make the statements true.[11]

Here's a quick example of this process at work; the details are a bit challenging, so let me encourage you to hang with me! It is typical for our best, contemporary biological understanding of the world to refer to biological species as the most basic unit of biological classification. As such, contemporary biologists often affirm the truth of species statements like, "There are humans that are *Homo sapiens*." To find out what must exist in order for this statement about humans and biological species to be true, we first need to formally clarify and simplify this statement (a process Quine calls "regimentation") by translating it into a particular formal-logical framework. Philosophers call this framework "first-order," "predicate," or "quantificational" logic, a form of logic that employs predicates, variables, and quantifiers. As a quick guide, the symbol $\exists$ is called the existential quantifier and should be read as "There exists at least one," "x" is a variable, "Hx" stands for "x is human," and "Sx" stands for "x is *Homo Sapiens*":

$$(\exists x)(Hx \ \& \ Sx)$$

This logical formula can be translated as "There exists at least one x, such that x is human and x is *Homo Sapiens*" or, more simply, "There exists a human that is *Homo Sapiens*." In predicate logic, what is called "the domain of quantification" is the relevant group of things the quantifier aims to single out for consideration (in our case the quantifier was $\exists$). This could include *everything* in the particular domain of quantification (e.g., all humans or all mammals) as with a quantifier that is unrestricted in scope (the universal quantifier $\forall$), or it could include *one particular thing* (or class of things) as with a quantifier that is restricted in scope, called the existential quantifier $\exists$, e.g., "There exists a black cat" as $\exists x(x$ is a cat and x is black). Our variable above, x, is said to be "bound" by the existential quantifier in the sense that it is not a free-standing variable but is linked with the existential quantifier $\exists$.

Most importantly (hang in there, we're almost finished!), according to a Quinean approach, in order for the above logical schema $(\exists x)(Hx \ \& \ Sx)$ to be true, the bound variable (x)—the one linked to the quantifier $\exists$—must have

---

[11]This has been adapted from Alyssa Ney, *Metaphysics: An Introduction* (New York: Routledge, 2014), 41.

a particular value, some *existing* thing that stands in for the variable and meets the relevant descriptions "is human" and "is *Homo Sapiens*." Thus, a human and biological species must really exist to stand in as the value of the bound variable in the above true logical schema. There you have it! With this three-step Quinean methodology, our best scientific theories about biological species ontologically commit us to the existence of biological species.

As Quine famously said, "to be is, purely and simply, to be the value of a variable."[12] One can derive one's ontological commitments from what must stand in for the value of the bound variable in true logical schemas like the one above. So, if biological species are needed to stand in as the value for the bound variable in a true, logical schema like the one above, then you are ontologically committed to the existence of biological species. Similarly, if electrons are needed to stand in as the value for bound variables in true, logical schemas like $\exists x$ (x is an electron and x is negatively charged), then you are committed to the existence of electrons.[13]

The careful reader will notice that step 1 of the Quinean method is restricted to true statements concerning our best, scientific theories of the world. What about other important truths about reality other than scientific truths? As a committed proponent of "naturalism," the philosophical view that all of reality is exhausted by the physical world, Quine was resolute that "it is within science itself, and not in some prior philosophy, that reality is to be identified and described."[14] Everything we currently know and can possibly know about reality in its totality (not just part of reality) is given to us by our best, scientific theories of the world. In this sense, Quine (though certainly not all Quineans, I might say)[15] aimed to naturalize metaphysics by making it more in line with

---

[12]Quine, "On What There Is," 32.

[13]The picture, as you can imagine, is a great deal more complex and nuanced that I let on here. In fact, Quine thinks that if even after this process of regimentation one finds such ontological commitments untenable, one can try to paraphrase claims about the purported existence of certain entities into claims that involve no such ontological commitment. For example, one might believe it's true that the average American family has 1.94 children (as of 2022), without believing that such talk commits one to the existence of 1.94 children. Rather, ordinary talk about the average number of children per US household can be paraphrased as talk about there being nearly two children per US household on average. Ordinarily, it is thought that a successful paraphrase in this sense must mean the same thing as the original statement it aims to paraphrase; if not, then the paraphrase is inadequate.

[14]W. V. Quine, *Theories and Things* (Cambridge, MA: Harvard University Press, 1981), 21.

[15]There are plenty of contemporary Christian metaphysicians who reject Quine's naturalism yet who generally embrace Quine's metaphysical method. Peter van Inwagen, for example, is a prominent Christian metaphysician who broadly follows Quine's understanding of the aim and

the empirical sciences and dislodging it from its more traditional footing in Aristotle's conception of metaphysics as "first philosophy," a nonempirical area of study that is conceptually prior to the empirical sciences.

METAPHYSICS AS CATEGORIAL ONTOLOGY

Let's now turn to our second contemporary characterization of the nature, aim, and methods of metaphysics, articulated and defended by E. J. Lowe and inspired by Aristotle and the Aristotelian tradition. According to Lowe, it is the primary task of metaphysics to "chart the possibilities of being, with a view to articulating the structure of reality as a whole, at its most fundamental level."[16] This view overlaps a great deal with Aristotle's being qua being approach outlined above in its focus on the most general categories of being. It differs in that it doesn't necessarily wed itself to Aristotle's own view that there are many senses of being, that is, the view that being is analogical (and not univocal).[17] Let's unpack this second characterization step-by-step, beginning with the latter notion that metaphysics aims to give an account of reality as a whole, at its most fundamental level.

In good Aristotelian fashion, when proponents of this view talk about a "fundamental level," they are referring to reality at its most general level (encompassing what is true of all things just insofar as they exist). As we have seen above with Aristotle's own view of metaphysics, the study of reality's most fundamental or general level in this sense has been traditionally called "categorial ontology," insofar as it aims to discover the most general categories of being and how those categories relate to one another.

The most bedrock categories of being—the ontological categories—have traditionally been understood to be ultimate and exhaustive. The categories are said to be ultimate in the sense that they aim to give the most fundamental, rock-bottom answer to the classification question "What, at bottom, *is* it?"

---

task of metaphysics. Interested readers will want to read van Inwagen's works "Metaontology," in *Ontology, Identity, and Modality: Essays in Metaphysics* (Cambridge: Cambridge University Press, 2001), and "Being, Existence, and Ontological Commitment," in *Existence: Essays in Ontology* (New York: Cambridge University Press, 2014).

[16] E. J. Lowe, "Metaphysics as the Science of Essence," in *Ontology, Modality, and Mind: Themes from the Metaphysics of E.J. Lowe*, eds. Alexander Carruth, Sophie Gibb, and John Heil (Oxford: Oxford University Press, 2018), 14.

[17] In fact, Lowe firmly maintains that while there are many different kinds of *beings*, there is only a single notion or sense of "being" (i.e., "being" is univocal). See Lowe's *More Kinds of Being: A Further Study of Individuation, Identity, and the Logic of Sortal Terms* (Chichester, UK: Wiley-Blackwell, 2009), 4.

Moreover, the categories are thought to be exhaustive in the sense that for absolutely any created entity that exists there is an answer to the classification question (i.e., every existing entity belongs to a fundamental ontological category, whether we know the answer or not).[18]

At its heart, the classification question ("What, at bottom, *is* it?") is a question about the nature or essence of a thing, what ultimately defines the thing in question and specifies *what it is*. Tulips, electrons, viruses, iPhones, and human beings all have an essence in the sense that there is a definite answer to the classification question for each of these existing things. A tulip, of course, has a very different essence than an iPhone and thus belongs to a distinct, fundamental ontological category; one is the type of thing that can naturally sprout roots, the other not—at least not yet! At one level, the classification question—and our deep desire to understand the essential nature of things—is a natural, untutored, and distinctively human posture.[19]

I will have much more to say about ontological categories and natures in chapters five and six, respectively. For our purposes here, it is crucial to point out that for proponents of this conception of metaphysics, discovering the natures of things as determined by their ultimate ontological categories is *prior* to merely itemizing what exists. "According to this conception of the aim and content of metaphysical theory," says Lowe, "metaphysics is above all concerned with identifying, as perspicuously as it can, the fundamental ontological categories to which all entities, actual and possible, belong."[20] This is in sharp contrast to the Quinean approach that places existence questions front

---

[18]Traditionally, God has not been thought to be a member of a genus or species in the strict sense that God is a member of an ontological category alongside of created things. According to older Christian thinkers, if God can be said to be a substance in any sense, it is only in an extended or analogical sense to the way in which creatures are substances. For example, see Augustine, *The Trinity* 5.8.9 (and books 5-7 in general) in *The Trinity*, trans. Stephen McKenna (Washington, DC: Catholic University of America Press, 2002), and Thomas Aquinas, *Summa Theologiae* Ia. q.13, a. 5. For more on Aquinas's view of the ontological categories, including the category of *Substance* and how it applies to God and creatures, see Jeffrey Brower, *Aquinas's Ontology of the Material World* (Oxford: Oxford University Press, 2014), chap. 2.

[19]In fact, there is interesting research in developmental psychology that indicates that children begin asking the classification question from a very young age. Anyone with young children knows how common questions of classification are: "What *is* that thing?" See Susan A. Gelman, *The Essential Child: The Origins of Essentialism in Everyday Thought* (New York: Oxford University Press, 2003), for psychological research on this natural, human posture.

[20]E. J. Lowe, "Metaphysics as the Science of Essence," in *Ontology, Modality, and Mind: Themes from the Metaphysics of E. J. Lowe*, eds. Alexander Carruth, Sophie Gibb, and John Heil (Oxford: Oxford University Press, 2018), 14.

and center in the task of metaphysics as the sole aim of metaphysical inquiry. In fact, Lowe sharply criticizes the Quinean approach to metaphysics by calling it a "pseudo-ontology" and a "no category ontology," insofar as it flattens the ontological structure of reality and construes beings as the values of variables (i.e., what we logically quantify over when we talk about the world.)[21]

According to Lowe and others in this Aristotelian camp, the essence of a (created) thing is prior to its existence, both in the order of reality and in the order of our knowledge of reality. To put it differently: *what* a thing is, is prior to *that* it is.

What exactly does this mean, and why think it's true? Lowe offers two reasons for thinking that essence is prior to existence. First, something can only actually exist if it's the sort of thing that could possibly exist. If something has a nature that precludes its existence, then you won't ever find that thing lying around, no matter how hard you look. Consider a round square as an example. Given that *roundness* and *squareness* both make up the nature of a round square, and no single, existing thing could possibly have both of these properties at the same time (since they preclude one another and are thus mutually contradictory), we know that there are no round squares in existence. Just by examining the nature of a round square by the light of reason we know round squares do not—indeed *cannot*—exist.[22]

The second reason Lowe gives as to why essence is prior to existence pertains to the order of knowing: How could we discover that something exists without having some initial grasp (however thin) of what it is in the first place? To illustrate, suppose I ask you: "Do you think furples exist?"[23] Yes, you heard me right, furples. How would you proceed to answer my question? Arguably, before you can adequately answer the existence question (do furples exist?), you must first get clear on the question of classification (what, at bottom, *is* a furple, and is its existence possible?); otherwise, you will have no idea whether

---

[21]For a sharp criticism of the Quinean approach to metaphysics, and the more logical-formal approach that Lowe calls "pseudo-ontology," see E. J. Lowe, "New Directions in Metaphysics and Ontology," *Axiomathes* 18 (2008): 273-88.

[22]Sometimes one hears it said, "It is impossible to prove a negative claim, like 'God does not exist.'" The apparent reason this is an impossible task is that one would have to explore every nook and cranny of reality in order to prove, without a doubt, that God is not there. But this is simply mistaken. If the essence of a thing is such that it involves predicating two incompatible properties of that thing, it is internally incoherent. Think: It makes no internal sense as it harbors an internal contradiction, such as something's being green all over and red all over at the same time.

[23]I owe this furple example to J. P. Moreland.

stumbling on something that exists, say a large, furry mammal lurking behind a tree, is a furple or something else altogether (a tiger). You can't discover that some particular thing is real if you have no idea what it is in the first place; that is, you can't make genuine ontological discoveries if you have no idea at all of what you are looking for.

We have seen, then, that for proponents of this neo-Aristotelian view of metaphysical inquiry, nonempirical or *a priori* knowledge (knowledge apart from sensory experience of the world) of natures by way of ultimate ontological categories is the central target of metaphysical inquiry. This also explains why, for Lowe, metaphysics aims to "chart the possibilities of being," as said above. According to Lowe, a thing's essence or nature ultimately explains what is or is not possible for that thing, as well as what is or is not necessary for it. For example, a tulip, being a material object by nature, must have some spatial dimension or other; it must have some determinate length, width, and height. Given what it is to be a material object (a thing extended in a certain way throughout space, perhaps), it is not possible for a tulip to lack spatial dimension altogether. Or, consider a more controversial matter: whether it is possible for a human being to exist without a brain. One's answer to this query will say a lot about what you think the essence of a human being is ("not possible" say those who think human beings are wholly material, perhaps just their brain; "possible indeed" say those who think humans are not wholly material). For Lowe, truths about possibility and necessity (what philosophers call "modal truths") are ultimately grounded in and explained by the essences or natures of things.[24]

So, we've seen that in Lowe's Aristotelian-inspired view, the aim of metaphysics is to "chart the possibilities of being, with a view to articulating the structure of reality as a whole, at its most fundamental level," which includes nonempirical knowledge of the natures of things as determined by their fundamental ontological categories.[25] It is important to point out that in contrast to the Quinean aim and task of metaphysics sketched above, Lowe's characterization does not restrict metaphysical inquiry to merely fleshing out the existence commitments of our best, scientific theories of the world. For Lowe, nonempirical knowledge of reality (knowledge apart from sensory experience of the world), including knowledge of the natures of things (and thus our

---

[24]See chaps. 5 and 6 for more on natures and essences.
[25]Lowe, "Metaphysics as the Science of Essence," 14.

knowledge of what is possible), is absolutely central to the aim and task of metaphysics and is conceptually prior to science.[26]

METAPHYSICS AND WHAT GROUNDS WHAT

A third contemporary way of characterizing metaphysics, also inspired by Aristotle and the Aristotelian tradition, is that metaphysics is "the study of what grounds what."[27] This approach, recently articulated and defended by philosopher Jonathan Schaffer, holds that the aim of metaphysical inquiry is not first and foremost to merely form "an unstructured list of existents" (what Schaffer calls "flat structure") as on the Quinean approach to metaphysics. Rather, the proper aim of metaphysics is to chart the hierarchical structure of reality—to explore what Schaffer calls "ordered structure"[28] in the world—and how certain categories of being depend on other categories of being, ultimately arriving at a category of being that in no way depends on any other (i.e., *Substance*). Informally, metaphysics is less like ontological bean counting and more like exploring an ontological construction site—no hard hat required!

As with Lowe's conception of metaphysics as categorial ontology (which shares a great deal in common with Schaffer's approach here), this neo-Aristotelian approach is in stark contrast to the Quinean approach to metaphysics outlined above, as we have seen already. To help illustrate this important difference, let's go back to the grocery list illustration I gave above. Let's once again compare my "flat structure" grocery list with my wife's "ordered structure" list, to use Schaffer's terminology.

As previously noted, my grocery lists are usually nothing more than itemized, unstructured lists of things to buy (deodorant, milk, Top Ramen, bread, eggs, spinach, etc.); they are as "flat" and one-dimensional as can be. So, figure 1.1 represents what my grocery list normally looks like:

---

[26]As suspected, Lowe's view is much more nuanced and multifaceted than what is articulated here by way of introduction. For more on Lowe's conception of the aim and task of metaphysics, see chap. 1 of his *A Survey of Metaphysics* (New York: Oxford University Press, 2002) or chap. 1 of his very challenging but rewarding book *The Possibility of Metaphysics: Substance, Identity, and Time* (New York: Oxford University Press, 1998).

[27]Jonathan Schaffer, "On What Grounds What," in *Metametaphysics: New Essays on the Foundations of Ontology*, eds. David Chalmers and David Manley (Oxford: Oxford University Press, 2009), 347-83. This essay is reprinted as chap. 7 in *Metaphysics: An Anthology*, 2nd edition, eds. Jaegwon Kim, Daniel Z. Korman, and Ernest Sosa (Malden, MA: Wiley-Blackwell, 2012).

[28]Schaffer, "On What Grounds What," 355.

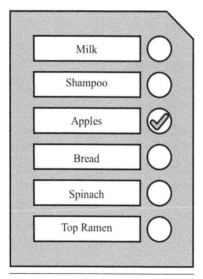

Figure 1.1. Ross's grocery list

My wife Suzanne's grocery list, by contrast, consists of a highly structured and ordered grouping of items that are related to one another in important ways; it exhibits "ordered structure" in Schaffer's terms. To add some flare to the illustration, suppose we assume, purely for the sake of illustration, that *Dairy* is the most fundamental or ultimate category on my wife's grocery list; all other categories of grocery items on her list revolve around and are subservient to *Dairy*. If so, then my wife's grocery list would have the following hierarchically ordered structure, with the category *Dairy* as primary and fundamental to all others (represented by both its size and the upward arrows), as depicted in figure 1.2:

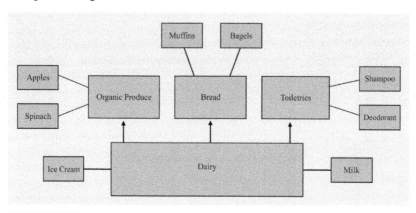

Figure 1.2. Suzanne's grocery list

If the aim of metaphysics was a bit like the aim of compiling grocery lists, it would be fair to say that I'd be more Quinean and my wife more Aristotelian, given the radical differences in our "flat" and "ordered" grocery lists.

Schaffer argues that metaphysics should aim to understand what is ultimate and most fundamental, and how every other category of being relates to what is fundamental. According to Schaffer (and Lowe), since what lie at the bedrock or foundation of all reality are what Aristotle called "primary substances" (Gk. *ousia*), metaphysics aims to investigate primary substances as beings that are primary, basic, or fundamental. For Aristotle, the things that belong to the elite category of *Substance* do not depend for their existence on any other kind of being. For Schaffer, while existence questions (what beings are there?) are still a key part of metaphysical inquiry, they are nowhere near as important as the question of what beings are fundamental, and they certainly should not be conceived of as the proper end of metaphysical inquiry.[29] To merely inventory the group of existing beings without describing the various dependence relations between such beings (and which sort of beings are independent of all else), is to miss a vitally important feature of metaphysical inquiry: metaphysical structure.

Notice that the main thrust of Schaffer's neo-Aristotelian view is not in tension with the previous Aristotelian-inspired views of the aim and task of metaphysics. In fact, Schaffer's characterization of metaphysics *presupposes* that there are objective categories of being, some being more fundamental than others; that these categories carve out various ways of being; and that the aim of metaphysics is to explore the categorial structure of reality. All of these tenets are deeply Aristotelian. As is the case with many of the main contours of Lowe's view, Schaffer's approach can be seen as a contemporary redressing of an important aspect of a broadly Aristotelian approach to metaphysics (with a few additional bells and whistles, I might add).[30]

A QUESTIONS-BASED APPROACH

A fourth characterization is what I'll call a "questions-based approach" to the nature and aim of metaphysics. A purely questions-based approach moves away from the attempt to draw clear-cut disciplinary boundaries in order to uniquely characterize the aim and scope of metaphysical inquiry. Rather, such an approach points to either a distinctive type of philosophical question that

---

[29]Schaffer, "On What Grounds What," 353.

[30]One such novelty of Schaffer's neo-Aristotelian account is his "permissivism" regarding what exists and his view that existence questions in general are trivial. For example, Schaffer, himself a self-declared atheist, believes that God exists. How might that be if he is an atheist, you ask? Well, for Schaffer, God is a fictional entity, like Harry Potter or Pegasus. For Schaffer, fictional entities *exist*, they are just *derivative* in so far as they are creations of the human mind and thus not fundamental (like substances are).

has historically been considered to fall within the purview of the discipline of metaphysics, or to questions that currently are being explored by contemporary philosophers working in the area of metaphysics. So, questions like the following are a sampling of what are typically considered to be distinctively metaphysical questions:

- What is time? Does time flow in one particular direction? Is time travel possible? Does the past or the future exist, in addition to the present?

- How do objects exist in time? Are they entirely present at a given moment in time, or are they spread out in time like a beaded necklace is spread out with different parts (beads) at different places?

- What is the nature of substance? Do individual substances exist? Or is the world exhausted by qualities or properties?

- What *is* existence?

- Are there properties, in addition to substances? If so, what are properties? Are properties universal or particular? Do they need substances to exist, or are they standalone sorts of beings? Where do they exist, if anywhere?

As a way of getting an initial grip on the subject matter of metaphysics, a questions-based approach can serve as a helpful handrail into some deep waters. But as a catch-all characterization of the discipline of metaphysics, such an approach has its limitations.

First, it may be the case that the sorts of questions that make it on the list are largely a reflection of what topics individual philosophers deem appropriate for distinctively metaphysical reflection. As these factors can often depend on shifting historical and cultural context, they provide a rather shaky conceptual ground as a way of characterizing the discipline of metaphysics. Second, we might ask: Why do these sorts of questions constitute distinctively metaphysical questions, and not others? Why not questions about the nature of knowledge, moral value, or the chemical composition of water? Do these questions not all have some common conceptual core? It may be that a questions-based approach already presupposes a particular view of the aim of metaphysics—it's the kind of inquiry that aims to explore *these* types of questions (and not *those* types of questions). It would be nice if we could get clear on the common conceptual core that unifies and classifies the above questions as distinctively metaphysical.

TOWARD A MIXED APPROACH

Toward this aim, let's consider one final approach to characterizing metaphysics as an area of inquiry, what I'll call a "mixed approach." The mixed approach takes aim at what is perhaps an underlying assumption of the above characterizations: that there is a single, uniform characterization of the discipline of metaphysics. But why think this? Why think that a proper characterization of metaphysics must be exclusively either the study of being qua being, categorial ontology, what grounds what, or a questions-based approach? Could not a characterization of metaphysics be multifaceted and incorporate many of these aims and methods?

This general, mixed approach has been put forward by Christian metaphysician Michael Rea. According to Rea: "(a) metaphysics is a non-empirical mode of inquiry, (b) it is partly about *what there is*, (c) it is partly about describing the essences or natures of things, and (d) it is concerned with what is possible, necessary, or impossible."[31] There's a lot here, but you can see the sizable overlap with the previous conceptions of metaphysics we've already discussed in this chapter.

First, echoing Aristotle and Lowe, Rea's characterization involves an epistemological claim regarding the proper method and ways of inquiring that are definitive of metaphysical inquiry. Clause (a) states that metaphysics is a distinctively nonempirical, *a priori* mode of inquiry. As we will see in detail in the next chapter, metaphysical knowledge, as with philosophical knowledge in general, is grounded in rational insight about reality (and not *a posteriori* empirical observation).[32] Second, this time echoing Quine, in clause (b) Rea maintains that metaphysics is also about what there is, that is, about answering existence questions (Does God exist? Does free will exist? etc.). But notice, in contrast to the Quinean approach, metaphysics for Rea is not *exclusively* about itemizing what there is and answering existence questions.

This brings us to clauses (c) and (d) of Rea's mixed characterization of the discipline of metaphysics. Clause (c) captures the Aristotelian notion, articulated in slightly different ways by Lowe and Schaffer, that metaphysical inquiry aims to explore the essential natures of things and how they are ordered

---

[31]Michael Rea, *Metaphysics: The Basics*, 2nd ed. (New York: Routledge, 2020), 10.
[32]Although, to be clear, Rea thinks that metaphysical inquiry is not "entirely free of empirical influence." See his *Metaphysics*, 10.

with respect to one another. While Rea considers both categorial analysis and the study of what grounds what to be vital aims that set metaphysics apart from other areas of philosophical inquiry, he is clear that he does not think that metaphysics can be *fully* captured by either of these tasks. As for clause (d), Rea is of the opinion that charting the domain of what is possible, necessary, and impossible is a characteristic feature of metaphysical inquiry. Clause (d) is closely aligned with Lowe's view that a primary aim of categorial ontology is to "chart the possibilities of being." However, for Lowe, there is a close connection between clauses (c) and (d) insofar as a thing's essence or nature ultimately explains what is possible, necessary, or impossible for that thing.

While there is much to explore about Rea's mixed characterization, we simply don't have the space to do so here. My aim is to give you just a taste of what a mixed approach to characterizing metaphysics might look like. The important point to make at this juncture is that in Rea's mixed approach, the discipline of metaphysics is not characterized solely by its method (clause (a)) or its subject matter (clauses (b), (c), (d)). Metaphysics can be a radiant, multifaceted jewel that is characterized by distinct and interlocking facets.

Let me close this chapter by taking stock of where we've been. My aim in this chapter has been to introduce you to several prominent characterizations of metaphysics as a subject of inquiry, both past and present. Remember, these are characterizations of the discipline of metaphysics, not clear-cut and airtight definitions. We've looked at Aristotle's time-tested view of metaphysics as the science of being qua being and how variations of his view have been articulated and defended by prominent contemporary metaphysicians like E. J. Lowe and Jonathan Schaffer. We have also explored the prospects and perils of a questions-based approach to characterizing metaphysics. All three Aristotelian characterizations of metaphysics—being qua being, categorial ontology, and the study of what grounds what—can be seen as complementary and mutually informative. Yet all three push back against the mainstream Quinean characterization of metaphysics as *solely* the task of discovering what exists by way of first-order canonical logic and our best scientific depictions of the world. So, now that you have an initial grasp of what metaphysics is, let's take a look at exploring the question whether metaphysical discoveries are even possible and, if so, how.

GOING DEEPER: WHAT IS METAPHYSICS?

Key Concepts in Metaphysics

- ontology
- essence
- criteria of ontological commitment
- Quine, W. V.
- conceptual analysis

Historical

- Aristotle, *Categories*; *Metaphysics*, book 4
- Immanuel Kant, *Prolegomena to Any Future Metaphysics*
- Thomas Aquinas, *On Being and Essence*

Contemporary

- W. V. Quine, "On What There Is"
- Jonathan Schaffer, "On What Grounds What"
- E. J. Lowe, "Metaphysics as the Science of Essence"

2

ARE METAPHYSICAL DISCOVERIES POSSIBLE?

ARE METAPHYSICAL DISCOVERIES POSSIBLE? IF SO, HOW?

Allow me to share with you one of my all-time favorite lines from a contemporary book on metaphysics: "Ontological discovery is not empirical. But ontologists[1] do make discoveries. Or so say believers in ontology. And I believe. If seeing were believing, then by the end of this book you would believe too. For—assuming my arguments are successful—ontological discoveries follow."[2] I too am a believer in ontological discovery. And by the end of this chapter, I hope you'll be a believer as well.

Initially, the idea of making ontological or metaphysical discoveries sounds strange to first-time philosophy students. When one talks or hears about "discoveries," one no doubt thinks of empirical discoveries in particular, discoveries made with the help of the five senses of sight, touch, hearing, taste, and smell. There are many different ways of making empirical discoveries, some more or less complicated. Some empirical discoveries are made by simple inspection with the naked eye, as one might discover that it rained last night simply by looking out the window, or how one might discover the best restaurants in one's new city of residence by tasting their respective cuisines. Discovering the sum total of one's liquid assets, by contrast, involves a more careful, empirical investigation, while William Gilbert's discovery of electricity in the seventeenth century involves a great deal more effort, inquiry, and sacrifice.

---

[1] "Ontologist" is another fancy name for those who do metaphysics (like "metaphysician").
[2] Trenton Merricks, *Objects and Persons* (New York: Oxford University Press, 2001), vii.

But what exactly are we to make of the traditional claim, explored in the previous chapter, that the study of metaphysics can yield genuine, albeit non-empirical, discoveries? What kinds of discoveries could there possibly be other than those that are made by way of empirical observation? It turns out that many philosophers in the early and mid-twentieth century were uneasy, even openly critical of the idea of making genuine discoveries about reality apart from sensory experience. It is important to first note that well into the twentieth century many influential philosophers, driven mainly by a view that restricts the scope of knowledge to what is sensory or empirical ("empiricism"), would have scoffed at the idea of nonempirical discovery (at least the kind that is informative, i.e., not trivially true or true by definition). We will look at this historically prominent objection to metaphysics in due course in this chapter.

For starters, why think empirical discoveries are the only kinds of discoveries that can be made? What, exactly, is the argument supposed to be here? To help initially open up space for the tenability of the idea of nonempirical discovery, and thus for genuine metaphysical discovery, we need to consider the following crucial question: Is the claim that empirical discovery is the only kind of discovery possible *itself* an empirical discovery? Did some fine-grained scientific instrument or sensory observation reveal this particular truth about the nature and scope of the types of discoveries that are possible? Does someone just "look and see" that this is true? Well, of course not. So, even at the outset, it is clear that while empirical discoveries are indeed important and make up our knowledge of one particular aspect of reality—namely the material world, the aspects of reality that exist in a sense-perceptible way—they certainly are not (cannot be!) the only kinds of discovery possible. And this is very good news for metaphysics!

What if there is such a thing as nonempirical discovery about reality, discovery that is not secured by the five senses but by rational insight alone? Historically, metaphysical discoveries about the nature and structure of being are made by way of pure rational insight. Here I want to defend the idea of metaphysical discovery and shore up the intellectual credentials of the discipline of metaphysics. First, I will briefly unpack the nature of rational insight itself. I'll then interact with a few well-known historical and contemporary objections to the intellectual credentials of metaphysics, namely, the idea that rational insight alone cannot reliably yield informative, nonempirical discoveries about reality.

Traditionally, metaphysical inquiry has been concerned with metaphysical *knowledge*. Going forward, I'll work with an informal characterization of knowledge as roughly *the ability to represent reality as it is on the basis of adequate grounds.*[3]

We commonly take ourselves to have knowledge in this sense about many mundane areas of life: I know that there is a coffee mug on the desk (perceptual knowledge), that 2+2=4 (mathematical knowledge), that electrons have negative charge (scientific knowledge), that there was an American Civil War and that Southeastern Seminary was founded in 1950 (historical knowledge), and so on. When I claim to know a matter of history or science, like there was an American Civil War or that electrons have negative charge, I claim to have the ability to represent the past and the physical world as they actually are (were), on the basis of some good reason or other. But what sort of adequate grounds or good reasons might legitimate these claims of historical and scientific knowledge? At least for most of us, when it comes to both historical and scientific knowledge in particular, it is pretty clearly the case that these claims to knowledge are supported by reliable testimony; I rightly claim to know (as opposed to merely believing them without adequate reasons) these historical and scientific matters precisely because I have it on reliable authority that there was a Civil War, or that electrons exist and have negative charge.

Claims to metaphysical knowledge, understood in this sense, should *also* be supported by adequate grounds or good reasons. Yet, the adequate grounds or reasons that have traditionally played a role in legitimizing metaphysical beliefs ("God exists," "human souls exist and are immaterial," "free will exists," etc.) are very different from grounds commonly thought to support ordinary beliefs about the physical world. From a Christian perspective, metaphysical knowledge—knowledge about the fundamental contour of reality—is available to us (at least in principle) both by virtue of our God-given intellectual capacities for rational thought and by way of divine testimony in Scripture.[4] In this way, metaphysics aims at genuine, nonempirical knowledge of

---

[3]This informal definition of knowledge is borrowed and adapted from Dallas Willard. See his *Knowing Christ Today: Why We Can Trust Spiritual Knowledge* (New York: HarperOne, 2009), a book that I would highly recommend you put on your summer reading list.

[4]Regarding metaphysical knowledge that comes by way of divine testimony, Hebrews 11:3 states, "By faith we understand that the universe was created by the word of God, so that what is seen was not made out of things that are visible."

reality, either by way of pure rational insight or by divine testimony. But what is this idea of knowledge by way of pure rational insight alone, apart from our sensory experience of the world?

Philosophers throughout the Western tradition have commonly distinguished between two different ways of knowing a particular proposition or statement. Consider the following statements that one might claim to know to be true:

(a) Wake Forest is a town in North Carolina.

(b) It is raining outside.

(c) The cheese is old and moldy.

(d) The grass is green.

(e) 3+2=5.

(f) If something is red, then it is colored.

(g) Nothing is blue all over and gold all over at the same time.

(h) Either A or B; not B; therefore A.

(i) I cannot be identical to a turnip.

When we carefully consider statements like (a)-(i), we are struck by the fact that they each seem to have something going for them epistemically; that is, they strike us as not only psychologically compelling but also as reasonably true and well supported on consideration. When a belief is reasonably well supported in this sense, when it is based on adequate grounds or evidence, the belief is what philosophers call "epistemically justified." The belief is above board intellectually, so to speak. What adequate grounds, we might ask, epistemically justify statements (a)-(i)?

I think it is reasonably clear that some of the above statements, such as (a)-(d), are epistemically justified by way of our sensory experience of the world; they are known in an *a posteriori* manner (a manner that is based on one's sense experience of the world), as philosophers like to say. Others, such as (e)-(i), are epistemically justified apart from sensory experience by way of rational insight alone; we can just intellectually "see" or "perceive" that they are true on thoughtful inspection. Statements such as (e)-(i) that are arguably known prior to or independent of sensory experience are thus known in an *a priori* manner, by simply thinking and reflecting on them. When we intellectually reflect on (e) and (h) in particular, a truth of arithmetic and logic respectively, they immediately strike us as being worthy of belief in that they are quite reasonable and epistemically justified. Or consider (i), that I cannot be identical to a turnip. When I reflect on what I am (a human person) and what a turnip is (a type of edible root), I see by the light of reason that it is impossible for me to be one and the same thing as an edible root; my nature, what I am essentially, seems to rationally preclude my being one and the same thing as a turnip. I think Aristotle was right when he said that thought is a bit like perception: "Thinking and understanding are regarded as akin to a form of perceiving; for in the one as well as the other the soul discriminates and is cognizant of something which is."[5]

Let me quickly clear up a common misunderstanding of nonempirical, *a priori* knowledge at this point. As Alvin Plantinga helpfully points out, the idea of *a priori* knowledge is not that such knowledge can be acquired without having any sensory experience *whatsoever*.[6] To see this, consider statement (f) above: If something is red, then it is colored. In order to understand this statement in the first place, I need to have had some sensory experience of color in general as well as the color red in particular. But saying that I need some minimal sensory experience of redness and color to *understand* what (f) means is very different from saying that sensory experience is what rationally *supports* or *justifies* (f). It would be odd to think that in order for me to reasonably believe (f), that generally if something is red then it is colored, that I actually have to visually inspect every existing red thing in question before inferring that it is also colored.

Why, then, should we trust rational insight as a source of epistemic justification and *a priori* knowledge of reality? Let me start by pointing out the obvious: You already *do* trust rational insight as a source of epistemic justification, at least to some degree and in particular areas of inquiry. How so? If you've ever successfully solved a proof in mathematics or logic, then you've relied on pure rational insight in doing so. If one rightly claims to know mathematical or logical truths, truths that are supported by *a priori* rational insight, then a wholesale skepticism about *a priori* knowledge is much too hasty.

---

[5]Aristotle, *De Anima* III. 3 427a 21, as quoted in Alvin Plantinga, *Warrant and Proper Function* (New York: Oxford University Press, 1993), 103.
[6]Plantinga, *Warrant and Proper Function*, 103-4.

The story of the intellectual credentials of rational insight and the *a priori* is a long and messy one that is well beyond the scope of our discussion here.[7] Let me gesture at a helpful place to start. Go back to statements (e)-(i) and take a moment to reflect on them once again. On carefully thinking about statements (e)-(i), do they strike you as worthy of belief, as reasonable? Do they seem true on reflection? If so, and apart from any good reason to think otherwise, it is perfectly reasonable to believe (e)-(i) are true on the basis of rational insight. So, perhaps our initial question of whether we should trust rational insight isn't the right question here. Perhaps the right question here is why *shouldn't* we trust rational insight as a source of epistemic justification? Why should we treat rational insight as guilty until proven innocent, instead of innocent until proven guilty? It is, after all, by way of rational insight into the nature and limits of human knowledge that critics of genuine meta-physical discoveries affirm that the only type of discoveries possible are em-pirical discoveries. Empirical discovery itself doesn't reveal that empirical discoveries are the only kinds of discoveries about reality that we can make. Ironically, it is *a priori* rational judgment into the nature and scope of human knowledge that drives this objection to the credibility of *a priori* rational judgment. Consequently, it seems that even the critic of rational insight cannot help but rely on at least some grasp of the way things are apart from empirical or sensory observation. Thus, the question is really: How can we *not* trust rational insight?

RATIONAL INSIGHT CHALLENGED

A well-known objection, past and present, to the aim and method of meta-physics stems from a particular family of views about the nature and scope of knowledge often referred to as "empiricism" or, in some contexts, "scientism." As an account of the nature and scope of epistemic justification and knowledge, empiricism has a long and complex history and admits of stronger and weaker versions.[8] For our purposes here, we can roughly characterize empiricism as the all-encompassing view that sensory experience is the only adequate basis or ground for *all* human knowledge; the only beliefs that can be epistemically

---

[7]An outstanding book, one of the best of its kind, that defends *a priori* knowledge and pure ratio-nal insight is Laurence BonJour's *In Defense of Pure Reason* (New York: Cambridge University Press, 1998).

[8]See BonJour's book *In Defense of Pure Reason*, chaps 1-3.

justified (and thus *known* to be true) are those that are derived from and based on our observation of the world by way of our five senses (*a posteriori*).

Scientism, which is based firmly on empiricism, claims that the empirical sciences in particular are the only way (or the most trustworthy way) to acquire knowledge about reality; the methods of the natural sciences are fully adequate to discover all there is to discover about all there is to reality; there's simply no room left for nonempirical, *a priori* metaphysical discoveries![9] It should go without saying that empiricism and scientism leave little or no room for robust, *a priori* rational insight into the nature of things and, consequently, robust metaphysical inquiry.

Let's briefly unpack the origin of this suspicion toward the *a priori* and rational insight in the early modern period and quickly trace its development throughout the twentieth century. The Scottish Enlightenment philosopher and historian David Hume (1711–1776) famously put forward what has become known as "Hume's Fork," that all human knowledge must fall into one of two categories, what he called "relations of ideas" and "matters of fact."[10] For Hume, relations of ideas are "discoverable by the mere operation of thought, without dependence on what is any where existent in the universe."[11] In other words, for Hume, there are things we can know by way of pure rational insight, apart from the deliverances of our senses.

The good news here is that Hume left a foot in the door for a sliver of *a priori* knowledge apart from sensory experience. The bad news is that Hume considered relations of ideas to be true merely in an "analytic" sense, that is, true only in virtue of the meaning of terms and concepts. Analytic truths are noninformative in that they do not aim to tell us what reality is really like (and thus do not, for Hume, tell us what *really* exists in the world, apart from how we think and speak about it). For instance, "all bachelors are unmarried" is analytically true in so far as it is true solely in virtue of the linguistic meaning of the word *bachelor* (unmarried male) and *unmarried*. The predicate *unmarried* is definitionally included in the subject *bachelor*. Hume considered truths of mathematics and geometry, indeed all "necessary truths" (truths

[9]For an accessible introduction to scientism and its rejection of traditional metaphysics or "first philosophy," see chaps. 1-10 of J. P. Moreland, *Scientism and Secularism* (Wheaton, IL: Crossway, 2018).
[10]See David Hume, *Enquiry Concerning Human Understanding*, IV.I (Indianapolis: Hackett, 1993), 15.
[11]Hume, *Enquiry* IV.I, 15.

regarding what *must* be the case), to fall within the category of relations of ideas and capable of being known *a priori*, apart from sensory observation. So while we can know some things *a priori*, even truths about necessity (about what *must* be, not just what *is*), the scope of this knowledge is severely limited to the way we define words and not about the world *itself*.

By contrast, Hume thought that "matters of fact" are true by virtue of the way the world is and can be known to be true solely on the basis of our sensory experience of the physical world. Consider the example of "snow is white" as a matter of fact for Hume. "Snow is white" is both "synthetic" and known *a posteriori*, on the basis of our sensory observation of the world. The statement "snow is white" is synthetic (that is, nonanalytic) precisely because it is true solely because of the way the world is and not by virtue of the meaning of the words in question (one could not discover that snow is actually white simply by the meaning of the terms *snow* and *white*). And the statement is known *a posteriori* since it can only be known by sensory observation (merely thinking hard about it will not lead to the discovery that snow is white). Here's the key point to take away from Hume's Fork: Only *a posteriori* knowledge can yield informative, nontrivial (synthetic) truths about the nature and contour of reality; *a priori* knowledge on the basis of rational insight can tell us nothing informative and substantive about the nature of reality.

What happens to metaphysical or even theological knowledge given Hume's Fork? Well, here I'm afraid there's only bad news. Since traditional metaphysical beliefs (i.e., "the soul exists," "there are immaterial substances") were based on pure rational insight and not sensory observation, they could not be matters of fact. And since metaphysical claims were not analytic truths (not true by definition), they could not be classified as relations of ideas nor known *a priori*, apart from sensory observation. So, metaphysical beliefs could be classified neither as relations of ideas nor matters of fact. Since, for Hume, all human knowledge must fall within one of these two categories, the implication is clear: Metaphysical claims cannot be *known* to be true; they do not make the cut as knowledge; opinion or belief, perhaps, but most definitely not genuine knowledge. Hume's Fork undergirds his famous remark in the final paragraph of his *Enquiry Concerning Human Understanding*:

> If we take in our hand any volume; of divinity [theology] or school metaphysics [traditional metaphysics], for instance; let us ask, Does it contain

any abstract reasoning concerning quantity or number? No. Does it contain any experimental reasoning concerning matter of fact and existence? No. Commit it then to the flames: for it can contain nothing but sophistry and illusion.[12]

There you have it, "Nothing but sophistry and illusion"; Hume's empiricist epistemology rules out the aim and methods of traditional metaphysics from the get-go (and theology to boot!).

Hume's staunch empiricism provided one of the chief intellectual pillars for an influential philosophical movement in the early twentieth century known as "logical positivism." The Vienna Circle—a group of European philosophers at the University of Vienna that included thinkers such as Moritz Schlick, Otto Neurath, Rudolph Carnap, and others—served as the fountainhead of an extreme form of empiricism that would dominate the analytic philosophical landscape for much of the early and middle part of the twentieth century. Logical positivism would cast a long, dark shadow over the study of metaphysics for decades to come.

Perhaps the clearest and most influential expression of logical positivism is found in A. J. Ayer's 1936 book *Language, Truth, and Logic*.[13] Ayer put forward a theory of linguistic meaning that was deeply influenced by Hume's empiricism that would subsequently hinder traditional, *a priori* metaphysical inquiry for years to come. The verification theory of meaning—"verificationism" as it is often called—was a philosophical theory about the linguistic meaning of statements. Ayer famously argued, with an eye on Hume, that all meaningful statements can be exclusively divided into two categories: analytic and synthetic. According to verificationism, all synthetic (nonanalytic) truths that are meaningful must be empirically verifiable, that is, capable of being verified by sensory experience (at least in principle). So, if synthetic statements such as "the human soul exists" or "God is triune" are not empirically verifiable on the basis of sensory experience, they are literally meaningless.

Pause and think for a moment about how strong of a claim this amounts to. Metaphysical and theological statements are literally nonsensical if they cannot be verified on the basis of the five senses. To press the point, consider the following example of a meaningless statement from Lewis Carrol's poem

---

[12]Hume, *Enquiry* XII.III, 114.
[13]A. J. Ayer, *Language, Truth, and Logic* (New York: Dover, 1952).

"Jabberwocky": "'Twas brillig, and the slithy toves / Did gyre and gimble in the wabe." A statement like this is pure nonsense and doesn't even rise to the level of being true or false; it is utterly meaningless and unintelligible. And if theology and metaphysics are in the same camp, who in their right mind would want to waste their time on such gibberish! You simply cannot assign a lower cognitive status to metaphysical and theological claims than what they were given by proponents of verificationism.

With respect to contemporary analytic philosophy, the ghost of Hume lingers still, even if just awkwardly in the background of contemporary metaphysical debates. A particularly sharp critique of the credibility of *a priori* rational insight in metaphysical inquiry is offered by James Ladyman, Don Ross, and David Spurrett, all self-proclaimed proponents of "scientism."[14] In a chapter titled "In Defense of Scientism," they launch a full-scale attack on what they take to be the shaky intellectual credentials of traditional metaphysics (what they pejoratively call "neo-scholastic metaphysics"), namely that rational insight is capable of delivering *a priori* knowledge of reality apart from the empirical sciences.

Ladyman, Ross, and Spurrett offer ground rules for what they see as a more responsible, scientifically governed approach to metaphysics that rejects rational insight as a source of *a priori* metaphysical knowledge. On their view, rational insight has proven to be a blind guide in the history of both philosophy and science and thus should be neither authoritative nor autonomous in its own right, apart from the natural sciences.[15] If metaphysicians want to keep their day job, they claim, they had better move to more stable, epistemological ground, namely by looking over the shoulders of scientists. In their view, metaphysical inquiry is only intellectually respectable if it helps unify and systematize various aspects of scientific theories; metaphysicians are mere intellectual bookkeepers for the scientists, nothing more.[16] While intellectual bookkeeping may sound appealing to bibliophiles

---

[14]James Ladyman, Don Ross, and David Spurrett, "In Defense of Scientism," in *Every Thing Must Go: Metaphysics Naturalized*, eds. James Ladyman, Don Ross, David Spurrett, and John Collier (New York: Oxford University Press, 2007), chap. 1.

[15]For an alternative take that ascribes both independent authority and autonomy to metaphysical inquiry in relation to the sciences, see George Bealer, "On the Possibility of Philosophical Knowledge," *Noûs* 30 (1996): 10. For a more accessible discussion of these same matters, see chaps. 9 and 10 of J. P. Moreland's *Scientism and Secularism*.

[16]On this point, see their "Principle of Naturalistic Closure," outlined in their chapter "In Defense of Scientism," 37.

and type A personalities, the fact is that scientism severely undercuts the privileged role that metaphysical inquiry has played throughout the history of Western philosophy.

This concludes our brief excursion into the historical origins regarding some of the suspicion we find today regarding the traditional aims and *a priori* methodology of metaphysics. We have seen that the antipathy toward metaphysical inquiry in general, and *a priori* rational insight in particular, has stemmed from an overarching theory of knowledge known as empiricism and scientism by extension. But are these good reasons for being suspicious of rational insight and the possibility of *a priori* knowledge about the nature of reality? Why think empiricism and scientism are true? Why restrict *all* epistemic justification and knowledge to what can be known empirically, or to what can be known on the basis of the natural sciences? Of course, *if* scientism is true, then the prospects of making informative discoveries about reality on the basis of pure rational insight are dim to nonexistent. But *is* scientism true? This is the key question to which we now turn.

WHY THINK SCIENTISM IS TRUE?

Let's slow down a bit and ask: What, exactly, is the argument supposed to be here in favor of scientism? Let's think together about two of what I take to be the clearest and strongest arguments for scientism and against traditional metaphysical inquiry on offer today.

The first argument is advanced by Ladyman, Ross, and Spurrett and considers the question of human origins to be central in answering the question of whether traditional, *a priori* metaphysical inquiry is a trustworthy route to genuine knowledge of reality. In their own words, "Attaching epistemic significance to metaphysical intuitions is anti-naturalist. . . . it requires ignoring central implications of evolutionary theory, and of the cognitive and behavioral sciences, concerning the nature of our minds."[17] In short: There's something about how our minds originated on the evolutionary scene that casts doubt on the reliability of pure rational insight and thus the metaphysical enterprise in its totality. To grasp this important objection, I'll need to do some stage-setting first (surprise, surprise!).

---

[17]Ladyman, Ross, and Spurrett, "In Defense of Scientism," 10.

Consider first a view that I'll call the "grand evolutionary story," a strictly scientific view about the origin and evolution of all living things that is widely accepted among mainstream contemporary philosophers and scientists:

> *The Grand Evolutionary Story*: All of life originated from inorganic matter and evolved from simple to more complex organisms (primarily) by means of natural selection operating on random genetic mutation.

Next, consider a philosophical view known as "metaphysical naturalism":

> *Metaphysical Naturalism*: The view that there is no God, nor anything like God; the space-time universe is all there is, was, or ever will be.

According to metaphysical naturalism, all that exists is complex, physical matter in motion governed by the laws of nature, nothing more. It is important to note that metaphysical naturalism is a *philosophical* view, not a *scientific* view; it is a metaphysical view about the extent and scope of all reality, namely, whether what exists includes God as well as the space-time universe. When we combine the grand evolutionary story and metaphysical naturalism we get a distinctively *philosophical* story about the origin and development of all living things, namely,

> *Evolutionary Naturalism*: The view that the grand evolutionary story is not orchestrated or superintended by God, nor any intelligent being like God.

What I'm calling "evolutionary naturalism" amounts to a commitment to a scientific, neo-Darwinian account of the origin and development of life, together with a metaphysical view that precludes the existence of God and thereby any divinely directed purposes or ends for the evolutionary process. But it is absolutely vital to note, and this is key, the claim that the grand evolutionary story is in no way guided or orchestrated by God is strictly a *metaphysical* and not a *scientific* claim.

With the above views on the table, let's consider how the origin and evolutionary development of human beings bears on the question of the reliability of rational insight to make genuine metaphysical discoveries about reality. Let's try to get inside the head of the evolutionary naturalist to see what follows from such a position. First, let's assume for the sake of argument that evolutionary naturalism is true. If evolutionary naturalism is true, human beings and their cognitive capacities (minds) are solely the products of unguided evolutionary processes. The process of natural

selection operating on random genetic mutations is in no way divinely orchestrated or aimed at specific, goal-directed outcomes. Evolutionary naturalist Richard Dawkins is crystal clear on this very point in his book *The
Blind Watchmaker*:

> Natural selection, the blind, unconscious automatic process which Darwin
> discovered, and which we now know is the explanation for the existence and
> apparently purposeful form of all life, has no purpose in mind. It has no mind
> and no mind's eye. It does not plan for the future. It has no vision, no foresight,
> no sight at all. If it can be said to play the role of watchmaker in nature, it is
> the blind watchmaker.[18]

This lack of foresight and directedness to the evolutionary process applies to
the origin and development of human beings along with their cognitive capacities to discover deep, metaphysical truths about the nature and structure
of reality. According to evolutionary naturalism, there is no sense in which
our capacity for rational insight evolved for the purpose of reliably discovering
deep, complex truths about the nature of ultimate reality.

Prominent atheist philosopher Thomas Nagel explicitly makes this point
about our theoretical beliefs about reality on evolutionary naturalism when
he says, "If we came to believe that our capacity for objective theory were the
product of natural selection, that would warrant serious skepticism about its
results."[19] Did you catch that? "Serious skepticism" about the results of our
complex, theoretical beliefs, if evolutionary naturalism is true. This is precisely because the only kind of adaptive advantage that matters in the everyday struggle for survival is what enables organisms to better fight, flee,
and reproduce, nothing more. As Patricia Churchland, a prominent metaphysical naturalist and neuroscientist at the University of California, San
Diego puts it:

> Boiled down to essentials, a nervous system enables the organism to succeed
> in the four F's: feeding, fleeing, fighting, and reproducing. The principal
> chore of nervous systems is to get the body parts where they should be in
> order that the organism may survive . . . Improvements in sensorimotor

---

[18]Richard Dawkins, *The Blind Watchmaker: Why the Evidence of Evolution Reveals a Universe Without Design* (New York: W. W. Norton, 1987), 5.
[19]Quoted in Alvin Plantinga, *Where the Conflict Really Lies* (New York: Oxford University Press,
2011), 315.

control confer an evolutionary advantage: a fancier style of representing is advantageous *so long as it is geared to the organism's way of life and enhances the organism's chances of survival.* Truth, whatever that is, definitely takes the hindmost.[20]

Don't miss the gravity of what Churchland is saying here: "Truth, whatever that is, definitively takes the hindmost." Truth, especially truth about deep metaphysical matters as is our sole concern here, is not only not front and center in the evolutionary process, but it takes the last seat at the very back of the bus.

How does this apply to the question of whether our cognitive faculties are reliable when it comes to *a priori* rational insight into the nature of reality? Of course, our ability to think deeply about high-level metaphysical matters such as the ontological categories, the nature of identity, numbers, properties, substance, and so on in no way confers on us a greater ability to feed, fight, flee, and reproduce. They have little to no selective advantage in the evolutionary process. Oddly enough, such a high-level cognitive ability to inquire into the complexities of the deep structure of reality may well *detract* from overall survival value. As Christian philosopher Alvin Plantinga humorously remarks, in true Plantingian style:

> After all, it is only the occasional assistant professor of mathematics or logic that needs to be able to prove Gödel's theorem in order to survive and reproduce. Indeed, given the nerdness factor, undue interest in such things would have been counterproductive in the Pleistocene. What prehistoric woman would be interested in some guy who prefers thinking about set theory to hunting?[21]

This is classic Plantinga. According to evolutionary naturalism, then, it is highly unreasonable to expect our cognitive capacity for rational insight apart from sensory experience to be systematically reliable in discovering truths about deep metaphysical matters in particular.

Now, with all of this as background, this is precisely the philosophical argument that Ladyman, Ross, and Spurrett press against metaphysical discovery by way of *a priori* rational insight. They say:

---

[20]Patricia Churchland, "Epistemology in the Age of Neuroscience," *The Journal of Philosophy* 84, no. 10 (1987): 548-49.

[21]Plantinga, *Where the Conflict Really Lies*, 133.

Proficiency in inferring the large-scale and small-scale structure of our immediate environment, or any features of parts of the universe distant from our ancestral stomping grounds, was of no relevance to our ancestors' reproductive fitness. *Hence, there is no reason to imagine that our habitual intuitions and inferential responses are well designed for science or for metaphysics.*[22]

Given that reproductive fitness requires little by way of cognitive complexity, we have no reason to expect that human mental capacities would be adequate for complex, theoretical tasks like metaphysical inquiry or theoretical science.

Here it is important to point out that at one level, I actually think Ladyman, Ross, and Spurrett are spot-on, *given evolutionary naturalism*. *If* evolutionary naturalism is true, then it is true that we have very little grounds to reasonably expect *a priori* rational insight to be reliable in making metaphysical discoveries. In evolutionary naturalism, apart from the natural sciences, there is no secure, intellectual ground for thinking that rational insight can provide reliable knowledge about reality. Consequently, the natural sciences are the only rock-solid, reliable way to secure genuine knowledge of reality. Ergo, scientism!

If you haven't already spotted it, there's really bad news lurking just around the corner for proponents of scientism (pause for few moments to see if you can spot it!). Evolutionary naturalism is the corrosive acid that fails to discriminate against the reliability of certain kinds of theoretical inquiry; that is, evolutionary naturalism doesn't just eat away at the reliability of some types of theoretical reflection and not others. Rather, it is a universal acid that undercuts the reliability of every area of complex, theoretical inquiry, *including the very natural sciences in which the proponent of scientism takes intellectual refuge.*

Carefully consider those last remarks from Ladyman, Ross, and Spurrett quoted above: "Hence, there is no reason to imagine that our habitual intuitions and inferential responses are well designed for science or for metaphysics." While the authors have only the "habitual intuitions and inferential responses" operative in scientific inquiry in mind here, it is not hard to see how the point generalizes to the entire theoretical enterprise of our scientific inquiry into the natural world.[23] As a key witness, let me once again call to the stand atheistic philosopher Thomas Nagel: "Evolutionary naturalism provides

---

[22]Ladyman, Ross, and Spurrett, "In Defense of Scientism," 2. My emphasis.
[23]Insofar as scientific reasoning involves, in part, inferential and probabilistic reasoning.

an account of our capacities that undermines their reliability, and in doing so undermines itself. . . . Mechanisms of belief formation that have selective advantage in the everyday struggle for existence *do not warrant our confidence in the construction of theoretical accounts of the world as a whole.*[24] Surely the scientific enterprise takes the "construction of theoretical accounts of the world as a whole" as a chief aim, does it not? So, the irony here is thick indeed. The very objection Ladyman, Ross, and Spurrett press against the reliability of *a priori*, rational insight, all under the banner of naturalizing metaphysics, turns out to undermine the intellectual credentials of the natural sciences as well. If successful, the argument digs not only the grave of metaphysics, but also the grave of theoretical science.

But wait, there's more! In pressing this argument for scientism and against *a priori* rational insight, Ladyman, Ross, and Spurrett, of course, assume the truth of evolutionary naturalism, that evolutionary processes can in no way be guided or orchestrated by God. This is precisely why they think there's no prior reason to expect that evolution would produce reliable human cognitive faculties equipped to make deep philosophical and empirical discoveries about reality. But remember that evolutionary naturalism is itself a *metaphysical* view that falls within the purview of traditional metaphysics, since it is based on *a priori* rational insight into the nature of reality apart from sensory experience (one can't just "look and see" or run an experiment to discover that the evolutionary process is not divinely guided or directed). Whether *metaphysical* naturalism—an essential ingredient of *evolutionary* naturalism—is true is a *metaphysical* discovery, not an *empirical* discovery.

So, here's the rub. If Ladyman, Ross, and Spurrett argue *for* scientism and *against a priori* metaphysical inquiry by assuming the truth of evolutionary naturalism, they inevitably rely on *a priori* metaphysical reflection in doing so, namely the truth of metaphysical naturalism as part and parcel of evolutionary naturalism. But to rely on *a priori* metaphysical reflection in an argument against the adequacy of *a priori* metaphysical reflection is a peculiar way to

---

[24]Thomas Nagel, *Mind and Cosmos: Why the Materialist Neo-Darwinian Conception of Nature Is Almost Certainly False* (New York: Oxford University Press, 2012), 27. My emphasis. This specific form of Plantinga's evolutionary argument against naturalism is also forcefully defended by Christian philosopher Thomas Crisp, "An Evolutionary Objection to the Argument from Evil," in *Evidence and Religious Belief*, eds. Kelly James Clark and Raymond J. VanArragon (New York: Oxford University Press, 2011).

argue, to say the least. It's a bit like using the air in your lungs to give a loud diatribe against the existence of oxygen, or sitting in a chair while arguing that no chairs are strong enough to support human beings.

This back-and-forth tells us two things. First, *a priori* metaphysical inquiry is simply indispensable; the very rejection of metaphysical inquiry involves heavyweight metaphysical commitments supported by *a priori* rational insight.[25] Second, the evolutionary argument for scientism given by Ladyman, Ross, and Spurrett cannot be consistently pressed by the die-hard proponent of scientism. Ironically, if the evolutionary argument against *a priori* metaphysical inquiry is sound (which relies on the truth of metaphysical naturalism), then scientism fails, since the truth of metaphysical naturalism presupposes *a priori* inquiry and is incapable of being supported purely by empirical observation alone. We should conclude, then, that this first philosophical argument for scientism (and against genuine metaphysical discovery) is in pretty bad shape indeed.

Before we move on to the second contemporary argument for scientism (and against *a priori*, metaphysical inquiry), let me conclude this section by pointing out the striking fit between human cognitive capacities and the structure of reality on the Christian story. According to historic Christian teaching, human beings were made to *know*. They are by nature divinely endowed with an intellect that is both hungry for knowledge of God and the natural order, and fit to reliably lay hold of them. There is, like a lock and key, a natural affinity between the human intellect and the fabric and structure of reality in all its glorious and wonder-filled dimensions. We were made to explore and delight in the many facets of being, first and foremost the triune God himself and secondarily the created order as it reflects the radiance of God like a mirror.[26]

Consequently, the fact that we can (and do!) come to a deeper theoretical understanding of the physical world (just think here of the twin pillars of twentieth-century physics: quantum mechanics and Einstein's general theory of relativity) lends credence to the idea that we are emphatically *not* cosmic

---

[25]On the indispensability of metaphysics, see E. J. Lowe, *A Survey of Metaphysics* (New York: Oxford University Press, 2002), chap. 1, in addition to just about everything that Lowe has written, God rest his soul.

[26]For more on the connection between wonder and the Christian philosophical life, see my *Christian Philosophy as a Way of Life: An Invitation to Wonder* (Grand Rapids, MI: Baker Academic, 2023), chaps. 1 and 2.

accidents. Rather, we've been intentionally placed here by a supremely intelligent being as emissaries, image-bearers if you will, to cultivate our knowledge of the created order for the glory of God and the good of others.

Let's turn to the second contemporary argument for scientism offered by philosopher of science Alex Rosenberg. According to Rosenberg, the strongest argument for scientism is the reliable track record of the natural sciences—physics in particular—to generate knowledge of the physical world. Rosenberg argues,

> If we're going to be scientistic, then we have to attain our view of reality from what physics tells us about it. Actually, we'll have to do more than that: we'll have to embrace physics as the whole truth about reality. Why buy the picture of reality that physics paints? Well, it's simple, really. We trust science as the only way to acquire knowledge.[27]

And,

> We have the best of reasons to believe that the method of physics—combining controlled experiment and careful observation with mainly mathematical requirements on the shape theories can take—are the right ones for acquiring *all* knowledge. Carving out some area of "inquiry" or "belief" as exempt from exploration by the methods of physics is special pleading or self-deception . . . The phenomenal accuracy of its prediction, the unimaginable power of its technological application, and the breathtaking extent and detail of its explanations are powerful reasons to believe that physics is *the whole truth about reality.*[28]

With descriptors like "phenomenal accuracy," "unimaginable power," and "breathtaking extent and detail," who wouldn't want to sign on the dotted line in favor of scientism!

Rosenberg clearly thinks that the sheer power and success of the natural sciences (modern physics in particular) compared to other areas of knowledge (esp. philosophy) offers good evidence that the natural sciences tell us the whole truth about reality. Keep that last phrase in mind going forward: *the whole truth about reality.*

According to Christian philosopher Edward Feser, Rosenberg's argument for scientism can be helpfully summarized as follows:

---

[27]Alex Rosenberg, *The Atheist's Guide to Reality: Enjoying Life without Illusions* (New York: W. W. Norton, 2011), 20.

[28]Rosenberg, *Atheist's Guide to Reality*, 24-25. My emphasis.

1. The predictive power and technological applications of physics are un-paralleled by those of any other purported source of knowledge.

2. Therefore, what physics reveals to us is all that is real.[29]

What are we to make of this argument? Is the inference from 1 to 2 a good inference? Does this argument undercut the possibility of making *a priori* metaphysical discoveries apart from the empirical sciences? It's hard to see how it does, really. To see why, consider the following parallel argument offered by Feser for the conclusion that what metal detectors discover about reality—metallic objects—is the whole truth about reality *full stop*:

3. Metal detectors have had far greater success in finding coins and other metallic objects in more places than any other method has.

4. Therefore, what metal detectors reveal to us (coins and other metallic objects) is all that is real.[30]

Should you believe that everything that exists is metallic based on the move from 3 to 4? Clearly not! Or at least I hope not since you yourself, the one carefully considering the argument, are clearly not metallic.

So, then, what's wrong with Rosenberg's original argument in favor of scientism? For one, there is a gaping hole between premise and conclusion, between 1 and 2. Just because a particular method is reliable in discovering truth about one particular part of reality, namely *physical* reality (1), doesn't at all suggest that therefore one part of reality encompasses *all* of reality (2). By analogy, a metal detector's failure to detect nonmetals would give you absolutely no reason whatsoever to think that nonmetals do not exist. This is because, as Feser helpfully points out, metal detectors *by their very nature* are designed to only track *certain kinds of things*, namely metals; they are not, for instance, designed to discover the life cycle of squirrels, Jell-O, or gum on the bottom of school desks across the country.

In the same way, the methods of the natural sciences (methods, not method[31])—which combine "controlled experiment and careful observation

---

[29]I borrow this formulation of the argument from Edward Feser, *Scholastic Metaphysics: A Contemporary Introduction* (Neunkirchen-Seelscheid: Editiones Scholasticae, 2014), 22.

[30]Feser, *Scholastic Metaphysics*, 22.

[31]The notion of *the* scientific method—a uniform approach to scientific theorizing that is applicable across the natural sciences—is much too simplistic. See Robert C. Koons, "Science and Theism: Concord, Not Conflict," in *The Rationality of Theism*, eds. Paul Copan and Paul K. Moser (New York: Routledge, 2003), for an excellent discussion of this important point.

with mainly mathematical requirements"—are by their very nature only attuned to the nature, structure, and laws that govern *physical* reality. The failure of a controlled experiment based on careful empirical observation to empirically detect nonphysical reality gives you no reason whatsoever to think that nonphysical reality does not exist (or positively, that physical reality is all there is). Such a sweeping metaphysical claim is just that, a *metaphysical* claim about the scope of existing things and about the total extent of reality.

I can imagine Rosenberg (and Ladyman, Ross, and Spurrett) giving the following little speech at this point,

> Okay, Mr. Metaphysician, why don't you give us an updated philosophical progress report on the predictive success and a list of technological innovations that have come from metaphysical inquiry? What sorts of *real* discoveries has metaphysics made, by way of *a priori* reflection, that have helped us predict and control the natural world for the purpose of bettering the human race (e.g., eliminating disease, prolonging human life, giving us an even more sophisticated version of the next iPhone)?

Of course, given such narrow requirements, the list provided by Mr. Metaphysician will come up very short indeed. But, of course, such a list will be near empty *by design*. Metaphysics by its very nature is simply not the sort of inquiry that is primarily attuned to these sorts of empirically quantifiable measures and outcomes in the first place. While metaphysical discoveries do indeed help us live more integrated and flourishing human lives and thereby "better" the human race in the truest sense of the word, their primary benefits are in no way scientific or technological.[32]

As Feser points out, the charge that metaphysics is devoid of technological innovation and is thereby useless misses the mark entirely. He notes, "This is about as impressive as demanding a list of the metal-detecting successes of gardening, cooking, and painting, and then concluding from the fact that no such list is forthcoming that spades, spatulas, and paint brushes are all useless and ought to be discarded and replaced with metal detectors."[33] The core assumption—the assumption on which this scientistic demand stands or falls—is that *the only kind of inquiry that can give us reliable knowledge of reality is*

---

[32]For more on the practical relevance of philosophical reflection for human life (including metaphysics), see my *Christian Philosophy as a Way of Life: An Invitation to Wonder* (Grand Rapids, MI: Baker Academic, 2023).

[33]Feser, *Scholastic Metaphysics*, 23.

the kind that can deliver predictive success and lead to technological innovation.
Since metaphysics has nothing to show for itself on this score, it certainly
looks rather anemic next to the "phenomenal accuracy" and "unimaginable
power" of the natural sciences.

But, as I hope you've already spotted at this point, this core philosophical
assumption that drives the entire argument simply restates what it is, in fact,
trying to prove. More plainly, it simply *asserts,* this time more loudly and
slowly, that there are no other ways of acquiring knowledge of reality other
than the empirical sciences. Again, this knee-jerk rejection of *a priori* rational
insight into the nature of reality is itself not a deliverance of the sciences.
Consequently, while there's certainly a lot of charged rhetoric in the vicinity
here, this assertion of scientism has very little going for it by way of substance;
in fact, it is entirely question-begging. So, perhaps the reasonable thing to
conclude at the close of this chapter is not "is there any good reason to trust
a priori rational insight as a reliable guide to reality?" Rather, it's better to ask:
"Assuming the truth of Christian theism, is there any good reason *not* to?"

GOING DEEPER: ARE METAPHYSICAL DISCOVERIES POSSIBLE?

Key Concepts in Metaphysics:

- *a priori*/*a posteriori*
- analytic versus synthetic truths
- David Hume
- Immanuel Kant
- realism and anti-realism (global)

Historical

- Aristotle, *Categories*
- Hume, *Enquiry Concerning Human Understanding*, sections II-IV
- Immanuel Kant, *Prolegomena to Any Future Metaphysics*, 4:255-80
- Bertrand Russell, "How *A Priori* Knowledge Is Possible," in *Problems of Philosophy*
- A. J. Ayer, *Language, Truth, and Logic*, chap. 1, "The Elimination of Metaphysics"

Contemporary

- Laurence Bonjour, *In Defense of Pure Reason*
- James Ladyman, Don Ross, and James Spurrett, "In Defense of Scientism," in *Every Thing Must Go*
- George Bealer, "*A Priori* Knowledge and the Scope of Philosophy"
- Edward Feser, "Prolegomenon," in *Scholastic Metaphysics*
- J. P. Moreland, *Scientism and Secularism*

3

DOING METAPHYSICS
AS A CHRISTIAN

Up to this point we have explored together several prominent historical and contemporary characterizations of the nature and aim of metaphysics as an area of philosophical study (chap. 1). We have also considered whether genuine metaphysical discoveries are indeed possible (chap. 2). In this chapter, I want to give you a sense as to how a distinctively Christian philosopher might go about the task of thinking metaphysically. I say "might" here since there are several viable ways one might approach the task of doing metaphysics from a Christian standpoint. My aim here is to simply give you a glimpse of how I go about the task of engaging in metaphysical reflection as someone who is a Christian first and a metaphysician second. My hope in articulating and modeling this posture is that you would at least try it on, so to speak, and see if it fits![1]

My students are often quite surprised to learn that many of the most influential philosophers in the Western tradition were metaphysicians and thus preoccupied with thoughtful reflection on the nature and structure of reality. Consider the following who's who list of metaphysicians in the history of Western philosophy: Parmenides, Heraclitus, Zeno, Plato, Aristotle, Saint Augustine, Boethius, Saint Anselm, Saint Thomas Aquinas, Peter Abelard, Duns Scotus, William of Ockham, René Descartes, Baruch Spinoza, John Locke, Gottfried Wilhelm Leibniz, George Berkeley, David Hume, Immanuel Kant, Georg Hegel, William Bradley, A. N. Whitehead,

---

[1]This account shares broad similarities with the account put forward by J. P. Moreland and William Lane Craig, *Philosophical Foundations for a Christian Worldview*, 2nd ed. (Downers Grove, IL: IVP Academic, 2017), 163-68.

Martin Heidegger . . . I could go on, really, but I won't. But check out that star-studded lineup!

My students are even more surprised to hear that many of these same Western philosophers who devoted themselves to metaphysical inquiry also identified with some form of historic Christian faith, such as Augustine, Boethius, Anselm, Aquinas, Scotus, Ockham, Descartes, Locke, Leibniz, Kant, and many others. There is a rich historical pedigree in the Christian tradition for engaging in careful, philosophical reflection on the nature of reality.

GETTING STARTED

I'm inclined to think that we should begin our metaphysical reflection with what we take ourselves to be reasonably justified in believing (at least initially), prior to our theoretical reflection on the ultimate nature and structure of reality. Prior to cracking open a metaphysics textbook for serious study, what do we reasonably take ourselves to know about reality?

What, exactly, do I mean here? Simply stated: Serious metaphysical reflection does not arise out of a vacuum; it starts with and is continuously shaped by what you already reasonably believe on the basis of other areas of inquiry. To be frank, it is hard to see where else one *could* start their serious study of metaphysics than from the standpoint of what they already reasonably believe to be true about the world. Even more, it is hard to see what is problematic with this methodological approach to philosophical study in general, and metaphysics in particular. If one holds reasonably justified beliefs regarding an area of inquiry, say theology or science or history, then shouldn't one bring those beliefs to bear on their serious study of metaphysics? It's hard to see why not, or at least it's hard for *me* to see why not. It strikes me as extremely naive to think that we can or even should bracket out all our prior, reasonably held beliefs about the world before we get on with the study of metaphysics. After all, we have to begin our serious metaphysical reflection *somewhere*, do we not?

More specifically, allow me to unpack two different categories of reasonable belief that I think should guide the Christian philosopher, at least initially, when doing philosophy in general, and metaphysics in particular: *pre-theoretical beliefs* and *Christian theological beliefs*.

PRE-THEORETICAL BELIEFS

We all come to our study of metaphysics with a host of beliefs about the world
that strike us as natural and intuitive; these beliefs just *seem* right on reflection.
Just as a sample, the following beliefs strike me as obviously true and intellectually "above board," we might say:

- I exist and am currently thinking.
- I have some degree of control over my actions.
- I could have been a truck driver.
- I am the very same person I was yesterday.
- I couldn't be one and the same thing as a turnip.
- It is impossible for God to cease to exist.
- I was once a teenager.
- My future grandchildren do not exist in any sense.

These are just a few of my "pre-theoretical beliefs," beliefs that seem true to me
on simple reflection, prior to my cracking open an introductory book on
metaphysics. These beliefs strike me as obvious, and they seem to fit my experience of the way the world truly is.

My initial acceptance of pre-theoretical beliefs of this sort is supported not
by philosophical argument, but by what some philosophers call "epistemic
seemings" or "rational intuitions." Many philosophers think that epistemic
seemings—the natural, intellectual pull that draws you toward these beliefs,
we might say—should be given (at least initial) weight in our theoretical reflection on the nature of reality. Unless we have some overriding reason to
cast these seemings aside, they should be treated as intellectually innocent
until proven guilty. This is one way of saying that epistemic seemings or intuitions, at least initially, should make a difference to *what* and *why* we believe
what we do about reality.[2] I'm inclined to think that pre-theoretical beliefs are
the sort of beliefs we are intellectually entitled to reason *from*; they are not

---

[2]See Michael DePaul and William Ramsey, eds., *Rethinking Intuition: The Psychology of Intuition
and its Role in Philosophical Inquiry* (Lanham, MD: Rowman & Littlefield, 1998), in general,
and in particular the essay by George Bealer, "Intuition and the Autonomy of Philosophy."
Richard Swinburne also defends what he calls "the principle of credulity" as a basic, *a priori*
epistemic principle that should guide our philosophical thinking. The principle of credulity
states that if it seems to S that P, and there are no known reasons to reject P, then S is epistemically justified in believing P. See Richard Swinburne, *Epistemic Justification* (Oxford: Clarendon,
2001), 141-49.

beliefs that we are required to reason *to* before we get going in the meta-physical task.[3]

I will draw heavily on a host of pre-theoretical beliefs in favor of certain metaphysical positions throughout the course of this book. For instance, one type of pre-theoretical belief that I think should be taken seriously in meta-physical reflection concerns various beliefs that I naturally hold about *myself*— namely, that I am a conscious, unified, embodied self that exists from one moment to the next and sees the world from a unique, first-person point of view. By my lights, I don't first argue for these straightforward beliefs about myself before I can reasonably believe them to be true (it would be odd to think that in order for me to reasonably hold these beliefs, I would first need to provide a philosophical argument to support them). Rather, these beliefs strike me as obvious, and many of them are so rudimentary to my ordinary experience of myself (kind of like the background music that sets the tone of a room) that it is difficult to imagine any of them being false. The pre-theoretical belief that I continue to exist in my entirety from one moment of time to the next (a view known in contemporary metaphysics as "endurantism" regarding how objects persist through time) is deeply entrenched and should only be given up at the greatest of costs. If a metaphysical view about how objects or persons in particular exist from one moment of time to the next were to cut against this well-grounded, pre-theoretical belief, it would be a serious mark against it, at least in my opinion.

A quick word of clarification is in order at this point. While pre-theoretical beliefs strike us as true and worthy of acceptance on their face, they are not infallible; that is, pre-theoretical beliefs are not *guaranteed* to be true, just because they seem to have the ring of truth to them. In fact, many things that seem obvious to us turn out to be false (beliefs about *perception*: I seem to see water on the road when there is not; beliefs about *memories*: I seem to re-member winning the state championship when I did not; beliefs about *logic* and *reason*: the argument seems to be impeccable, when it is not; beliefs about the *testimony* of others: that person seems to be credible and honest, when they are not; etc.). While pre-theoretical beliefs (and the epistemic seemings

---

[3]One of the chief exemplars of this model in contemporary metaphysics was Roderick Chisholm in his book *Person and Object* (La Salle, IL: Open Court, 1976). For a discussion of this general methodological approach in Aristotle, see Christopher Shields, "The Phainomenological Method in Aristotle's Metaphysics," in *Aristotle on Method and Metaphysics*, ed. Edward Feser (New York: Palgrave MacMillan, 2013).

or rational intuitions that support them) may be innocent until proven guilty, it is possible for them to be proven guilty, at least in principle. Taking these beliefs seriously when doing metaphysics doesn't mean that we uncritically lean on them come what may, that is, without the possibility of such beliefs being mistaken. While these beliefs (and how things seem to us initially) serve as helpful guides along the way, they are not infallible indicators of the truth. But, in my view, in order for such beliefs to be reasonably overturned it would take a substantive amount of philosophical evidence to do so.

One theological reason for taking pre-theoretical beliefs seriously when doing metaphysics is the fact that God has purposefully created human beings in his image with intellectual capacities that are aimed at the truth and designed to make contact with reality in its various dimensions.[4] This point was raised in the previous chapter about the general reliability of human cognitive faculties to make contact with the world as God created it. We were not only created to understand reality in its intricate complexity—even nonphysical reality such as the human soul as well as God himself as our true and highest good (John 17:3)— we were also created in the divine image to rule and exercise dominion over the created order (Genesis 1:27-28). The creation mandate itself assumes God has equipped human beings with the relevant cognitive equipment to be God's vice-regents on earth and to intelligently steward the creation well (evidenced in rightly ordered science, art, technology, and humanities). While things aren't so hopeful on evolutionary naturalism (see chap. 2), I think the doctrine of the *imago Dei* provides reasonable grounds to expect at least some of our higher-order cognitive capacities to be generally reliable (all things considered)—even those faculties that are relevant to our discovering deep metaphysical truths about reality (e.g., truth, created natures or essences, laws of nature).

CHRISTIAN THEOLOGICAL BELIEFS

The second category of reasonable belief that I think Christians should bring to bear on metaphysical reflection is Christian theological belief, beliefs about the nature and activity of the triune God and all things in relation to God, grounded in the authority and testimony of Holy Scripture.[5] One's

---

[4]This is not to deny the distinctively noetic effects of sin, the corruptive effects of sin on human intellectual faculties and their operations.

[5]For an excellent treatment of Scripture as divine testimony that interacts with contemporary work in the epistemology of testimony, see Mats Wahlberg, *Revelation as Testimony: A Philosophical-Theological* Study (Grand Rapids, MI: Eerdmans, 2014).

metaphysical views—whether about existence itself, the nature of truth, properties/universals, substance, time, God, consciousness, free will, the human person, etc.—should at the very least be in accord with (and not inconsistent with) the explicit or implicit teaching of Scripture. As distinctively Christian philosophers, we ought to take the deliverances of the consensual Christian theological tradition as a genuine body of justified true belief that we reason *from*, and not necessarily *to*, before we engage in formulating metaphysical views about the fundamental structure of reality.[6]

Let me briefly say a word about the interplay between metaphysics and Christian theology as two vital areas of inquiry. First, well-grounded theological beliefs can serve as the conceptual backdrop by which one can evaluate conflicting metaphysical views about the nature of reality. For example, a robust Christian doctrine of God and creation—which entails a commitment to both material and immaterial reality—can help guide the Christian in rejecting views of ultimate reality that restrict what exists to what is physical or material (more on this in chap. 4). Likewise, a robust theological anthropology—where human beings are uniquely created in the divine image and are morally responsible for their actions—can serve as a guardrail against a certain metaphysical picture that rejects outright the existence of free will or affirms the view that human beings are nothing more than electrochemical machines fit for propagating DNA.[7] Thus, well-grounded Christian theological beliefs should both guide and guard the Christian philosopher when doing metaphysics.

It may be helpful to know that this standpoint—starting one's metaphysical inquiry with well-grounded Christian belief—is by no means unique to the *Christian* metaphysician. Even naturalist metaphysicians, those philosophers who think the natural world is all that exists and thus there is no God (classically defined) nor any being sufficiently like God, are upfront about their background *anti-theological* beliefs that they freely bring to the table. David Armstrong, an ardent metaphysical naturalist and one of the most influential metaphysicians of the latter half of the twentieth century, begins his small

---

[6]This is not to say that such theological beliefs are incapable of being reasoned *to* in some sense, not at all. Rather, it is to make the point that before we get to thinking metaphysically, Christians need not rationally justify their background theological beliefs; they are well within their intellectual rights to bring such beliefs with them to the metaphysical table.

[7]See Richard Dawkins, *River out of Eden: A Darwinian View of Life* (New York: Basic Books, 1995), 133.

volume *Sketch for a Systematic Metaphysics*—indeed is the very first sentence of the book—with the following assertion:

> I begin with the assumption that all that exists is the space-time world, the physical world as we say. What argument is offered for this assumption? All I can say is that this is a position that many—philosophers and others—would accept . . . So let us start from this position and see if a coherent metaphysical scheme, one that gives a plausible answer to many of the great problems of metaphysics, can be erected on this relatively narrow foundation.[8]

Consequently, while the informed Christian metaphysician can certainly supply a host of philosophical reasons in favor of their Christian theological beliefs, the point here is that they are not *required* to do so before they begin serious metaphysical reflection as a Christian (no more than a metaphysical naturalist is *required* to do so before they get on with serious metaphysical reflection as a naturalist).[9]

Turning now to the second way in which metaphysics and Christian theology interact, it is often the case that adequately formulating certain core Christian doctrines is aided by the use of fine-grained metaphysical concepts and distinctions. An old, now long-dead Christian theologian once put it like this, "A theologian can miss metaphysics and logic no less than a carpenter a hammer and a soldier weapons."[10] Hammers help carpenters do what they do with precision and care. While a carpenter may certainly use another object like a steel-toed shoe to eventually get the job done, it would be much less precise and less adequate to the task. And what is true of carpenters and hammers is also true of theologians and metaphysics.

This is perhaps most clearly the case regarding the use of distinctively metaphysical terms and concepts like essence, substance (Gk. *ousia*), and person (Gk. *hypostasis*; *supposit*) in formulating an orthodox doctrine of the Trinity as defined by the Nicaean-Constantinopolitan Creed in 381. This standard symbol of sound biblical teaching states that Christ, the eternal Word, is of the very *same* essence or substance as the Father (Gk. *homoousios*),

---

[8]D. M. Armstrong, *Sketch for a Systematic Metaphysics* (New York: Oxford University Press, 2010), 1.

[9]For more on this idea of a Christian's bringing their theological commitments to the philosophical table, see the now classic address by Alvin Plantinga, "Advice to Christian Philosophers," in *The Analytic Theist: An Alvin Plantinga Reader*, ed. James F. Sennett (Grand Rapids, MI: Eerdmans, 1998).

[10]This quote is from seventeenth century Dutch Reformed theologian Gisbertus Voetius. Quoted in Herman Selderhuis, *A Companion to Reformed Orthodoxy* (Leiden: Brill, 2013), 33.

and not of merely a *similar* essence or substance as the Father (Gk. *homoiousios*); "Light from Light, true God from true God, begotten not created, of the same essence [*homoousion*] as the Father, through whom all things came into being," as the creed beautifully puts it.[11] Thus, the historic Christian church believed that certain metaphysical concepts and distinctions were a help (not a hindrance) in adequately conveying sound biblical teaching concerning the full divinity of the Son and his ontological equality with the Father (Colossians 1:15; Hebrews 1:3).

The very same applies to the formulation of a historic, orthodox doctrine of the incarnation. According to Scripture and authoritative church teaching as expressed in the Chalcedonian creed in 451, Jesus Christ has two distinct natures, one human and one divine, that are inseparably united in a single person (Gk. *hypostasis*). As the Chalcedonian creed puts it, Jesus Christ is:

> of the same reality [*homoousion*] as God as far as his deity is concerned and of the same reality [*homoousion*] as we are ourselves as far as his humanness is concerned . . . in two natures; without confusing the two natures, without transmuting one nature into the other, without dividing them into two separate categories, without contrasting them according to area or function. The distinctiveness of each nature is not nullified by the union. Instead, the properties of each nature are conserved and both natures concur in one person and in one *hypostasis*.[12]

Note the distinctively metaphysical concepts at play in the creed: Jesus is one in *being* with the Father as to his divine nature and one in *being* with us as to his human nature, and his two natures were mysteriously *united* in his single person or *hypostasis*. As those familiar with their church history know, the Chalcedonian creed is carefully crafted—metaphysical concepts and all—to safeguard against certain views about the person of Christ that fell short of sound biblical teaching (Eutychianism, Nestorianism, etc.).[13] The key point here is to note that the church fathers were keen to employ distinctively *metaphysical* terms and concepts (being/essence, nature, person, *hypostasis*) as

---

[11]"The Constantinopolitan Creed," in John H. Leith, *Creeds of the Churches*, 3rd ed. (Louisville, KY: John Knox, 1982), 33.

[12]"The Definition of Chalcedon," in Leith, *Creeds of the Churches*, 36.

[13]The christological heresy known as Eutychianism (also known as Monophysitism) is the view that there is only a single nature in the person of Christ, a blend of humanity and divinity. Nestorianism is the view that there are two distinct persons in Christ, one human person and one divine person.

guardrails against aberrant teaching and thus adequately steward right biblical teaching about the very *identity* of Jesus of Nazareth. All in all, metaphysics and Christian theology can mutually inform and reinforce one another in the task of understanding the ultimate nature of reality.

THEOLOGICAL HABITS OF MIND FOR CHRISTIAN METAPHYSICIANS

We've looked at some general methodological considerations regarding how a Christian might approach the serious intellectual study of metaphysics. In addition to these more formal, methodological considerations, I want to draw your attention to three habits of mind or intellectual character traits that I think should aptly describe the Christian metaphysician: Theo-Centric, Scriptural, and Creedal.

To start, what exactly is a "habit of mind"? It may be helpful to think of a habit in general as an ingrained tendency to think or behave in a particular way. For example, somewhere along the way I've acquired the bad habit, or the ingrained tendency, of picking my fingernails. I'm far beyond having to consciously think about picking my nails; it has become automatic for me, or second nature as Aristotle would have said. The bad habit remains even when I currently am not picking my nails. Thus, habits are not to be equated with how one thinks or acts on any given occasion. Rather, habits are much more settled aspects of the person as they help explain how one thinks or acts on any given occasion. In this way, habits are like deep grooves or ruts that have been developed over time by repeated patterns of thinking and acting, just like water's continually running down a hill will eventually produce a deep groove in the hillside. Once the grooves are carved out, they explain why all subsequent water flows in the direction that it does. Your moral and intellectual character is the sum total of your moral and intellectual habits, and your character constitutes the kind of person you are and governs how you think and act.

In his insightful and deeply pastoral essay "Letter to an Aspiring Theologian," Christian theologian Kevin Vanhoozer responds to a reader's question about the best route to becoming a Christian theologian.[14] In his response, Vanhoozer commends several habits of mind that he thinks ought to

---

[14]Kevin J. Vanhoozer, "Letter to an Aspiring Theologian: How to Speak of God Truly," *First Things*, August 2018, www.firstthings.com/article/2018/08/letter-to-an-aspiring-theologian.

characterize the Christian theologian in the undertaking of the theological task. In a similar spirit, I'd like to lay out three habits of mind—ingrained tendencies regarding how to conduct oneself intellectually—that, I think, aspiring Christian metaphysicians should strive to cultivate and deepen as much as they can this side of heaven.

A THEO-CENTRIC HABIT OF MIND

First, I think the Christian metaphysician should strive to cultivate a distinctively *theo-centric* habit of mind. While the word "theo-centric" can be overused in certain contexts, by a theo-centric habit of mind I mean one whose center of intellectual gravity is oriented toward the triune God and how all things are "*from* him and *through* him and *to* him. . . . To him be glory forever. Amen" (Romans 11:36, my emphasis).

More concretely, adopting a theo-centric posture when doing metaphysics means that one's learned default intellectual posture should be the tendency to situate any existing entity whatsoever (other than God), E, in light of E's ultimate source in God, E's original and continual existence as caused by God, and E's being finally ordered to God. When done well, the Christian's exploration of ultimate reality in light of the triune God ought to eventually lead, at some point or other, to praise and adoration ("To him be glory forever. Amen" [Romans 11:36]). Well-formed Christian metaphysical inquiry, indeed *all* intellectual inquiry, ought to culminate in doxology and praise.

Let me put an even finer point on the matter, and perhaps risk being overly technical at this point. By my lights, inhabiting a theo-centric posture when doing metaphysics (both in *method* and in *content*) involves taking God's nature, existence, and activity (who God *is* and what he *does*) as explanatorily relevant in some way or other to the nature, existence, and activity of *all* beings that are not God. If E is not God, then God will be relevant in the explanation of the existence, nature, and activity of E, in some way or other. I will say more in a bit about the scriptural foundation for this theo-centric posture, and why a Christian metaphysician ought to strive to cultivate a theo-centric habit of mind in their metaphysical study. We will also have the chance to explore particular, concrete examples of this posture throughout the course of the book when it comes to various issues in contemporary metaphysics. Suffice it to say at this point that I first and foremost have in view a stable, settled posture that instinctively approaches all of creaturely reality, as well as every metaphysical issue that pertains to creaturely reality, in light of its relation to the triune God.

A SCRIPTURAL HABIT OF MIND

Second, I'm inclined to think that a Christian philosopher, one who takes Holy Scripture to be authoritative on all matters to which it speaks, should aim to embody a *scriptural* habit of mind. But what, exactly, does a scriptural habit of mind consist in? As with "theo-centric," the label "scriptural" is often bandied about without ever being defined in any substantive sense. Here it may be helpful to first try to unpack a clear and concise way of understanding a view's being scriptural, with an eye toward developing this sense into a full-blown habit of mind.

In my estimation, one of the most helpful discussions concerning what it means for a belief or view to be scriptural comes from the work of Thomas McCall, a Christian theologian who is sure-footed in the analytic philosophical tradition.[15] McCall seeks to get clear on what, exactly, we mean when we say our favored theological view is "scriptural." He offers the following precise categories as to the various ways in which a theological proposition P (e.g., that God is triune, that salvation is by grace alone through faith alone, etc.) may be considered scriptural ("S"):

S1: The Bible, properly (and theologically) interpreted, contains sentences that explicitly assert P.

S2: The Bible, properly interpreted, contains sentences that entail P.

S3: The Bible, properly interpreted, contains sentences that are consistent with P and suggest P.

S4: The Bible, properly interpreted, contains sentences that do not entail ~P (the negation of P), and are consistent with P (but does not suggest P; merely is neutral with respect to P).[16]

S1 and S2 capture the notion that a theological position P is scriptural in the strongest sense of the word, in that scriptural teaching requires the affirmation of P. For example, if the Bible explicitly (S1) or even implicitly (S2) teaches the

[15]See Thomas H. McCall, *An Invitation to Analytic Christian Theology* (Downers Grove, IL: IVP Academic, 2015), 55-56.
[16]McCall, *Invitation to Analytic Christian Theology*, 55-56.

deity of Christ (P), then the Christian philosopher who gives pride of authoritative place to Scripture ought to affirm the deity of Christ (P). Or, more indirectly and perhaps more controversially, if Jesus' teaching about God's judgment in the life to come entails a view about the metaphysical makeup of human beings as including body *and* soul (Matthew 10:26-33), then the Christian metaphysician ought to affirm such a metaphysical view of the human being as well.[17]

By contrast, S3 and S4 capture a weaker sense in which a theological position P can be considered scriptural. S3 claims that P is scriptural if Scripture is both *consistent* with P and includes teaching that *suggests* P (though Scripture does not strictly *entail* P).[18] S4 is weaker still in saying that P is scriptural if Scripture is *merely* consistent with P,[19] and Scripture nowhere explicitly or implicitly denies P.

With the distinctions among S1-S4 in hand, let's turn to molding these insights into a scriptural habit of mind, as I recommend above. I want to suggest that Christians engaged in the study of metaphysics should strive to cultivate a certain scriptural posture of mind, a settled tendency to conform their metaphysical beliefs about the nature and structure of reality as closely to scriptural teaching as possible. The default posture of the Christian metaphysician (or at least one who takes Scripture to be authoritative) should be one of actively leaning into scriptural teaching about the reality of God and all things in relation to God, striving to identify the metaphysical commitments of Scripture (S1), to draw out the metaphysical commitments that Scripture *entails* (S2) and *suggests* (S3), and to identify what metaphysical views are *minimally consistent* with scriptural teaching (S4).

---

[17]Both S1 and S2 are arguably in view when the *Westminster Confession of Faith* (1646) 1.6 states, "The whole counsel of God concerning all things necessary for his own glory, man's salvation, faith and life, is either expressly set down in Scripture [S1], or by good and necessary consequence may be deduced from Scripture [S2]." See "The Westminster Confession," in Leith, *Creeds of the Churches*, 195.

[18]I admit that the difference between Scripture's *entailing* P and *suggesting* P is not clear on its face. Let's try an example. The claim "The apple is red" entails (and does not merely suggest) the further claim that "the apple is colored." To be red is to *necessarily* be colored; it simply can't be true that a thing is red without it also being true that it is colored. However, the claim "Tim is tall" *suggests* (but doesn't at all entail) the further claim "Tim is at least 5 feet 5 inches." There is no entailment here since the claim "Tim is at least 5 feet 5 inches tall" does not *necessarily* follow from the claim "Tim is tall." He could be some other exact height under 5 feet 5 inches that the speaker or the relevant community considers tall (e.g., where someone's being 5 feet tall is considered tall relative to the wider community).

[19]I say merely consistent with P since Scripture doesn't teach anything that is indicative or suggestive of P. As McCall points out, Scripture "does not suggest P; merely is neutral with respect to P."

This is certainly no easy task in practice, I might add. Scripture doesn't always wear its metaphysical commitments or entailments on its sleeve, we might say. Nevertheless, it is important to keep in mind that I am commending here a general posture toward doing metaphysics as a Christian, an ingrained habit of mind first and foremost. As such, the intellectual reflexes of the Christian metaphysician should involve, whenever possible, the attempt to conform their metaphysical views to scriptural teaching in the most robust sense possible, in particular along the lines of S1-S3.

As contemporary issues in metaphysics are often far removed from the explicit or implicit teaching of Scripture (think of the nature of time, modality, substance, parts and wholes, etc.), conforming one's metaphysical views to Scripture along the lines of S1-S3 may not be feasible in every case. After all, what, if anything, does Scripture have to say about natures or essences, about metaphysical necessity and possibility, or about the nature of creaturely persistence through time? For what it's worth, I tend to think that Scripture has a great deal more to say on metaphysical matters than most realize, assuming a view of what it means to be scriptural along the lines of S1-S3 (but alas, you'll have to wait and see exactly what these matters are in the chapters to follow). But in cases where Scripture is largely silent about teaching that bears directly or indirectly on a particular metaphysical topic, the Christian metaphysician should strive, at the very least, to hold metaphysical views that are minimally consistent with the scriptural teaching in terms of S4; that is, Scripture should not explicitly or implicitly teach anything contrary to one's stated metaphysical views. If Scripture does so teach, this is a decisive reason to abandon the metaphysical view in question.

What might it look like for scriptural teaching to authorize a particular metaphysical view along the lines of S1-S3? A quick example here might help. It is interesting to note that Scripture clearly employs the terms "nature," "natural," "being," or "form" to express the idea that some features, aspects, or behaviors of a thing are more central than others in accounting for what that thing *is*—its *essence*. Scripture clearly attributes one or more of these terms to God,[20] nonhuman beings,[21] human beings,[22] and certain human behaviors.[23]

---

[20]"[His] invisible attributes, namely, his eternal power and divine nature [*theiotēs*]" (Romans 1:20); "partakers of the divine nature [*physeōs*]" (2 Peter 1:4); "[Jesus Christ], who, though he was in the form [*morphē*] of God" (Philippians 2:6).

[21]"[You] were enslaved to those that by nature [*physis*] are not gods" (Galatians 4:8).

[22]"Gentiles, who . . . by nature [*physis*] do what the law requires" (Romans 2:14).

[23]Some are "contrary to nature [*physikōs*]" and others "natural [*physis*]" (Romans 1:26-27).

Although I can't make the full case here, I think these passages harbor significant metaphysical commitments and implications about the way reality is structured in a basic, metaphysical sense. These scriptural passages either explicitly (S1) or implicitly affirm (S2) or suggest (S3) that there are deep truths about what things are (and are not) in the most basic ontological sense, and such truths are not made true by mere human convention or social agreement (or products of the way we use language). However the Christian philosopher unpacks the details concerning essences or natures (see chap. 6), this is an example of how scriptural teaching can shape one's metaphysical views about essence and modality.[24]

A CONFESSIONAL HABIT OF MIND

Let me conclude this section with a third and final habit of mind, what I'll call a *confessional* habit of mind. Christian metaphysicians operating out of a confessional habit of mind see themselves as thinking alongside of and in service to the Christian tradition, both past and present. More than anything, this posture aims to capture the insight that the Christian metaphysician does not do metaphysics in a historical and theological vacuum, nor do they undertake metaphysical inquiry solely for the purpose of the individual benefit of a deeper understanding of reality. For the Christian, metaphysical inquiry is communal in the sense that it should always be directed toward the good of the other, from beginning to end. Let's look at these two facets of a confessional habit of mind in turn.

In the broadest sense, a confessional habit of mind involves a settled awareness that one is standing—indeed thinking—on the shoulders of Christian intellectual and spiritual titans that have gone before. We are part of an age-old conversation that is filled to the brim with Christian wisdom and insight about the nature and structure of ultimate reality. This collective repository of Christian wisdom about metaphysical matters should be carefully consulted and engaged (whether critically or constructively) in one's own contemporary metaphysical reflection. A confessional habit of mind actively leans into this repository of philosophical wisdom, at times for insight and at other times for scrutiny.

---

[24]For an example of a metaphysical view's failing to meet even the weak, minimal standard for being scriptural laid out in S4, see the discussion on "Some Naturalist-Friendly Theories of Existence" in chap. 4.

More specifically, operating out of a confessional habit of mind involves reasoning within a particular, theological context. The Christian philosopher will, at the very least, faithfully operate within the theological parameters that mark out mere historic, orthodox Christianity, as expressed in the ecumenical creeds and councils of the undivided Christian church. To inhabit a confessional posture in this sense is to be a faithful recipient and ardent defender of historic, orthodox Christian teaching.

One's metaphysical views about reality should adhere to and not be in tension with orthodox Christian teaching about God and all things in relation to God. The Christian metaphysician should humbly strive, when possible, to accurately characterize the nature of reality along the grain of orthodox Christian teaching, and not against it. This confessional habit of mind, this humble and receptive posture of the Christian philosopher, is illustrated nicely by the following words from Anselm of Canterbury (1033–1109):

> With witless arrogance they judge that what they cannot understand is in no way possible, rather than acknowledging in humble wisdom that many things are possible that they are unable to comprehend. Indeed, no Christian ought to argue that something the Catholic church believes with her heart and confesses with her lips is not true. Instead, always holding that same faith unswervingly, loving it, and living in accordance with it, a Christian ought to seek the reason of its truth as humbly as he can. If he is capable of understanding, let him give thanks to God. If he is not, let him not brandish his horns to scatter, but instead let him bow his head in reverent submission.[25]

Overall, this confessional posture—embodied in Anselm himself and his metaphysical and theological reflection—captures an old, tried-and-true way of thinking about of the relationship between Christian theology and philosophy. Historically, philosophy (perhaps especially metaphysics) has been understood to be the handmaiden and servant of Christian theology. At least in relation to the Christian theological tradition, the metaphysician is a humble servant in the house of the great Christian tradition, not a lord or master. Metaphysical categories and distinctions can serve the theological tradition by aiding precision, clarity, and a deeper conceptual understanding of

---

[25]Anselm, *On the Incarnation of the Word* in *Anselm: Basic Writings*, trans. Thomas Williams (Indianapolis, IN: Hackett Publishing, 2007), 215.

Christian doctrines, and therein help draw out the conceptual implications of God's revelation in Scripture for all of human life.

In this way, the Christian metaphysician inquires not simply for the sake of a deeper and more robust understanding of the nature of reality. This aim, mind you, is well and good and indeed commendable for its own sake. However, the intellectual labor of the Christian metaphysician should also aim to benefit the entire Christian community. One way of doing so involves deepening and strengthening the intellectual foundations of "the faith that was once for all delivered to the saints" (Jude 3). More specifically, the Christian metaphysician can serve the church by helping the saints come to a deeper and fuller understanding—by way of careful, metaphysical reflection on the great truths of the Christian faith—of the God they confess in prayer, praise, and proclamation.

THEOLOGICAL METAPHYSICS AND GOD OVER ALL

In the final section of the chapter, and in the spirit of my remarks above about the three habits of mind that I think should guide Christian metaphysical inquiry, I want to unpack a particular and vitally important theological truth about God that, I believe, should anchor and guide our metaphysical inquiry going forward.

The doctrine of divine aseity (*a se* means "from himself" in Latin), roughly the view that God is absolutely self-existent and the ultimate source of all that is not God, has been monumentally influential in the history of Christian thought. According to the doctrine of divine aseity, the triune God does not receive his existence and life from anyone or anything else (John 5:26). On the contrary, the triune God is the originating fount and giver of existence and life to absolutely everything that is not God. "The God who made the world and everything in it," the apostle Paul states in Acts 17:24-28, "he himself gives to all mankind life and breath and everything. . . . 'In him we live and move and have our being.'"

I offer the doctrine of divine aseity here as a metaphysical anchor and guide or, to use a more archaic yet fitting term, a "lodestar." According to the *Oxford English Dictionary*, the word *lodestar* originated as a navigational term that meant "a star that shows the way" and referred primarily to the North Star (a.k.a. Polaris).[26] Before the invention of the compass, sailors used the North

---

[26]*Oxford English Dictionary,* s.v. "lodestar (n)."

Star as a fixed point of reference to navigate the seas at night. This is because the North Star is located nearly at the point around which the entire Northern sky turns, the north celestial pole, which is why the North Star is also called the "pole star." In short, the North Star signals the way due north.

In the same way, I want to suggest that the doctrine of divine aseity be due north theologically for the Christian metaphysician; all our metaphysical theorizing should turn on this vitally important theological truth. Let me briefly turn to saying a bit more about the scriptural, theological, and historical aspects of divine aseity and the role I see it playing in metaphysical inquiry.

One striking feature of the scriptural narrative from beginning to end is that it paints a composite picture of the utter completeness and sufficiency of the being of the triune God in himself, as well as the independence of God's existence in relation to creatures. God is the rock-bottom metaphysical reality; the existence of every other thing derives or borrows its existence from God, the fount and foundation of all created being.

From Genesis to Revelation, we find the triune God speaking all creaturely reality into existence, freely entering into covenantal relationships with some of those created beings, and bringing creation to its completion in loving fellowship with God. There is an inexhaustible metaphysical depth to who God is that radically sets him apart from his creatures (Job 11:7-10; Romans 11:33; 1 Corinthians 2:10; 1 Timothy 6:15-16).

Throughout Isaiah 40–48 we find the constant refrain in the mouth of God (six times in eight chapters), "To whom then will you compare me, that I should be like him?" (Isaiah 40:25) and "To whom will you liken me and make me equal, and compare me, that we may be alike?" (Isaiah 46:5). God is, we might say, utterly dissimilar to his creatures in that God is not of the same metaphysical order as created beings. While human beings may be like God in important ways (Genesis 1:27-28), God in himself is in no way like creatures.

And this is not an uncommon theme throughout Scripture, I might add. Rather, there are pervasive patterns of biblical discourse that attest to God's primacy as the fount and ontological source of everything other than himself. The apostle Paul emphasizes that there are "all things" (Gk. *ta panta*) and then there is God: "From him and through him and to him are all things [*ta panta*]" (Romans 11:36), and "God . . . from whom are all things [*ta panta*] . . . through whom are all things [*ta panta*] and through whom we exist" (1 Corinthians 8:6), and "he is before all things, and in him all things [*ta panta*] hold together" (Colossians 1:17). Likewise, the apostle John, listening in on the heavenly liturgy, hears the angelic hosts proclaim, "Worthy are you, our Lord and God, to receive glory and honor and power, for you created all things [*ta panta*], and by your will they existed and were created" (Revelation 4:11). The biblical pattern, then, is this: There is God, and there are all things. In this specific sense, God is not a "thing" alongside other things; rather, there is a clear metaphysical priority and supremacy to God in relation to every being that is not God. This sizable, indeed incommensurable, metaphysical gap between God and creatures serves as a kind of intellectual guardrail—a metaphysical and theological grammar, we might say—for thinking and speaking about God and all things in relation to God.[27]

Isaiah 40–48 further illustrates this metaphysical gap between God and creatures by considering the folly and futility of idolatry. Isaiah 44:9-20 vividly describes the created and utterly dependent nature of idols who owe their very existence to the ingenuity and handiwork of human craftsmen. Every aspect of the idol, its existence, shape, material makeup, position, and so on, is derived from the creator of the idol.

In sharp contrast to the Babylonian idols that have neither breath nor life, God is the absolute and all-sufficient Creator and giver of life, "who created the heavens and stretched them out, who spread out the earth and what comes from it, who gives breath to the people on it and spirit to those who walk in it" (Isaiah 42:5). The utter, metaphysical absurdity of idolatry is brought to light even further by the fact that God himself is the giver of life to the very ones who fashion lifeless idols and fall at their feet in worship (compare with Jeremiah 10:1-10). Just as every aspect of an idol is derived from the creative activity of creatures, so too every aspect of creatures is derived from the creative activity of God. Idol worship is utterly futile, precisely because it is, in part, a failure to properly align oneself with ultimate reality; a misdirected metaphysics guides and governs misdirected worship.

---

[27]In fact, from these patterns of biblical speech about God, Augustine infers the following rule when speaking of the triune God, "Whatever is said of a nature, unchangeable, invisible and having life absolutely and sufficient to itself, must not be measured after the custom of things visible, and changeable, and mortal, or not self-sufficient." See Augustine, *The Trinity* 5.1.2, trans. Stephen McKenna (Washington, DC: Catholic University of America Press, 2002), 175-76. For an extremely helpful introduction to theologically informed biblical exegesis, see R. B. Jamieson and Tyler R. Wittman, *Biblical Reasoning: Christological and Trinitarian Rules for Exegesis* (Grand Rapids, MI: Baker Academic, 2022).

In fact, in sharp contrast to idols and those who create them, there is absolutely nothing about God that is derived from another, whether God's existence, understanding, justice, knowledge, life, and so on. For "whom did he consult, and who made him understand? Who taught him the path of justice, and taught him knowledge, and showed him the way of understanding?" (Isaiah 40:14) No one, of course! The idea that God's nature and existence are not explained by anything that is not God is a constant refrain throughout Scripture. The self-existence of the triune God is on display in the revelation of God's name to Moses in the burning bush, "I AM WHO I AM" (or "I WILL BE WHAT I WILL BE"; Exodus 3:14), which has historically been understood as saying (at least in part) that God alone accounts for God's existence, nature, and action. The apostle Paul, alluding to Job 41:11, says, "'For who has known the mind of the Lord, or who has been his counselor?' 'Or who has given a gift to him that he might be repaid?' For from him and through him and to him are all things" (Romans 11:34-36).

In fact, Paul is even more emphatic on this point about the metaphysical gap between God and creatures in his address to the intellectual elite of the Areopagus in Athens: "The God who made the world and everything in it, being Lord of heaven and earth, does not live in temples made by man, nor is he served by human hands, as though he needed anything, since he himself gives to all mankind life and breath and everything. . . . 'In him we live and move and have our being'" (Acts 17:24-28). Paul's point is clear: In contrast to the localized and finite "deities" that were worshiped among the Athenians, there is absolutely no need or lack in the true and living God.

It is precisely due to this fullness of being, this lack of need or deficiency in the life of the triune God, that God can so freely give of himself without being diminished or depleted in the least. God is the ever-full and ever-flowing fountain of being (Psalm 36:9), and we are the glad recipients of his free and gracious overflow.[28] God freely gives from the depths and abundance of who God is (Ephesians 3:7-21). In light of all God's gracious saving action toward us in the gospel, Paul erupts in doxology: "Oh, the depth of the riches and wisdom and knowledge of God! How unsearchable are his judgements and how inscrutable his ways!" (Romans 11:33).

---

[28]Of course, those in Christ share in the full and everlasting life of God in a unique way that is salvific and sanctifying (John 11:25).

As for everything other than the triune God, the apostle John is clear in the prologue to his gospel that: "In the beginning was the Word, and the Word was with God, and the Word was God. He was in the beginning with God. All things were made through him, and without him was not any thing made that was made" (John 1:1-3). According to John, there is the triune God, and there is everything else: "*All things* were made through him, and without him was not any thing made that was made" (John 1:3, my emphasis) and, elsewhere, "you created *all things*, and by your will they existed and were created" (Revelation 4:11, my emphasis).

Every thing that is not one and the same being as the triune God has been created by the triune God. *All* things. As if to rule out any existing entity (other than God) from finding its metaphysical source in anything but God, the apostle Paul clearly echoes this refrain when he says, "For by him all things were created, in heaven and on earth, visible and invisible, whether thrones or dominions or rulers or authorities—all things were created through him and for him" (Colossians 1:16). Don't miss this: for Paul and John, other than God himself, no existing entity whatsoever is excluded from God's creative activity. If something exists and is not God, its existence and nature is ultimately explained by God, for "there is one God, the Father, from whom are *all things* and for whom we exist, and one Lord, Jesus Christ, through whom are *all things* and through whom we exist" (1 Corinthians 8:6, my emphasis).

Divine aseity has been a center piece of an orthodox view of God throughout the Christian tradition. An aspect of divine aseity, namely God's being the source of all that is not God, finds support in the very first ecumenical council, the Council of Nicaea in 325, and is later reaffirmed at subsequent ecumenical councils such as First Constantinople (381), Ephesus (431), and Chalcedon (451).

Reflecting the biblical witness of the apostles John (John 1) and Paul (Colossians 1:16) in particular, the Council of Nicaea in 325 states, "We believe in one God, the Father, All Governing, creator of all things visible and invisible."[29] What's more, Christian theologians in the early church understood this aspect of God's aseity as unique to God *alone*. Everything that exists, other than God, is brought into existence by God; God is the *sole* uncreated reality.[30] As the

---

[29]"Creed of Nicaea," in Leith, *Creeds of the Churches*, 30.
[30]William Lane Craig, *God Over All: Divine Aseity and the Challenge of Platonism* (Oxford: Oxford University Press, 2016), chap. 2. See also G. L. Prestige, *God in Patristic Thought* (Eugene, OR: Wipf & Stock, 2008), chap. 2.

early church father Irenaeus (ca. 120–ca. 200) so clearly put it, "In all things God has the pre-eminence, who alone is uncreated, the first of all things, and the primary cause of the existence of all."[31]

We also find divine aseity enthusiastically reaffirmed across the wide spectrum of Christendom in various confessions, whether Roman Catholic, Reformed, Lutheran, Baptist, or Anglican. *The Westminster Confession of Faith* (as well as *The Second London Baptist Confession*) beautifully echoes a long-standing Christian tradition: "God has all life, glory, goodness, and blessedness in and of himself. He alone is all-sufficient in and unto himself, nor does he need any of his creations or derive any glory from them. Rather, he manifests his own glory in, by, unto, and on them. He is the only source of all being, by whom, through whom, and to whom everything exists."[32] In light of what I've said thus far, and for the sake of clarity going forward, I want to offer (and not argue for) a characterization of divine aseity that I consider to be theologically, scripturally, and historically well attested. But the reader needs to be aware that there is a great risk here of over-simplifying a complex, rich, and indeed ongoing discussion in contemporary theistic metaphysics about how best to characterize divine aseity. Take what I offer here as one particular way of thinking about divine aseity—a way that I believe best fits with Scripture and the ecumenical Christian tradition—and examine these issues for yourself.

With humility and trepidation, then, I offer the following twofold characterization of divine aseity:

Divine Aseity: (i) God alone is the ontologically sufficient condition for God's existence and nature, and (ii) everything that is not the same being as God is brought into existence and sustained in existence by God.[33]

The first clause, (i), means that nothing other than God himself suffices to explain *that* God is (God's existence) and *what* God is (God's essential nature). The second clause, (ii), conveys that everything other than God

[31]Irenaeus, *Against Heresies* 4.38.3, cited in Craig, *God over All*, 33.

[32]*The Westminster Confession of Faith in Modern English* (Orlando, FL: Evangelical Presbyterian Church, 2010), 6.

[33]This twofold characterization of divine aseity in terms of God in himself as well as God's relation to creatures (if there are any) is unpacked nicely in John Webster's essay "Life in and of Himself," in *God Without Measure: Working Papers in Christian Theology*, vol. 1 (London: Bloomsbury T&T Clark, 2018). For an excellent historical treatment of this concept of aseity, see Anselm of Canterbury, *Monologion 7*, in *Anselm: Basic Writings*, 13-15.

himself is created by and continually sustained in existence by God. It's important to point out that this characterization of divine aseity says something about how God is in himself as he is apart from creatures (clause (i)), as well as something about God in relation to creatures, everything that is not God (clause (ii)).

A Christian metaphysician operating out of theo-centric, scriptural, and confessional habits of mind will aim to ascribe metaphysical pride of place to God and God alone when engaged in metaphysical reflection. After much reflection (and change of mind, I might add), my own particular way of unpacking these particular methodological commitments leads me to adopt the above characterization of divine aseity (or something very similar) as a guide in my metaphysical reflection. Thus, as we will see in more detail in the chapters to follow, divine aseity is a theological lodestar that will shape and govern our thinking about the nature and structure of created reality in its various dimensions as freely willed by God.

GOING DEEPER: DOING METAPHYSICS AS A CHRISTIAN

Key Concepts in Metaphysics

- Moorean facts
- theoretical virtues

Historical

- Christopher Shields, "The Phainomenological Method in Aristotle's Metaphysics"
- Augustine, *The Trinity*, books 5-7
- Anselm of Canterbury, *Monologion*, chapters 1-17

Contemporary

- Roderick Chisholm, "Introduction," in *Person and Object*
- Mats Walberg, *Revelation as Divine Testimony: A Philosophical-Theological Study*
- Garrett DeWeese, *Doing Philosophy as a Christian*, chapters 2-4
- Ross D. Inman, *Christian Philosophy as a Way of Life: An Invitation to Wonder*

- Alvin Plantinga, "Advice to Christian Philosophers"
- William Lane Craig, "God: The Sole Ultimate Reality," in *God over All*
- W. Matthews Grant, "Aseity," in *The Routledge Encyclopedia of Philosophy*
- John Webster, "Life in and of Himself," in *God Without Measure: Working Papers in Christian Theology*, vol. 1
- R. B. Jamieson and Tyler R. Wittman, *Biblical Reasoning: Christological and Trinitarian Rules for Exegesis*, chap. 4

4

CREATURELY EXISTENCE

THE WONDER OF EXISTENCE

Pause, put this book down, and take a quick look around you. Look up, look down, and look side-to-side; and don't forget to look within too! All these things you are likely immediately aware of—the ceiling of the room you inhabit (or the sky if you're lucky), your shoes, yourself—exist. For all but the entrenched philosophical skeptic, this much seems right to us (could you be genuinely aware of them if they didn't exist?). It is also quite natural for us to make claims about the *nonexistence* of things, such as "unicorns do not exist" or "Harry Potter does not exist." Both existence and nonexistence claims of this sort are so mundane that many of us rarely, if ever, stop to ponder what it is we are actually saying when we speak this way.

Beyond existence or nonexistence claims, have you ever wondered about the mind-boggling notion of existence *itself*? Not just the various created things that exist and whether they could fail to exist, but about what it is for a creature to be or exist in the first place? What exactly *is* creaturely existence? What's the fundamental difference between creatures that exist and creatures that do not exist, such as Harry Potter and unicorns (spoiler alert: neither exists)?[1] Is it even coherent to talk and think about things that do not exist?

A FEW GUIDING QUESTIONS ABOUT EXISTENCE

While we often find ourselves wondering about the various things that exist (just hang around kids long enough and you'll see!), few of us rarely focus our

---

[1]"Not so," say some philosophers who hold that fictional entities like Harry Potter really do exist, but they're not the kind of entities you might expect. Fictional entities are abstract objects, objects that exist outside of space and time (like numbers and other mathematical entities). Harry Potter, on such views, exists but isn't the walking, talking, glasses-wearing, wand-wielding, flesh-and-blood wizard you might think he is ("He's" not even a person!). What a letdown!

wonder on the notion of existence or being *itself*.[2] What exactly *is* the nature of creaturely existence or being?

Notice that this question is to be distinguished from two very similar questions. First, it is a different type of question than another metaphysical question, the question "*What* exists?"—a question about the scope and extent of existing things. This latter question is a question about what belongs to the group of existing things, we might say. Rather, in asking what it is to *be* or *exist* in the first place, we are after something much deeper. It's a bit like the difference between asking a bouncer at a nightclub who is on the VIP list and who is not, and asking the bouncer what it takes to get on the VIP list in the first place.

Second, our guiding question here is different from the epistemological question "How do we *know* what exists?" This latter question is one about how we reliably determine what exists (say, on the basis of sound rational inference, empirical observation, or reliable testimony, including divine testimony in Scripture). Rather, our target metaphysical question ("What *is* existence?") is a much deeper question about the nature of existence itself.

In this section I want to explore several key questions about the contour of existence itself. In particular, we will look at the following guiding questions together:

1. *The Ways of Being Question*: Is there more than one way *to be* or *exist*?
2. *The Degrees of Being Question*: Is being or existence degreed? Can some things exist more or less than others?
3. *The Theory of Existence Question*: What is the best account of the nature of existence?

As we have seen, philosophical reflection on the nature of the various kinds of beings that purportedly exist—cats, numbers, persons, souls, and tulips—has taken center stage in a traditional approach to metaphysics in terms of categorial ontology. While it may be clear that there are various kinds of *beings* that exist, is it equally clear that there are various kinds of *being* as well? Is there more than one way to *be*? This is the "Ways of Being Question."

THE WAYS OF BEING QUESTION

In the Western philosophical tradition, by far the most common way of answering the Ways of Being Question has been in the affirmative: There is

---

[2]Unless otherwise noted I will use "existence" and "being" interchangeably.

more than one way to be.[3] Recall Aristotle's understanding of metaphysics
as the study of being qua being from chapter one, which included a study of
the various ways things exist. For Aristotle and later Aristotelian-minded
metaphysicians, "Being is divided into the ten categories not univocally, as
a genus into its species, but according to distinct modes of being."[4] This
means that for each different kind of being there corresponds a distinct way
or mode of being. These distinct ways of being are united by analogy, in the
same way that a gymnast, a schedule, and a rubber chicken can all be flexible
but not in exactly the same sense. Things that belong to the category of *Substance* for Aristotle, such as living organisms, exist in a primary or fundamental sense. In fact, substantial being is the primary or focal sense of being,
and entities that belong to other categories exist in a derivative way, as qualities or characteristics are derivative on substances (e.g., the redness of an
apple or the biological health of an organism). Aristotle underscores both
the many senses of being and the primacy of substantial being in particular
as follows:

> There are many senses in which a thing is said to be, but all refer to one
> starting-point; some things are said to be because they are substances, others
> because they are affections of substance, others because they are a process
> towards substance, or destructions or privations or qualities of substance, or
> productive or generative of substance, or of things which are relative to substance, or negations of some of these things or of substance itself.[5]

This Aristotelian view dominated the Western metaphysical landscape for
many centuries.

In the main, however, the vast majority of metaphysicians today emphatically reject the idea that there are various ways of being; they answer the Ways
of Being Question firmly in the negative. This is just to say that for many
contemporary philosophers, there is only one sense of being or existence;

---

[3]For a helpful overview of a ways of being ontology in contemporary metaphysics, see Joshua
Spencer, "Ways of Being," *Philosophy Compass* 7 (2012): 910-18. For a more classical, theological
treatment of this concept, see Steven Duby, *God in Himself: Scripture, Metaphysics, and the Task
of Christian Theology* (Downers Grove, IL: IVP Academic, 2019).
[4]See Aristotle, *Metaphysics* 4.2 (1003a33-1003b18), in *The Complete Works of Aristotle*, trans. Jonathan Barnes (Princeton, NJ: Princeton University Press, 1991), 2:42. The quote is from Thomas
Aquinas, *Physics* 3.5.15, in *Commentary on the Physics*, trans. Richard J. Blackwell, Richard J.
Spath, and W. Edmund Thirlkel (New Haven, CT: Yale University Press, 1963).
[5]Aristotle, *Metaphysics* 4.2 (1003b5–10).

everything that exists does so in precisely the same sense. While there may be various kinds of things that exist, there is only one way to exist.

What accounts for this sharp departure from the classical, Aristotelian answer to the Ways of Being Question? Many contemporary philosophers think there is something fundamentally defective about the very idea that there are different ways of being. Others report that they reject ways of being not on the basis of a philosophical argument but simply because of their extreme puzzlement over the concept itself and the lack of reasons given in its favor. Indeed, one well-known metaphysician has even said the view is an "extremely attractive position," one that "undergraduates fall effortlessly into. . . . But it is false."[6] Sorry undergraduates, this is not very high praise. However, there have been a number of philosophers who have offered substantive philosophical arguments against the view.[7]

The ways of being approach has, however, seen recent signs of new life in contemporary metaphysics in the form of what is called "ontological pluralism," the view that there are various ways of being (and not just a single way to be). Contemporary metaphysicians such as Kris McDaniel, Jason Turner, and Jeffrey Brower have aimed to restate and defend anew an affirmative answer to the Ways of Being question by interacting with contemporary objections to the view.[8]

While space does not allow me to unpack a detailed articulation and defense of ontological pluralism, let me gesture toward several reasons that have been offered in its defense. Kris McDaniel points out that there are several types of reasons one might give in favor of ontological pluralism. First, there may be distinctively *theological* reasons to think that there is more than one way to be or exist. This approach has significant historical precedent in the

---

[6]The quote is from Peter van Inwagen, "Meta-ontology" in *Ontology, Identity, and Modality: Essays in Metaphysics* (Cambridge: Cambridge University Press, 2001), 16-17. See also J. P. Moreland and William Lane Craig, *Philosophical Foundations for a Christian World*view, 2nd ed. (Downers Grove, IL: IVP Academic, 2017), 172-73; and E. J. Lowe, *More Kinds of Being: A Further Study of Individuation, Identity, and the Logic of Sortal Terms* (Malden, MA: Wiley-Blackwell, 2009), 4.

[7]See Peter van Inwagen, "Modes of Being and Quantification," *Disputation* 6 (2013): 1-24, and "Meta-Ontology," in *Ontology, Identity, and Modality*; and Trenton Merricks, "The Only Way to Be," *Noûs* 53, no. 3 (2019): 593-612.

[8]See primarily Kris McDaniel, "Ways of Being," in *Metametaphysics: New Essays on the Foundations of Ontology*, eds. David Chalmers and David Manley (New York: Oxford University Press, 2009), and "A Return to the Analogy of Being," *Philosophical and Phenomenological Research* 81, no. 3 (2010): 688-717; Jason Turner, "Ontological Pluralism," *Journal of Philosophy* 107, no. 1 (2010): 5-34; Jeffrey Brower, *Aquinas's Ontology of the Material World* (New York: Oxford University Press, 2014), section 2.4.

history of Christian thought in particular. Thomas Aquinas, for instance, followed the common medieval view that Aristotle's ten categories of being only strictly applied to *created* beings.[9] On this view, God is not on ontological par with creatures as God, strictly speaking, is not a common member of an ontological category (the category of *Substance*, to be exact) alongside created beings.[10] As such, while God and created beings can both be loosely called "substances," it is only in a highly qualified sense that this is the case.[11]

Interestingly enough, in this classical view, God's complete self-sufficiency and metaphysical independence was understood as a fundamentally different mode of being altogether, a mode of being that was unique to the triune God and thus radically different from creaturely categories as derivative modes of being. While the modes of being unique to God and creatures may be united by way of analogy (there must be something that makes them both modes of being, after all), God and creatures strictly do not exist in precisely the same way.

A second reason one might offer in favor of the classical ways of being approach is *phenomenological*. According to McDaniel, following German philosopher Martin Heidegger, we can arguably be phenomenologically aware of various ways of existing, that is, in our experience of reality as it presents itself to us.[12]

What, exactly, does this mean? Let me try to explain by way of an illustration. Consider the following two existing things as they present themselves to you in perceptual experience: clouds and oak trees. My own experience of a cloud, for example, is rather limited to my observation of them high above the earth and occasionally passing through them while flying in an airplane. Clouds appear to us as ephemeral beings, beings whose existence is radically thin and tenuous. The physical boundaries of a cloud

[9]Thomas Aquinas, *Summa Theologiae* I, q. 13. Jeffrey Brower points out that it is "the standard medieval view that the ten Aristotelian categories apply only to *created beings*." *Aquinas's Ontology*, 45.

[10]In *Summa Contra Gentiles* 1.25, Aquinas outright denies that God is strictly a substance for this reason. See Thomas Aquinas, *Summa contra Gentiles*, trans. Vernon J. Bourke (Notre Dame, IN: University of Notre Dame Press, 1975), 1:126-28. Again, Brower notes, "Insofar as God is an absolutely independent being, Aquinas insists that he exists in a way that is radically different from creatures—so different that he cannot be said to fall under any genus or species associated with the Aristotelian categories." *Aquinas's Ontology*, 44.

[11]See Aquinas, *Summa Theologiae* 1.13.5.

[12]McDaniel, "Return," 694-701.

strike us as nebulous and in constant flux; it is not always clear where one cloud ends and another begins.

Now, compare your experience of a cloud with your experience of a mature oak tree. Oak trees appear to us as living and stable beings; they are dynamic yet substantive and enduring beings. The physical boundaries of an oak tree strike us as stable and clear-cut; it is normally clear in our perceptual experience where one oak tree ends and where another begins. The idea here is supposed to be that our different phenomenological experiences of the being of clouds and oak trees convey not only that they are different kinds of *beings*, but that they have different kinds of *being*. Clouds and trees both exist, but they seem to exist in different ways.

Let's look at another example, one a bit closer to home we might say, to illustrate how one might have a phenomenological grasp of various ways of being. Consider a thinker and their thoughts, say, you and your current thoughts about whether there are various ways of being. You have a basic yet intimate awareness of yourself as a thinker, as well as a basic awareness of what you are thinking at present, your thoughts. Now, your basic, phenomenological awareness of yourself will likely convey to you something whose existence is stable and enduring, namely *you* as the stable and enduring subject of experience.

Contrast this basic awareness of yourself with your awareness of your thoughts, what it is that you are thinking *about* at present. Your awareness of your many thoughts will likely convey to you the existence of entities that are fleeting and perhaps "less substantial" than you as the stable subject of experience. Thoughts are, after all, radically dependent on thinkers from moment to moment; no thinkers, no thoughts, we might say. I think about God's goodness at one moment, my wife's tireless patience at another, and my three young children's boundless energy at another, and so on. Thoughts come and go, but the very same stable being—me, the thinker—remains the same through it all.

Might the fact that our first-person, phenomenological experience presents thinkers and thoughts to us in such radically different ways—thinkers as having an independent and stable sort of being, and thoughts having a dependent and fleeting sort of being—suggest that there are, in fact, different kinds of *being*, rather than just different kinds of *beings*? Perhaps. While there are some vocal contemporary critics of ontological pluralism, it is important to note that such an ontology has both rich historical precedent and some able contemporary proponents. And for these reasons, it should at the very least not be ignored or dismissed outright.

THE DEGREES OF BEING QUESTION

Next, we come to the "Degrees of Being Question": Is being or existence degreed? Can some things exist more or less than others? Some qualities come in degrees, like sweetness. Tea, for example, can be more or less sweet (depending on where you are in the country, perhaps). Is existence in any way like sweetness in this sense, admitting of degrees or gradations?

Note that this question is distinct from, yet not unrelated to, the Ways of Being Question. Most contemporary metaphysicians who answer in the negative to the Ways of Being Question do the same with respect to the Degrees of Being Question.[13] Existence is an all-or-nothing affair, they claim. In this way, existence is more like a traditional on-off light switch than a gradual dimmer switch. For many metaphysicians, the idea of having more or less light makes sense; the idea of having more or less being, not so much.

But is this really the case? Is being necessarily an all-or-nothing affair? There's a lot to say here, and I encourage you to dive in deeper beyond this chapter if you are interested (see the Going Deeper resources at the end of this chapter). Suffice it to say, at least historically, many philosophers and nonphilosophers alike have reached a different conclusion from most contemporary metaphysicians. Again, all I can do here is quickly gesture toward some initial considerations in favor of an affirmative answer to the Degrees of Being Question.[14]

Many (if not most) non-Christian and Christian philosophers in the premodern philosophical tradition, dating from Plato on up to the early modern period (roughly the seventeenth through the first half of the eighteenth century), were of the opinion that reality consisted of a great chain or "hierarchy of being." According to this view, being admits of different grades or

---

[13]Interestingly enough, as McDaniel points out, one could reject a ways of being ontology (ontological pluralism) yet still affirm that there are different degrees of the singular sense of existence. According to Richard Cross, medieval philosopher Duns Scotus, the Subtle Doctor as he is often called, arguably held just this view. See Richard Cross, *Duns Scotus* (New York: Oxford University Press, 1999), 31-39.

[14]See Kris McDaniel, "Degrees of Being," *Philosophers Imprint* 13, no. 19 (2013): 1-18, for a further explication and defense of the view that existence is degreed.

levels; some beings exist in a greater, fuller sense than others. Alexander Pope states this classical notion beautifully in his "Essay on Man": "Vast chain of being which from God began natures ethereal, human, angel, man, beast, bird, fish, insect, what no eye can see. No glass can reach, from infinite to thee. From thee to nothing."[15]

Atop the hierarchy or chain of being is the triune God, the supremely existing being who exists in the fullest possible sense. The hierarchy then continues downward to creatures, both immaterial and material, who exist in a lesser, attenuated sense, and finally terminates in that which has the lowest degree of being, almost nothingness.[16] As Augustine aptly puts it in his classic *City of God*, "To some He [God] gave Being more fully, and to others he gave it in a more restricted way; and so he arranged natural entities according to their degrees of being."[17] On this classical view, while all existing things have being in some sense and to some degree or other, some have being by the skin of their teeth, we might say (perhaps shadows, holes, cuts, and clouds).[18]

For some classical Christian thinkers such as Boethius (477–524) in his timeless book *The Consolation of Philosophy*, the degree to which a human has being, a being endowed with an intellect and a will, depends on the degree to which their will is aligned with that which is truly good and perfective of human nature.[19] So, those who give themselves over to that which is less than what they morally ought to be by divine design, to that which is truly morally evil and base for humans, diminish the degree to which they are truly human (they remain human, but become dehumanized in a sense). By contrast, the human being who orders their will around that which is truly good and fulfilling can be said to be more fully human, true to what human beings ought

---

[15]Alexander Pope, "An Essay on Man: Epistle 1," *Poetry Foundation*, n.d., https://www.poetry foundation.org/poems/44899/an-essay-on-man-epistle-i.

[16]Indeed, in his *Monologion* 28, the great medieval Augustinian theologian Anselm of Canterbury thought that creatures in general "barely exist" in comparison to the supreme being, who alone exists in an absolute, unqualified sense.

[17]Augustine, *City of God*, trans. Henry Bettenson (New York: Penguin Books, 2004), XII.2. For a robust contemporary analytic defense of the great chain of being (with some important qualifications), see David Oderberg, "Restoring the Hierarchy of Being," in *Neo-Aristotelian Metaphysics and the Theology of Nature*, eds. William M. R. Simpson, Robert C. Koons, and James Orr (New York: Routledge, 2021), and his *The Metaphysics of Good and Evil* (New York: Routledge, 2020), 208-12.

[18]Kris McDaniel refers to these very items as examples of what he calls "almost nothings." See McDaniel, "Being and Almost Nothingness," *Noûs* 44, no. 4 (2010): 628-49.

[19]Boethius, *The Consolation of Philosophy*, trans. Victor Watts (New York: Penguin Books, 1999), book IV.

to be by nature (again, they remain human, but they become more truly and authentically human, in a sense).[20]

To further illustrate, consider two fictional inhabitants of Middle-earth from the creative genius of J. R. R. Tolkien in *The Lord of the Rings*, the Nazgûl and Gollum (Sméagol). For those who need a quick refresher, the Nazgûl (or better known as Ringwraiths) are the dark and creepy (and ear-piercingly loud) ephemeral servants of Sauron who have become mere shadows of the beings they once were. Though they were once human kings, their excessive and destructive lust for power has transformed them into mere ontological shadows. In precisely the same way, Gollum, the once beloved hobbit (Sméagol), gradually ontologically dwindles into something less than what he once was, a shriveled parody of a hobbit. Both C. S. Lewis and J. R. R. Tolkien, it turns out, read Boethius carefully and were both steeped in a classical metaphysical worldview with the notion of a hierarchy of being at its foundation.[21]

While this, of course, all sounds a bit weird to the contemporary ear (does it, though?), for nearly two thousand years the notion of a hierarchy of being was the primary way in which philosophers made intelligible sense of reality in all of its complex layers and dimensions.[22] And for this reason, wherever one lands on this question, an affirmative answer to the Degrees of Being question should not simply be ignored or dismissed outright by contemporary metaphysicians.

THE THEORY OF EXISTENCE QUESTION

Let us move, then, to our third question, the "Theory of Existence Question," which asks, "What is the best account of the nature of existence?" Let me encourage you at the outset to not get spooked by the word "theory" or "theorizing"; it's harmless, really, at least once it is understood properly. When a

---

[20]For one of the most remarkable passages on this idea, see Boethius, *Consolation of Philosophy* IV.3.

[21]One could also point to further fictional examples of the great chain of being in the ontologically parasitic characters of Voldemort and the dementors in J. K. Rowling's Harry Potter series. Also, consider the enhanced ontological status of the residents of heaven, as well as the diminished ontological status of the heavenly visitors in C. S. Lewis's wonderful fictional work *The Great Divorce*.

[22]See Arthur Lovejoy's now classic *The Great Chain of Being* (Cambridge, MA: Harvard University Press, 2001) as well as a rigorous contemporary explication and defense of the view by Christian philosopher David Oderberg in his "Restoring the Hierarchy of Being." For Christian authors who are steeped in this classical, Christian metaphysical framework, see the work of C. S. Lewis and J. R. R. Tolkien, as mentioned.

philosopher sets out to develop a theory of X (whether a theory of existence, properties, knowledge, truth, goodness, beauty, etc.), what they are aiming at is a general and wide-ranging account of the various essential dimensions of X, what those dimensions are, and how they fit together. Moreover, it is important to keep in mind that philosophical theories are ultimately for the purpose of helping us better understand the way things are. Though the human intellectual capacity is remarkable in its power and scope, it nevertheless remains finite and severely limited in a host of ways. At their best, philosophical theories can help expand the scope of our cognitive grasp of reality and ready us for properly ordered action by providing us with the conceptual handles needed to better get a grip on reality—what is, what is true, and what is good—and to orient our lives accordingly.[23]

With that said, an adequate theory of existence itself should arguably aim to do several things.[24] First, it should fit with what we already take ourselves to reasonably believe about what does and does not exist; call this *the fittingness condition*. The careful reader may notice that the fittingness condition regarding an adequate theory of existence is a natural application of a methodological principle I articulated in chapter two, namely that we ought to at least begin our metaphysical theorizing with what we are already reasonably justified in believing to be the case.

Second, an adequate theory of existence should arguably account for what *could* exist, even if that thing doesn't *actually* exist (or is believed to not actually exist); call this *the possibility condition*. In other words, an adequate theory of existence should have the breadth to account for both the realm of what *is* and the realm of *what could have been*. For example, while gremlins (scaly and mischievous little creatures who like to wreak havoc) and unicorns do not actually exist, they conceivably *could* have, had God decided to bring them into existence.

Third, an adequate theory of existence must arguably be conceptually coherent; call this *the coherence condition*. What exactly do I mean here? For starters, a theory of existence (or any philosophical theory for that matter) should not be in tension with basic, fundamental laws of reality. The basic laws

---

[23]For more on the notion of philosophy and its essential role in living well in light of the gospel of Christ, see my *Christian Philosophy as a Way of Life: An Invitation to Wonder* (Grand Rapids, MI: Baker Academic, 2023).

[24]I owe these preliminary insights regarding an adequate theory of existence to Moreland and Craig, *Philosophical Foundations for a Christian Worldview*, 173-74.

of reality I have in mind here include the law of identity (A is identical to A), the law of excluded middle (for any proposition P, P must be either true or false), and the law of noncontradiction (P cannot be both true and false at the same time and in the same sense).

These three principles are called "laws" precisely because they ground and govern the very intelligibility of reality itself. They are basic or fundamental in the sense that all rational and intelligible thought is predicated on these three principles; even in arguing against them one must employ them (exercise: try to refute the above three basic laws of reality without putting them to use). Philosophical theories, including one's theory of existence, should aim to focus on a coherent understanding of the way things are. Since a theory of existence is just that, a philosophical theory, it should likewise aim for conceptual coherence and thus strive to be in line with the intelligible grain of reality. By extension, a theory of existence should also be internally consistent (not self-refuting). It must not rule out the existence of the very conditions in which existence itself is defined or analyzed.

One last preliminary remark before we turn to examine some individual theories of existence. Since the Theory of Existence Question is, fundamentally, a question about what it is to exist or be in the first place, an adequate answer will take the form of what philosophers call an "analysis" of existence itself. Simply stated, to analyze a particular notion, like existence, in this sense is to roughly ask: Under what conditions or circumstances is it true of something that it exists?

Thus, for each theory of existence that follows, we will attempt to offer an analysis of existence by filling in the following existence condition:

Existence Condition: Something, *x*, exists if and only if _____.

I hope you love fill-in-the-blank because here we go!

SOME NATURALIST-FRIENDLY THEORIES OF EXISTENCE

"Seeing is believing," says the train conductor from the movie *The Polar Express* (voiced by actor Tom Hanks), "but sometimes the most real things in the world are the things we can't see."[25] Who would have guessed it: Tom Hanks, a metaphysician! Every December as I watch, re-watch, re-re-watch (ad infinitum; I have three young kids) *The Polar Express*, I'm overjoyed by the above,

---

[25] *The Polar Express*, directed by Robert Zemeckis (Warner Bros., 2004).

deeply metaphysical line in what is otherwise a rather unusual children's Christmas movie. While this small line from the Polar Express expresses a historically prominent view of both the extent of reality as well as the nature of existence itself (including an affirmative answer to the Degrees of Being Question), it is radically at odds with a metaphysical picture that currently holds captive the collective imagination of modern Western culture. As we have seen in the previous chapters, this metaphysical story is called "metaphysical naturalism," the view that roughly the material universe is all that exists, has existed, or ever will exist.

It may be helpful to first consider the following group of theories of existence that bear a family resemblance to one another and that are a natural fit with metaphysical naturalism:[26]

Space-Time Theory of Existence: Something, x, exists if and only if x is located in space and time.

Matter Theory of Existence: Something, x, exists if and only if x is material.

Perceptual Theory of Existence: Something, x, exists if and only if x is sense-perceptible.

As one can see, all of the above views are relevantly similar in how they fill in Existence Condition. Each view analyzes existence exclusively in terms of some naturalist-friendly condition, whether space, time, matter, or sense-perceptibility. In these views, to *be* is either to be somewhere in space and time, to be made of material stuff, or to be sense-perceptible (i.e., to be the kind of thing that can be perceived by the human senses). In short, according to the metaphysical naturalist, the train conductor in *The Polar Express* is deeply misguided; what is real and what it means to exist can be exhaustively accounted for in terms of what is spread out in space and observable with the five senses. Hollywood should stick to storytelling and leave the serious metaphysics to the pros, or so we are told.

If metaphysical naturalism is true and everything that does in fact exist is either within space and time, is material, or is sense-perceptible, then it is a

---

[26]I should note that depending on other philosophical factors, these theories may be defined or analyzed in terms of one another. For example, if something is sense-perceptible if and only if it is material, then the Perceptual Theory of Existence collapses into the Matter Theory of Existence. And if something is material just in case it is located in space, then the Matter Theory of Existence collapses into the Space-Time Theory of Existence.

short step to further analyze existence itself in terms of one of these naturalist-friendly conditions (thus not only all that does in fact exist but all that could *possibly* exist must be either material, spatial, or sense-perceptible).[27]

But it is not just contemporary naturalistic philosophers that have been sympathetic to one or more of the above theories of existence. It is interesting to note that none other than the great Christian theologian Saint Augustine (354–430) himself was once in the grip of something like a combination of the above three naturalist-friendly theories of existence prior to becoming a Christian. In recounting his pre-conversion struggle to conceive of the triune God as immaterial or nonphysical, Augustine pinpoints a deeper, metaphysical assumption about the nature of existence at the root of this theological struggle (exercise: try to spot each of the three naturalist-friendly theories of existence in the following quotations):

> But the older I became, the more shameful it was that I retained so much vanity as to be unable to think any substance possible other than that which the eyes normally perceive.

> I nevertheless felt forced to imagine something physical occupying space diffused either in the world or even through infinite space outside the world.

> But I thought that anything from which space was abstracted was nonexistent, indeed absolutely nothing, not even a vacuum, as when a body is removed from a place.

> I though simply non-existent anything not extended in space or diffused or concentrated or expanding, which does not possess, or is incapable of possessing, such qualities.[28]

Notice carefully: It was in part an underlying *metaphysical* view about the nature of existence itself that prevented Augustine from properly conceiving of God as he truly is, as immaterial and transcendent, and orienting his life accordingly.[29]

---

[27]Arguably something like this posture is on display in the opening remark (cited in chap. 2) by David Armstrong in his book *Sketch for a Systematic Metaphysics* (New York: Oxford University Press, 2010), 1: "I begin with the assumption that all that exists is the space-time world, the physical world as we say. What argument is offered for this assumption? All I can say is that this is a position that many—philosophers and others—would accept. Think of it this way. This is a *hypothesis* that many would accept as plausible. The space-time entity seems obviously to exist. Other suggested beings seem much more hypothetical."

[28]Augustine, *Confessions*, trans. Henry Chadwick (Oxford: Oxford University Press, 2009), 7.1-21.

[29]See my *Christian Philosophy as a Way of Life: An Invitation to Wonder* (Grand Rapids, MI: Baker Academic, 2023), 169-73.

What are we to make of the above naturalist-friendly theories of existence? Well, most importantly, if Christianity is true, then all three of the above naturalist-friendly theories of existence are deeply misguided from the get-go. Since the historic Christian faith is metaphysically committed to the existence of intrinsically nonspatial/immaterial/non–sense perceptible beings like God, angels, and arguably human souls, then existence itself cannot be defined in terms of spatiality/materiality/sense-perceptibility. In this sense, all three theories of existence fail *the fittingness condition*. Given the truth of Christianity, it is not only *possible* that there is much more to reality that meets the eye, there actually exists a realm populated with beings that are neither confined in space, made up of material stuff, nor accessible by way of one's ordinary sensory faculties (cf. 2 Kings 6).

Let's go further and take a look at a specific philosophical worry that pushes against each of the above three naturalist-friendly theories of existence. First, a case can be made that all three theories arguably fail to meet *the coherence condition* stated above. Recall that *the coherence condition* stated that a theory of existence must not rule out the existence of the very conditions in terms of which existence itself is analyzed. Consider the human mind itself that deliberates about whether to adopt the Space-Time Theory of Existence, the Matter Theory of Existence, or the Perceptual Theory of Existence. Does the human mind itself exist? Surely it does. But is the human mind itself in space, material, or sense-perceptible? Not a few philosophers of mind, both Christian and non-Christian alike, have made the philosophical case that for a host of reasons the mind cannot be spatial (at least in the same way that material objects are spatial), material, and perhaps by extension, sense-perceptible. If not, and since the Matter Theory of Existence and the Perceptual Theory of Existence analyze existence in terms of matter and sense-perceptibility, it follows that the mind does not exist. If the mind does not exist, then it's hard to see how one could mentally affirm the truth of either theory of existence. So, if either theory of existence is true, then they are incapable of being mentally affirmed.

Here Augustine can be of some help to us once again. Augustine tells us how exactly he was eventually able to wiggle out of the tight and alluring grip of these naturalist-friendly theories of existence.[30] He says in no

---

[30]For the alluring nature of a materialist metaphysics, see Letter 1 of C. S. Lewis, *The Screwtape Letters* (New York: HarperOne, 2015).

uncertain terms: "So my heart had become gross and I had no clear vision even of my own self. . . . I did not see that the mental power by which I formed these images does not occupy any space, though it could not form them unless it were some great thing."[31] For Augustine, at the heart of the problem with the underlying theory of existence he once held is that it excluded the very thing he was using to ponder the nature of existence itself, his own mind, as immaterial and nonspatial. The point, of course, generalizes to both the Matter Theory of Existence and the Perceptual Theory of Existence. If the mind itself exists and is neither spatial, made of material stuff, nor sense-perceptible, then each of the above naturalist-friendly theories of existence is deeply misguided.

Yet another philosophical worry with these naturalist-friendly theories of existence is that each arguably fails *the possibility condition*. Each of the above theories rules out not only the actual existence of things that are non-spatial, immaterial, and non–sense perceptible, they also rule out their very possibility. Entities like numbers, God (classically conceived), angels, and human souls cannot possibly exist since on many accounts such items, if they existed, would not be confined to space and time, made of material stuff, or sense perceptible.

But, intuitively, even apart from theological considerations, this exclusion seems much too strong. Does it not seem possible that reality *could* include things that are (in principle) incapable of being detected by the human senses (even with the most fine-tuned scientific equipment)? Even assuming the truth of metaphysical naturalism, could it not have been the case that reality included more than meets the eye? Surely, even the ardent metaphysical naturalist who rejects the *actual* existence of abstract objects that exist outside of space and time and immaterial human souls and angels might think that these things arguably *could* have existed. To limit all that *is* to material, spatial, or sense-perceptible being is one thing; to limit all that could *possibly* exist in this way seems entirely too narrow and restrictive.

So, while one might think that being material or sense-perceptible, or existing in space and time is one particular mode or manner of existence (with being immaterial as another mode), it arguably cannot account for the nature of existence *itself*.

---

[31]Augustine, *Confessions* 7.2.

THE PROPERTY THEORY OF EXISTENCE

Let's consider yet another theory of existence. Take the simple statement: "The cat is black." Here we have a straightforward case of a subject, "the cat," and a predicate, "is black." According to a well-known theory of existence in the history of Western philosophy, *existence* itself is a property or feature that is predicated of everything that is. Take the simple positive existence claim, "The cat exists." Again, the grammatical form of such a claim is exactly like the claim above, a straightforward case of subject, "the cat," and predicate, "exists."

According to the "Property Theory of Existence," *existence* is itself a property that is predicated of everything that exists. Just like *redness* can be predicated of all red things (red apples, red fire engines, and the giant red bow on that shiny new Lexus that you'll never receive for Christmas), so too *existence* is predicated of all existing things, and is not accurately predicated of things that do not exist (e.g., Harry Potter, unicorns, goblins). What distinguishes you from a nonexistent object like Harry Potter, then, is that you have something fictional entities do not, the property *existence*.

In terms of its philosophical and historical street cred, the Property Theory of Existence is no slouch; the view has been defended by formidable philosophers throughout history such as Plato (ca. 428–ca. 348 BC), René Descartes (1596–1650), and Alexius Meinong (1853–1920). And it's not hard to see why such a view has been attractive in the history of philosophy. The view is a natural one to hold, given the surface grammar of existence claims. The view can be clearly stated as follows:

Property Theory of Existence: Something, *x*, exists if and only if x has the property *existence*.

Yet, since the early modern period of Western philosophy, the Property Theory of Existence has been dogpiled on by the likes of David Hume, Immanuel Kant, and others. Why? For starters, think again about the alleged property of *existence*. If *existence* and *nonexistence* are properties, they clearly are not like ordinary properties like *redness*, *wetness*, *sweetness*, etc. While attributing *sweetness* to the apple may add something to your concept of an apple, attributing *existence* does not, or at least so Kant thought.[32] Thus,

---

[32]Immanuel Kant, *Critique of Pure Reason*, trans. Werner S. Pluhar (Indianapolis: Hackett, 1996), A 600/B 628.

existence (and *nonexistence*) doesn't seem to be like an ordinary property like *sweetness*. The jury is still out on whether Kant's objection here is a good one.[33]

But the Property Theory of Existence is not out of the woods yet. In fact, things get weird fast in this view, especially for claims about the nonexistence of things. To set up this notable worry in the history of metaphysics, consider the following positive statement about Fido the dog: "Fido is furry." Suppose this is a true statement about Fido. If so, then it's plausible to think that there must be some existing thing that makes such a statement true (arguably Fido and his furriness); that is, if "Fido is furry" is true, there exists something that is furry, namely, Fido. This seems natural enough, doesn't it? Many are of the natural opinion that *truth* should be appropriately connected, in some way or other, to the way things *are*.

But now consider the following statement, what philosophers call a negative existential statement, "Harry Potter's glasses do not exist." This is a true statement as neither Harry Potter nor Harry Potter's glasses exist. If this negative statement is true (and it clearly is) and given that there needs to be an appropriate connection between truth and the way things are in reality, there must be a thing (Harry's glasses) that exists with the property *nonexistence* that thereby makes such a statement true. But what could possibly make this statement true? Surely, Harry's glasses can't exist and be the bearer of the property *nonexistence*? Do you spot the problem? This would be tantamount to affirming the following contradiction: There is some existing thing (Harry's glasses) that has the property *nonexistence* (after all, how can something have a property if it doesn't exist in any sense?). Thus, Harry's glasses both exist and do not exist (since they have both the property of *existence* and *nonexistence*)! And, of course, no contradiction can be true. A big problem!

As the issue of nonexistent objects and negative existentials has loomed large in the history of metaphysics, I can only give you but a taste of how some proponents of the Property Theory of Existence might reply to this thorny problem.

One potential solution here would be to adopt an ontology that distinguishes between various modes or ways of being (see earlier section "The Ways of Being Question"). One might say, with famous twentieth-century British philosopher Bertrand Russell (1872–1970), that some things *exist*, such

---

[33]For a critique, see Reinhardt Grossman, *The Existence of the World: An Introduction to Ontology* (New York: Routledge, 1992), 98-99.

as trees, poodles, people (things that are in space and time), while other things *subsist* like the number 2 or fictional entities like Sherlock Holmes or Harry Potter (things that are not in space and time). While Harry Potter's glasses do not *exist* strictly speaking (they are purely fictional after all), they nevertheless *subsist* as they have some type of being or other. After all, the proponent of this modes of being view might claim, we can surely talk or think about Harry's glasses, perhaps even attribute features to Harry's glasses (round, shiny, breakable, etc.). If so, then surely Harry's glasses must *be* in some very minimal sense. As Russell himself put it, "For what does not exist must be something, or it would be meaningless to deny its existence; and hence we need the concept of being, as that which belongs even to the non-existent."[34] However, as you might imagine, many have found the distinction between existence and subsistence difficult to make sense of.

There is also a notable theological worry with the Property Theory of Existence. As we have seen in chapter three, according to classical Christian theism, God is metaphysically ultimate and rock bottom; there is nothing behind or in back of God that explains what or how God is in himself. More technically, for any explanatory claim of the general form "God is *F* (wise, good, powerful, etc.) in virtue of _____" (where F is some feature that God has in himself, apart from standing in relations to creatures), there can be nothing that is not identical to God that can possibly fill in the blank. Neither God's existence nor God's nature is (or can be) explained by something that is not God.

In the Christian tradition, one natural metaphysical implication of this particularly robust view of God's aseity and ultimacy is a version of divine simplicity that maintains that God does not possess distinct, intrinsic (nonrelational) properties.[35] Properties, as we will see in more detail in chapter seven, play the role of metaphysically explaining what a thing is like, its qualitative character (the apple's being appropriately related to the properties *redness* and *sweetness* metaphysically explains its being red and being sweet). Of course, saying that God does not have properties does not mean (nor has it ever meant, contrary to some contemporary critics) that God is utterly devoid of an

---

[34]Cited in Chris Daly, "To Be," in *The Routledge Companion to Metaphysics*, eds. Robin Le Poidevin, Peter Simons, Andrew McGonigal, and Ross P. Cameron (New York: Routledge, 2009).
[35]This view of divine simplicity, of course, allows God to stand in various relations to creatures like Creator and Redeemer. This is because divine names such as "Creator" and "Redeemer" are true of God as God is in relation to creatures.

essential, qualitative character; that God is utterly nondescript. Rather, at bottom, it means that in contrast to what explains the qualitative character and nature of creatures (possessing properties and kinds), God himself is the sole sufficient ground of his own qualitative character and nature; God isn't good in virtue of being appropriately related to the property *goodness*, God *is* the Good, we might say. And here's the kicker: If God does not strictly have properties in this sense, God does not have the property of *existence*. According to the Property Theory of Existence, then, it follows that God does not exist (since God does not have the property of *existence*). In short, the Property Theory of Existence, together with a robust view of divine simplicity, entails the nonexistence of God. For Christian philosophers committed to more classical forms of Christian theism that include a strong view of divine simplicity, the Property Theory of Existence fails *the fittingness condition* and *the possibility condition* regarding God. And for Christian philosophers, any theory of existence that entails that God does not exist is a big problem, to put it mildly.

THE EXEMPLIFICATION THEORY OF EXISTENCE

Another historically prominent theory of existence that has received robust defense in contemporary metaphysics is the "Exemplification Theory of Existence": that existence is *the having of a property* (or the property of *being had*). In the nineteenth and twentieth centuries, philosophers such as G. E. Moore, Edmund Husserl, Roderick Chisholm, Dallas Willard, and J. P. Moreland have articulated and defended such a view.[36] We can state the view as follows:

> *Exemplification Theory of Existence*: Something, *x*, exists if and only if <u>*x* has at least one property (or *x* is a property that is had by something)</u>.

It is important not to confuse the Exemplification Theory of Existence with the Property Theory of Existence. According to the Exemplification Theory of Existence, existence does not amount to having the property of *existence*. Rather, existence amounts to *the having of some property or other*. The core idea here is that something exists if and only if it "enters into the nexus of exemplification," as one prominent defender of the view has put it.[37] Let me explain. Properties, characteristics, or features (I use all these synonymous for our purposes here), in general, contrast with the objects that have or exemplify

---

[36]J. P. Moreland, *Universals* (Montreal: McGill-Queen's University Press, 2001), 134-39.
[37]Moreland, *Universals*, 137.

them, for example, the redness of the apple, the hardness of the metal, the roundness of the frisbee, the mass of an atom, and so on. A red apple has the property of *being red*, and thus is said to exemplify *redness*; put differently, the property *redness* belongs to the apple. This "belongs to" or "having" relation is what philosophers call the relation of "exemplification."

Take the property of *being a unicorn*. The nonexistence of unicorns amounts to the fact that the property of *being a unicorn* is not had by anything, that there is nothing that exemplifies this property. But what about the property of *being a unicorn* itself? Does it exist? It certainly does in this particular theory of existence. Why? The reason is that properties themselves have or exemplify properties. On one prominent account of properties that we will encounter in chapter seven (inspired by Plato and considering properties as necessarily existing beings that are abstract in the sense of existing beyond space and time), for example, the property of *being a unicorn* itself has the property of *being abstract*. Thus, even though unicorns do not exist, the property of *being a unicorn* certainly does as it enters into the exemplification relation insofar as it has at least one property. But what about the exemplification relation itself, does it exist? Yes, indeed it does, insofar as it too has properties, such as *being a relation* and *being abstract*.

"But wait just a minute," you might say. You might think that it's obvious that unicorns have properties. What about the properties of *being a one-horned horse* or *being mythical*? The proponent of the Exemplification Theory of Existence has a ready response. Statements about nonexistent objects like unicorns or Harry Potter's glasses are best understood as counter-to-fact (counterfactual) statements such as "If unicorns *were* to exist, they *would* have the properties of being a one-horned horse and being mythical" and "If Harry Potter's glasses *did* exist, they *would* be round, shiny, breakable, etc." But neither unicorns nor Harry's glasses *actually* have these properties; if they did, they would exist, or so says the proponent of the Exemplification Theory of Existence.

Another interesting point to make about the Exemplification Theory of Existence is that nonexistence (nothingness) is just that, the total absence of properties altogether. Contrary to rather wild and muddled claims in popular philosophy and science writing today,[38] "nothing" is not something with a few

---

[38]No, sadly, I'm not kidding. Laurence Kraus confidently asserts that "surely 'nothing' is every bit as physical as 'something'" and that we should "understand precisely the physical nature of both

properties peppered about here and there. Nothingness is not even a strange something like a sea of fluctuating quantum energy. Absolute nothingness does not exist, period. In this view, to say that nothing "exists" is just downright confused.

The Exemplification Theory of Existence has a lot going for it. It seems to align with both *the coherence condition* and *the possibility condition* in a way that the other theories of existence do not. First, since existence is the entering into the relation of exemplification, and the exemplification itself exists (it has the properties of *being a relation* and *being abstract*), the Exemplification Theory of Existence does not undermine itself in the way the above naturalist-friendly theories do. Nor does the Exemplification Theory of Existence preclude the mere *possibility* of immaterial objects such as abstract objects, immaterial souls, and angels. All of these objects *could* exist insofar as they could enter into the relation of exemplification, even if one thinks they don't actually exist (if nothing has the property *being an abstract object*, or *being an immaterial soul*, or *being an angel*).

The view, however, does suffer from the same theological worry raised against the Property Theory of Existence noted above. If God's metaphysical ultimacy is thought to entail a version of divine simplicity that says that God necessarily fails to exemplify intrinsic properties of any kind, this also means that God does not, strictly speaking, enter into the exemplification relation. If divine aseity and divine simplicity are true, then God is not the way God is *by virtue of* having or exemplifying various properties or characteristics. Again, it is important not to confuse this rather nuanced, theological claim—that God strictly doesn't exemplify intrinsic properties—with the deeply unbiblical claim that God has no qualitative character of any kind, that God is utterly nondescript. Once again, the claim is that God's nature is the way it is by virtue of God and God alone; God is not explanatorily dependent for his qualitative character on anything that is not God.

The careful reader will note that this route is an application of pressing divine aseity into service as a metaphysical lodestar and guiding light when doing metaphysics as a Christian. If God does not strictly exemplify properties in order for him to be what he is (and God is not a property that is had

---

these quantities." Kraus himself protests that philosophers and theologians deem this "scientific" understanding of "nothing" as muddleheaded. Indeed! See Lawrence Kraus, *A Universe from Nothing: Why There Is Something Rather Than Nothing* (New York: Atria, 2012), xiv.

by anything), and if the Exemplification Theory of Existence is true, then it follows God does not (and cannot) exist. Again, a big problem for the Christian philosopher. This is to say that the Exemplification Theory of Existence arguably fails *the fittingness condition* and *the possibility condition* for God, at least from the standpoint of a historically prominent understanding of the nature of God in the Christian tradition.

Of course, the theological shortcoming here of the Exemplification Theory of Existence only stems from a commitment to a classical conception of God along the lines of a strong view of divine aseity and divine simplicity. For those Christian metaphysicians who reject this full-throttle view of divine aseity as well as divine simplicity, the Exemplification Theory of Existence fairs quite nicely. But, here again, for Christian metaphysicians who are inclined to favor a more traditional doctrine of God like myself, a robust form of divine aseity will lead away from these theories of existence.

PRIMITIVE EXISTENCE

The final view that I'd like to briefly consider calls into question the entire project of trying to find a clear-cut and precise answer to Existence Condition in the first place. Recall our original statement of Existence Condition:

Existence Condition: Something, *x*, exists if and only if _____.

Recall also that what we are looking for in answering Existence Condition is an informative, philosophical *analysis* of existence itself, an answer to the question, "Under what conditions or circumstances is it true of something that it exists?" So far, we've examined three naturalist-friendly theories of existence (Space-Time Theory, Matter Theory, Perceptual Theory), the Property Theory of Existence, and the Exemplification Theory of Existence and have found that all have various shortcomings, some much more severe than others. Some of these theories of existence straightforwardly violate one or more of our three guiding conditions (the *fittingness, possibility,* and *coherence* conditions), others face theological problems that those with more traditional theological sensibilities about the nature of God (robust divine aseity and robust divine simplicity) will find problematic.[39]

---

[39]For more on these theories of existence (and more theories besides) as well as their respective costs and benefits, see Chris Daly, "To Be." For a defense of yet another popular theory of existence among philosophers known as the *Causal or Eleatic Theory of Existence* (a.k.a. "Alexander's

But perhaps our quest here for an airtight analysis or definition of existence is misguided from the start (likewise, our quest for a full-blown comprehensive theory of existence); after all, as we pointed out in chapter one regarding the prospects of defining "metaphysics," complete and precise real definitions are very hard to come by for most things, let alone something as basic to reality as existence itself.

For this reason, not a few contemporary metaphysicians, E. J. Lowe, David Oderberg, Trenton Merricks, and Reinhard Grossman among them, have argued that there is arguably no deeper, noncircular analysis of existence itself.[40] Some concepts are so metaphysically rock bottom or fundamental that they cannot be analyzed in terms of any other concepts. After all, all building projects, whether physical or metaphysical, must ultimately rest on some foundation or other, whether concrete or conceptual. Philosophers refer to such foundational concepts as "primitive." In philosophy, primitive concepts are concepts that cannot be broken down into any more basic or fundamental concepts. As metaphysicians are quick to admit, there are no bottom-less metaphysical theories; all theories must hit the rock bottom of the well of metaphysical explanation somewhere. And existence is, say these thinkers, very likely one of these primitive, foundational concepts.[41]

To take existence itself as primitive, or incapable of being further analyzed, doesn't at all mean that we are confined to silence about the nature of existence; far from it. Up to this point in the chapter, we've said a lot about what existence itself may or may not be (e.g., analogical/univocal and degreed/nondegreed). This is all entirely consistent with saying that there is, at the end of the day, no clear-cut and informative (noncircular) definition of existence itself. So, even if the Christian metaphysician takes existence itself to be primitive, this doesn't mean they can't rule out other inadequate theories of existence, such as the naturalist-friendly theories of existence we discussed above. While we can say a lot about the nature of existence, whether we can land on a clear-cut and informative (noncircular) definition of existence is another matter.

---

dictum")—to be/exist is to have causal powers—see D. M. Armstrong, *A World of States of Affairs* (Cambridge: Cambridge University Press, 1997), 41.

[40]For philosophers who are sympathetic to a primitive view of existence, see Garrett Deweese, *Doing Philosophy as a Christian* (Downers Grove, IL: IVP Academic, 2011), 121; Trenton Merricks, *Truth and Ontology* (New York: Oxford University Press, 2007), 186; David Oderberg, *Real Essentialism* (New York: Routledge, 2007), 124; Grossman, *Existence of the World*, 106-12; and E. J. Lowe, "How Real Is Substantial Change?," *The Monist* 89, no. 3 (2006): 278.

[41]Merricks, *Truth and Ontology*, 186.

Getting Theological: The Mystery of Creaturely Being

In the spirit of doing metaphysics from a theo-centric habit of mind (see chap. 3), there's one last marvel of existence that I'd like to consider with you before we close this chapter. Think about this striking fact: There exist some things, rather than no things. While this fact may seem rather mundane, and indeed it is, it generates what some philosophers consider to be the one of the most fundamental enigmas of metaphysics, *why is there something rather than nothing?* If there could have been nothing at all, then *why* is there anything at all? What's the explanation for why anything exists in the first place? This is the question I want to consider here; call it the "Mystery of Creaturely Being Question."

As Aristotle pointed out long ago, we humans are "meaning-seeking animals";[a] we strive for intelligibility in our desire to know and understand reality. The Mystery of Creaturely Being Question is perhaps the most basic, rock-bottom question of meaning we could possibly ask. Following an argument originally put forward by seventeenth-century Christian metaphysician Gottfried Wilhelm Leibniz in his essay "On the Ultimate Origination of Things," I'd like to explore an age-old answer to this question by way of a step-by-step argument in favor of the existence of a necessary being (a being whose nonexistence is impossible) at the foundation of contingent reality (all beings whose nonexistence is possible).

Let's ease in here with a commonsensical claim about what exists:

Contingency: Some beings exist that could have failed to exist.[b]

Contingency states that there are beings that exist but could have not existed. Traditionally, beings like these are called "contingent beings." Consider a car, a cat, an iPhone, and this book. Each of these items exists. This much is clear. Yet each of these items not only exists but could also have *not* existed; there's no sense in which a particular iPhone (or the entire collection of iPhones) *had* to be, come what may.

Let's take another small step. It seems obvious to us that the existence of some contingent being has an explanation, that is, that there is an explanation (whatever it might be) for why some contingent being *is*, rather than *not*. Why does this book exist? Ultimately, because I wanted to explore with you the contemporary metaphysical landscape from a Christian perspective. Why does a company like Apple exist? Well, because of the creative and entrepreneurial spirit of Steve Jobs and other tech pioneers. And so on. At bottom, this is a point about the intelligibility of reality; contingent beings don't just exist inexplicably, without any explanation whatsoever.

We've arrived, then, at the first small step in our argument:

1. For any contingent being or group of contingent beings, there is an explanation as to why those beings exist.

Let's take a second small step on our quest to answer the Mystery of Creaturely Being Question. Call the group of all contingent beings that currently exist—every last one of them—*Totality*. There's really no significant metaphysical difference between one contingent being and a group of contingent beings. And as Leibniz pointed out long ago, we can even grant the possibility that *Totality* consists of a chain of contingent beings with no first link in the chain (for every link on the chain there is a prior link). We've come, then, to the second small step in the argument:

2. *Totality* exists.

A third small step in the argument follows immediately from steps 1 and 2:

3. Therefore, there is an explanation as to why *Totality* exists.

If it makes sense to ask of any one contingent being why it exists rather than not (as in premise 1 above), does it not equally make sense to ask why the plurality of all contingent beings, *Totality*, exists rather than not (3)? Certainly, it does; given that *Totality* is nothing more than the group of all contingent beings that exist, there should be an explanation as to why this group exists—these very contingent beings—rather than not.

Here things get interesting, since it would seem that any explanation of the existence of *Totality* cannot itself be a contingent being and thus a member of *Totality*. Think about it: What could possibly explain the existence of the group of all contingent beings like *Totality*? Suppose I ask you for an explanation for why the group of all existing red things happens to exist (rather than a group of existing red things made up of slightly or entirely different assortment of red things)? Why *these* red things when there could have been *other* red things? Here's an inadequate reply to my question: The group of all existing red things happens to exist because some existing red thing made it so. This response is woefully inadequate since the red thing that allegedly explains the existence of all red things is itself part of the group of all red things, the very thing we are seeking to explain. More generally, a genuine explanation of why a particular group of Fs exist cannot appeal to something among the Fs, otherwise we would have a circular explanation, an explanation that circles back on itself and doesn't close the explanatory gap as needed (which is bad news philosophically!). So, if the group of existing red things has an explanation of its existence, the explanation must be the existence of a thing that isn't itself in the group of red things.

In the same way, if there is an explanation for why *Totality*, the collection of contingent beings, exists—those very contingent beings and not others—then such an explanation must appeal to some thing that isn't itself in the group of contingent beings, that is, a noncontingent or necessary being. Thus, our fourth small step:

4. If there is an explanation of why *Totality* exists, that explanation is found in a necessary (noncontingent) being.

If *Totality* has a (noncircular) explanation of its existence, then the explanation of its existence must lie *outside* of the realm of contingent beings and in some necessary being (or group of necessary beings). Just as the explanation of the existence of all red things cannot itself be a red thing (on pains of circularity), so too the explanation of the existence of all contingent beings cannot itself be contingent (on pains of circularity). Thus, in just a few small but intuitive steps, we've reached our final destination, the existence of a necessary, noncontingent explanation for all contingent reality (*Totality*):

5. Therefore, the explanation of why *Totality* exists is found in a necessary (noncontingent) being.[c]

So, in sum, if reality is intelligible at both the level of particular contingent beings as well as at the level of all contingent reality itself

(*Totality*)—then there is reason to think that a necessary, noncontingent being exists that provides an ultimate and complete explanation for all of continent reality, *Totality*. In Christian theism, the Mystery of Creaturely Being Question—why there is something rather than nothing—finds its deepest answer in the existence and good pleasure of the triune God, the necessarily existing, uncreated Creator of all things "in heaven and on earth, visible and invisible" (Colossians 1:16).

[a] I borrow the wonderful phrase "meaning-seeking animals" from David McPherson, *Virtue and Meaning: A Neo-Aristotelian Perspective* (New York: Cambridge University Press, 2021), who in turn borrows it from Jonathan Sacks, *The Great Partnership: God, Science and the Search for Meaning* (London: Hodder & Stoughton, 2011), chap. 1.

[b] By "beings" here I mean concrete beings, those that have the power to cause something.

[c] I owe this formulation of the argument from contingency to Alexander Pruss and Joshua Rasmussen in their technical book *Necessary Existence* (New York: Oxford University Press, 2018). See also Rasmussen's more popular-level works defending a necessary foundation to existence, *The Bridge of Reason: Ten Steps to See God* (n.p: Great Legacy Books, 2018) and *How Reason Can Lead to God: A Philosopher's Bridge to Faith* (Downers Grove, IL: IVP Academic, 2019).

GOING DEEPER: CREATURELY EXISTENCE

Key Concepts in Metaphysics:

- existence
- nonexistence
- primitive
- exemplification
- properties
- negative facts

Historical

- Plato, *Republic*, books 4-5
- Aristotle, *Metaphysics*, book 4
- Thomas Aquinas, *On Being and Essence*
- Jeffrey Brower, Section 2.4, "Types vs. Modes of Being," in *Aquinas's Ontology of the Material World*

- Duns Scotus, "Concerning Metaphysics," in *Duns Scotus: Philosophical Writings*
- Gottfried Wilhelm Leibniz, "On the Ultimate Origination of Things," in *Philosophical Essays*
- Bertrand Russell, *The Problems of Philosophy*, 91-100
- Alexius Meinong, *On Assumptions*, 49-62
- Franz Brentano, *On the Several Senses of Being in Aristotle*
- Edmund Husserl, *Logical Investigations*, 2:249-50
- Martin Heidegger, *Being and Time*
- Peter Coffey, *Ontology or the Theory of Being: An Introduction to General Metaphysics*, chap. 1

Contemporary

- Roderick Chisholm, "Coming to Be and Passing Away: Can the Metaphysician Help?," in *On Metaphysics*
- Chris Daly, "To Be," in *The Routledge Companion to Metaphysics*
- Graham Priest, "Not to Be," in *The Routledge Companion to Metaphysics*
- Kris McDaniel, *The Fragmentation of Being*; "Ways of Being," in *Metametaphysics*
- Joshua Spencer, "Ways of Being," in *Philosophy Compass*
- J. P. Moreland, *Universals*, 134-39
- William Vallicella, *A Paradigm Theory of Existence*

5

CLASSIFYING CREATURELY REALITY

IDENTITY AND ONTOLOGICAL CATEGORIES

THE WONDER OF SAMENESS AND DISTINCTNESS

When we slow down and carefully attend to the intricacies of created reality, we are struck by the fact that the objects of our immediate awareness are distinct from one another; they are not one and the same. For example, ceilings, shoes, people, and my current thought of my three young children are all distinct things; each exists but is not one and the same with any of the others. Shoes are clearly not people, and ceilings are not human thoughts. We are aware of distinctness in reality, we might say, and this distinctness resides not simply in the way we speak, think, or talk about reality but, rather, in the very shape of reality itself.

Again, this much seems evident to us on simple reflection. Yet, it is also evident to us that many objects of our present experience and from one moment to the next are indeed one and the same object; they are what philosophers call "numerically identical." The bonsai tree you pruned last night is the very same bonsai tree you behold today; the piece of chalk you wrote on the chalkboard with last week is the very same piece of chalk you write with today; the unborn child in your mother's womb many years ago was the very same human being that is currently reading this sentence (Psalm 139:13-16). You get the idea. Just as we are aware of *distinctness* in reality, we are also aware of *sameness*. Indeed, our ability to make coherent and intelligible sense of reality, including God and all created things, relies on reality's being structured along the lines of sameness and difference as it is in itself.

To illustrate, consider the following rather mundane statements concerning sameness and difference:

(a) I am the same person as the husband of Suzanne Inman.

(b) The Morning Star is the same as the Evening Star.

(c) Superman is Clark Kent.

(d) I have the exact same shirt!

(e) This is the same class I took last semester.

(f) You've changed; you're different. You're not the same person I once knew.

(g) My body is made up of different cells than when I was a kid.

Pause and think carefully about (a)-(g); think about each statement individually, as well as each in relation to one another. On reflection, you will notice rather quickly that the concepts of sameness and difference are used in a variety of ways. First, some of the statements involve sameness or difference *at a point in time*. Philosophers call statements about sameness or difference at a time, "synchronic identity statements" (Gk. *syn*, "at/with," and *chronos*, "time"). Statements (a)-(d) are all synchronic identity statements in this sense.

Other statements involve sameness or difference *through time*, what philosophers call "diachronic identity statements" (Gk. *dia*, "through," and *chronos*, "time"). Statements (e)-(g) are all diachronic identity statements in this sense since they pertain to sameness and difference over or through time. Questions about personal identity through time—whether you are strictly one and the same person as the child in your baby pictures—is a question of diachronic sameness.

Another way that the concepts of sameness and difference are used throughout (a)-(g) involves the distinction between a strict, philosophical sense and a loose, popular sense of sameness/identity and difference.[1] Let me explain. We very often speak in such a way that we do not intend to communicate fine-point metaphysical views about sameness and difference. So, take statements (d) and (f). It would be rather silly to interpret these two statements as strict, philosophical statements about sameness (d) and difference (f).

---

[1]Joseph Butler, *The Whole Works of Joseph Butler* (London: Thomas Tegg, 1839), 263-70. See also Roderick Chisholm, *Person and Object* (La Salle, IL: Open Court, 1976), chap. 3.

Rather, a more plausible way to read (d) and (f) would be as merely ways of speaking about relevant degrees of similarity or dissimilarity. When someone claims to have the exact same shirt as you, they probably mean that they have a shirt that highly or even exactly resembles the one you are wearing (they don't mean that your shirt is *strictly one and the same* as their shirt!). Likewise, if one claims that you're not the same person they once knew, they probably mean to convey the fact that you have changed in important ways, perhaps for the better or worse (they don't mean to deny that you are *strictly one and the same* person they once knew in high school).

This leads us to another important distinction involving sameness and identity that is important to grasp going forward. Traditionally, philosophers have distinguished between what they call "qualitative sameness" and "numerical sameness." Two things, say two coffee mugs, are *qualitatively* the same if they highly (or exactly) resemble one another with respect to their characteristics or features. So, if the features of coffee mug A are highly similar to or exactly resemble the features of coffee mug B (color, shape, height, logo, capacity, etc.), then they are qualitatively identical.

However, there remains the further question whether coffee mug A and coffee mug B are *numerically* the same, that is, to be counted as one and the same coffee mug. The reason this question still remains is that, according to many metaphysicians, two numerically distinct things (things that are not numerically one and the same) can exactly resemble one another in their characteristics or features.[2]

To illustrate, suppose you leave your eight-ounce plain white coffee mug on a table in the student lounge on Friday, perhaps after a long and gruesome study session in preparation for your upcoming metaphysics exam. When you return to the lounge on Monday to retrieve your coffee mug, you see a freshman philosophy major sitting at the same table drinking coffee from an eight-ounce plain white mug, one that looks *exactly* like the one you left behind on Friday. You are left with the pressing question: Is that *the very same* mug as mine? Is the mug in the hand of the freshman *one and the same* mug that belongs to me? This question pertains to whether the freshman's mug is

---

[2] The idea that if object x and object y share all their qualities then they are identical is known as the principle of the "Identity of Indiscernibles." This principle is widely rejected in contemporary metaphysics, largely due to the work of philosopher Max Black in his famous essay "The Identity of Indiscernibles," *Mind* 61, no. 242 (1952): 153-64.

numerically identical to your mug, the question of strict numerical sameness. If the two mugs really are numerically the same mug, then of course they are strictly identical and there are not two mugs here, there's only one: yours (so get ready to make a scene!).

For the most part, it is numerical sameness and difference in the strict, philosophical sense (whether *at a time* or *through time*) that has occupied the attention of metaphysicians, past and present. What exactly *is* numerical sameness and difference in this strict, philosophical sense? How are we to understand the notion of numerical sameness, exactly? What makes it the case that *x* and *y* are numerically one and the same entity, both synchronically (at a time) and diachronically (across time)? These are all very difficult yet immensely important questions that extend well beyond the reach of metaphysical reflection and into the areas of theology, ethics, and the natural sciences.

A CLOSER LOOK AT NUMERICAL IDENTITY

Let's turn now to explore in more detail the notion of numerical sameness or identity, understood in a strict, philosophical sense. For starters, it is vitally important to get clear on what identity *is not* before we focus on what it *is*.

First, identity is a different notion from that of *inseparability*. Just because two things are incapable of being separated from one another doesn't amount to their being numerically one and the same thing. Water's wetness and its being a solvent are seemingly inseparable in this sense, yet these are arguably two distinct (nonidentical) features of water.

Second, identity is a different notion from that of *co-extensionality*. Let me pause and unpack this one a bit. Philosophers distinguish between the "intension" and "extension" of a concept. For example, consider the concept *ship*. The *intension* of the concept *ship* is its formal definition or meaning, in this case "a vehicle for conveyance on water." The *extension* of the concept *ship* includes the group of objects that satisfy (or could satisfy) the intension of the concept. Thus, battle ships, cruise ships, and cargo ships are all included in the extension of the concept *ship* since they are all vehicles for conveyance on water.

Now, two things are co-extensional if they have the very same extension, that is, if they have the very same objects that satisfy the intension of their respective concepts. So, the features of *being triangular* and *being trilateral* are co-extensional in this sense; everything that is triangular is also trilateral. Even more so, these two features are *necessarily* co-extensional: In every possible scenario, if something is triangular it will also be trilateral.

To say that identity is different from mere co-extensionality—even necessary co-extensionality—is to say that two features, like *being triangular* and *being trilateral*, can have (even necessarily!) the exact same extensions and still not be numerically one and the same thing. The features being triangular and being trilateral are not numerically identical, precisely (as we will see in more detail below) because there are things that are true of the former that are not true of the latter (namely, the former has the further property of *being an angle* where the latter does not).[3]

Last, identity is not mere *correlation*. Two things can be correlated in the sense that one always shows up with the other (whether as a causal effect or just always follows the other in time), even necessarily so, and yet not be numerically one and the same thing. So, simply because smoke always accompanies fire does not mean that smoke *just is* fire, that smoke and fire are one and the same thing. Another example here may be instructive. Even if we were to stipulate that every embodied human thought is or can be accompanied by a particular physical state in the brain, this doesn't (on its own) mean that human thoughts *just are* physical states of the brain. Identity is one thing and correlation is quite another; they should not be confused. I hope you now see that identity is a very strong relation that must be distinguished from other kinds of relation that lurk in the neighborhood.

Let's turn to a positive characterization of the notion of numerical identity. Consider once again the statements (a)-(c) noted above, with the additional theological statement (h):

   (a) I am the same person as the husband of Suzanne Inman.

   (b) The Morning Star is the same as the Evening Star.

   (c) Superman is Clark Kent.

   (h) Jesus of Nazareth is the Eternal Word of the Father.

Each of these statements are statements concerning numerical sameness or identity in the strict, philosophical sense. Statement (a) claims that I am identical to the husband of Suzanne Inman—I am numerically one and the

---

[3]J. P. Moreland, *Universals* (Montreal: McGill-Queen's University Press, 2001), 31.

same person as the person who is currently married to Suzanne Inman. Statement (c) also conveys the notion that Superman is not numerically distinct from Clark Kent; indeed, they are, according to the comic, one and the same person. Clark Kent just is Superman, and Superman just is Clark Kent.

On a more theological note, statement (h) makes a claim concerning the identity of Jesus of Nazareth as one and the same person as the eternal, divine Word of the Father (John 1:1-18; Hebrews 1:1-3). In other words, Jesus of Nazareth—the person who was born of a virgin, ate, bathed, and walked the Palestinian countryside—is *the very same person* as the eternal Word, the divine Son (John 1:1-18). Contrary to the ancient heresy known as Nestorianism, there are not two numerically distinct persons here, the person of Jesus of Nazareth and the person of the divine Word. Rather, it is precisely *because* it is numerically one and the same divine person who "was with God, and . . . was God" (John 1:1), who "became flesh and dwelt among us" (John 1:14), and who definitively accomplished our redemption that we can "with confidence draw near to the throne of grace" and "receive mercy and find grace to help in time of need" (Hebrews 4:16).

NUMERICAL IDENTITY IS A RELATION

Metaphysicians have thought long and hard about the nature of numerical sameness and identity.[4] What, exactly, *is* numerical identity? There are several features that are commonly assumed to characterize the relation of numerical identity in contemporary metaphysics. At rock bottom, numerical identity is a certain kind of relation. Informally, relations among creatures in general can be thought of as the ontological glue that binds them together. Relations have what philosophers call "relata" (singular: relatum), the things that the relation links together. So, in the case of my standing in *the brother of* relation to my older sister, my sister and I are the relata of this relation; we are what the relation ontologically links together (represented as "xRy," or, put differently: x stands in the relation R to y).

Traditionally, there are all sorts of relations, some much stronger than others (just like there are different strengths of glue; gorilla glue is much stronger than a kid's blue glue stick). There are *logical* relations (P logically

---

[4]I'll use "numerical sameness," "identity," and "numerical identity" synonymously, unless otherwise noted.

follows from P & Q), *causal* relations (causes are related to their effects), *spatial* relations (to the left of, etc.), *formal ontological* relations (exemplification, instantiation, inherence, composition, identity, etc.), and more besides.[5] Identity is standardly thought to be the strongest type of formal ontological relation on the books; it is the gorilla glue of all relations, we might say. Identity may well be the strongest and most fundamental type of relation—it's hard to conceive of another relation as ontologically bedrock—in that it necessarily carves out the most basic ontological joints of reality and provides reality with its deepest metaphysical infrastructure. Arguably, all facts about sameness and difference are ultimately grounded in relations of numerical identity and distinctness (the latter when a relation of numerical identity fails to obtain).

As a relation that applies to every existing entity, numerical identity is standardly thought to exhibit the following logical features:

1. *Reflexive*: xRx

2. *Transitive*: xRy, yRz, xRz

3. *Symmetrical*: xRy, yRx

A "reflexive" relation is one that relates one of the relata to itself. To get a grip on a relation's being reflexive, it may be helpful to first consider an "irreflexive" relation, by contrast. An irreflexive relation is one that does *not* relate one of the relata to itself. So, the relation *being the brother of* is an irreflexive relation since no one can be their own brother. Further, no matter what White Goodman (Ben Stiller) says at the end of the movie *Dodgeball* when he triumphantly declares, "I created myself," the relation *being created by* is irreflexive; absolutely nothing can create itself as the very idea of bringing oneself into existence is intrinsically nonsensical.[6] The identity relation is reflexive in that, as we will see shortly, every existing thing is identical with itself (self-identical); everything is what it is in particular and it is not something else.

---

[5]See E. J. Lowe, *Four-Category Ontology* (Oxford: Oxford University Press, 2006), chap. 3.

[6]*Dodgeball*, directed by Rawson Marshall Thurber (Twentieth Century Fox, 2004). Consider the following quick reason why self-creation is impossible: For x to create itself, arguably x would need to exist in order to bring itself into existence (which is what creation is). If self-creation were possible, then something would need to exist for it to bring itself into existence. But it's impossible for something to both exist and not exist at the same time. Thus, self-creation is impossible.

A "transitive" relation is one that carries over to other things that are related by the relation in question. For example, the *greater than* relation is transitive in the sense that if 5 is greater than 3, and 3 is greater than 1, then 5 is greater than 1. We could multiply examples here (taller than, being part of, slimier than). The relation of identity is a transitive relation in that if Clark Kent is identical to Superman, and Superman is identical to the husband of Lois Lane, then Clark Kent is identical to the husband of Lois Lane.

Finally, a "symmetric" relation is a relation that is a two-way street in that it applies to both relata that stand in such a relation. The *brother of* relation is a symmetric relation in that if Hudson is the brother of Declan, then Declan is the brother of Hudson. An "asymmetric" relation is one that is only a one-way street in that it does not apply to both relata that stand in the relation. *Being created by* is an asymmetric relation that humans stand in to God: Humans are created by God, but God is in no way created by humans. However, numerical identity is a symmetric or "two-way street" relation in that if Jesus Christ is identical to the divine Word ($x = y$), then the divine Word is identical to Jesus Christ ($y = x$).

NUMERICAL IDENTITY IS ABSOLUTE:
THE INDISCERNIBILITY OF IDENTICALS
(A.K.A. "LEIBNIZ'S LAW")

Among most (though certainly not all) contemporary metaphysicians, identity statements such as "$x = y$" are considered to be "absolute" in the sense that they are not to be understood in a relativized or qualified fashion; that is, you don't need to ask, "In what respect are x and y identical?" Suffice it to say here that a widespread assumption among contemporary metaphysicians about the absoluteness (nonrelativity) of identity amounts to the claim that all meaningful identity statements take the absolute form of "$x=y$."

Along these lines, a principle or law of identity that has been foundational to the intelligibility of created reality is known as "The Indiscernibility of Identicals," or "Leibniz's Law" for short, and is named after seventeenth-century German Christian philosopher Gottfried Wilhelm Leibniz (1646–1716). A bona fide genius, polymath, and Christian metaphysician par excellence, Leibniz helped clarify this fundamental insight into the nature of identity.

Without further ado, here's a very important law of identity that will guide a lot of our discussion throughout the book:

Indiscernibility of Identicals (a.k.a., Leibniz's Law; "LL"): For any entities *x* and *y*, if *x* and *y* are numerically identical (i.e., one and the same), then *x* and *y* have all the same features.

Another way of saying this is that if *x* is one and the same as *y*, then everything that is true of *x* is also true of *y*, and vice versa. So, for any things *x* (Ross Inman) and *y* (the husband of Suzanne Inman), if *x* is numerically one and the same thing as *y* (symbolized by the = sign), then whatever features *x* has *y* will also have, or whatever is true of *x* will also be true of *y*.

The reasoning here is straightforward, and the merits of the principle should be obvious on reflection. If Ross Inman *just is* the very same person as the husband of Suzanne Inman, then everything true of the former should also be true of the latter. So, if Ross Inman is currently six feet tall and if Ross Inman is numerically identical to the husband of Suzanne Inman, then the latter will also be six feet tall at present. If the two had different heights at the same time, then, by Leibniz's Law (LL), it would follow that Ross Inman is not one and the same person as the husband of Suzanne Inman; that is, they are numerically distinct. In general, if two things are exactly one and the same, then everything true of the one should also be true of the other (namely because there are not strictly two things at all, just one). Again, it is hard to see how this intuitive principle about identity could fail to be true. To deny the principle would be to believe that one and the same thing can have different heights at one and the same time, which seems absurd.

It is important to point out that LL is not intended as a (real) definition of numerical identity. Rather, it is a true principle that accompanies the relation of numerical identity whenever it shows up, we might say. Recall that an adequate definition of a thing must be noncircular, that is, it cannot refer to the very thing that it aims to define. Now, look carefully again at LL as formulated above. LL states what *follows* from *x* and *y* being numerically identical, not *what it is* for *x* and *y* to be identical. That's the first reason LL is not proposed here as a definition of numerical identity, strictly speaking. Notice also that the very notion of numerical sameness shows up in the formulation of LL when it says that sameness of features follows from numerical identity ("then *x* and *y* have all the same features"). Since the notion of "sameness" shows up in LL, LL itself cannot be an airtight definition of numerical sameness. Most analytic metaphysicians are content with the view that numerical identity is primitive and metaphysically rock bottom; identity is a fundamental piece of the furniture of reality that is incapable of being further defined in terms of some deeper notion.

The absurdity of denying LL (and thus the obviousness of LL on its face) is grounded in a deeper bedrock law of reality: "that everything is what it is and is not something else," in the words of English clergyman and metaphysician Joseph Butler (1692–1752).[7] Everything is (indeed *must* be) identical with itself; more formally, everything is necessarily self-identical. Whether a tulip or a tiger, a person or a pebble, every existing entity whatsoever is what it is and is not something else; every created being has a delimited nature or essence. As we will see shortly, truths about numerical identity and distinctness are ultimately closely tied to the natures or essences of things.

If LL is true and identity is absolute (as most contemporary metaphysicians think), we have the following handy diagnostic test regarding how to tell if two things are not numerically one and the same, whether they are numerically distinct in the strict, philosophical sense.

> *Diagnostic Test for Numerical Distinctness*: If we know that x and y do not share all of the same features, we therefore know, by LL, that x and y are not numerically identical or one and the same.

Let me quickly apply this little diagnostic test to a perennial issue in metaphysics, the question: *what am I?* Am I numerically identical to my body, a purely physical biological organism, or perhaps my brain (as materialists have long argued)? Well, by LL, if I were numerically identical to my body as a living, biological organism, then I would need to have all of the same features as my body. Or, to put it differently, everything that is true of me will be true of my body as a purely physical biological organism. But is that true? Do I share all of the same features as my body? Well, arguably no, I do not.

While there's a lot to say here, let me just point the reader to the words of 2 Corinthians 5:6-8, "We know that while we are at home in the body we are away from the Lord . . . we would rather be away from the body and at home with the Lord." So, there seems to be something true of *me* that is not true of my body, namely this: that I can be away from my body (while at home with the Lord). Of course, it would be hard to make any coherent or

---

[7]See Joseph Butler, *The Whole Works of Joseph Butler* (London: Thomas Tegg, 1839).

meaningful sense of the idea that my body can be away from itself. But it sure seems like 2 Corinthians 5:6-8 teaches that *I* can be away from my body. If so, then by LL, I am not (indeed cannot be) one and the same thing as my body. Consequently, if LL is true and this really is true of me and not my body, then any version of materialism that says I am numerically identical to my body is false.

Getting Theological: Relative Identity and the Doctrine of the Trinity

The doctrine of the Trinity is one of the central mysteries of the Christian faith. Scripture teaches that God is both absolutely *singular* and one (Deuteronomy 6:4) and that God eternally exists as a triunity of distinct divine persons; the Father, the Son, and the Holy Spirit are all equally and fully God. As the Athanasian Creed so aptly puts it: "The Father is God, the Son is God, the Holy Spirit is God . . . yet there are not three gods; there is but one God."

The historic orthodox doctrine of the Trinity seems to put pressure on standard ways of counting solely by way of Leibniz's Law (strict, absolute numerical identity and distinctness). Let me explain. For example, consider how we normally count that there are three human beings in the room, Tim, Ted, and Tina: Tim, Ted, and Tina are all human and all three humans are numerically distinct (nonidentical) from one another; thus, there are three human beings in the room. But, as the Athanasian Creed points out, this ordinary way of counting by numerical identity/ distinctness in a trinitarian context is woefully misguided; indeed, it is a grave theological error. While the Father, Son, and Spirit are all God, and all are numerically distinct (nonidentical) persons from each other, we emphatically do *not* count three gods. Doing so would land us squarely in the heretical camp of tritheism.

One traditional way of avoiding these counting problems with respect to the Trinity is to broaden the standard notion of identity or sameness to include different types of identity or sameness relations. Perhaps a creedally orthodox doctrine of the Trinity metaphysically requires a species of sameness that is *relative* and not absolute. This is in stark contrast to the now canonical view that claims that *all* sameness relations are absolute or nonrelative (see above). Perhaps the

doctrine of the Trinity demands that some identity or sameness relations can be relative to kinds or sortals, say kinds F and G. On this view,
x can be the same F as y but not the same G as y. Again, the view that
identity or sameness is always absolute will have none of this talk of
sameness relative to a kind—if x is identical or numerically the same as
y then, by Leibniz's Law, everything that is true of x will be true of y (and
vice versa).

What might an appeal to a type of identity or sameness relation that
is relative look like in the case of the Trinity? Here's a sneak peek: The
Father is one and the same *God* (F) as the Son, but not one and the
same *person* (G) as the Son. In other words, when we count according
to the kind *God* (F) we count one (securing monotheism and avoiding
tritheism), but when we count according to the kind *divine person* (G)
we count three (securing triunity of persons and avoiding the heresy of
Sabellianism). Broadening the notion of identity or sameness to include a species of relative identity need not, on its own, entail that all
forms of sameness are relative; it is perfectly compatible with some
sameness relations being absolute and characterized by Leibniz's Law.
Nevertheless, this move has struck many contemporary Christian
metaphysicians as a difficult ontological pill to swallow. Be that as it
may, expanding the metaphysics of identity or sameness in light of the
doctrine of the Trinity has deep historical precedent in the thought of
Augustine, Anselm, Abelard, Aquinas, Scotus, and others besides, and
deserves serious consideration.[a]

---

[a]See Anselm of Canterbury, "On the Incarnation of the Word," in *Anselm: Basic Writings*,
trans. Thomas Williams (Indianapolis: Hackett, 2007), chaps. 9 and 13; and Jeffrey
Brower, "Trinity," in *The Cambridge Companion to Abelard*, eds. Jeffrey E. Brower and
Kevin Guilfoy (New York: Cambridge University Press, 2004), chap. 7. Consider the
following remarks from Christian philosophers Jeffrey Brower and Michael Rea: "As is
well known, respected Christian philosophers and theologians—such as Augustine,
Anselm, and Aquinas—habitually speak of the Trinity in ways that require the introduc-
tion of a form of sameness that fails Leibniz [sic] Law." See Jeffrey Brower and Michael
Rea, "Material Constitution and the Trinity," *Faith and Philosophy* 22, no. 1 (2005): 68.

THE NECESSITY OF NUMERICAL IDENTITY

Another important feature of numerical identity is the notion that if x and y
are in fact numerically identical, then it couldn't be otherwise. That is, x and

y do not just happen to be one and the same thing; rather, it is impossible for *x* and *y not* to be one and the same thing. This pertains to the fact that identity statements, if true, are true of necessity; that is, if true, they couldn't fail to be true.

The majority of contemporary metaphysicians think that numerical identity is necessary in this sense, and that it's impossible for contingent (nonnecessary) identity statements to be true.[8] So, if "the Morning Star" is in fact numerically identical to "the Evening Star" (both historically refer to one and the same planet, Venus), then "they" are really one and the same thing; there are not two things here, only one. To say that the Morning Star could fail to be identical to the Evening Star (and, say, be identical to the planet Mars) is tantamount to saying that something could be fundamentally other than what it, in fact, is. Or, if I am one and the same thing as a human person, then I couldn't fail to be identical to a human person; it's not even possible, in the broadest metaphysical sense, for a human being to be identical to a turnip or a Thanksgiving cornucopia.

As with LL, the necessity of numerical identity rests on a deeper insight into reality: that every entity has a nature or essence, or, everything is what it is and is not something else.[9]

CARVING REALITY AT ITS JOINTS: DEEP AND SHALLOW CLASSIFICATION

With the various formal features of identity in place, let's now turn to the idea of carving up reality at its joints. Suppose you were given the task of compiling an inventory of absolutely every created entity that exists. Yes, that's right, every existing creature of God. Your task—if you choose to accept it—is to provide an exhaustive inventory of created being. Are you up for the task? Setting aside whether comprehensively carrying out such a task is humanly possible, let's ask the following guiding question: How should you go about the task of compiling an exhaustive inventory of creaturely being? Should you just start randomly listing things that exist? Or should you seek to sort or categorize existing things into various kinds of being?

---

[8]Largely due to the arguments of Saul Kripke in his technical but very influential book *Naming and Necessity* (Cambridge, MA: Harvard University Press, 1980).

[9]David Oderberg helpfully points out the connection between essences and numerical identity in his book *Real Essentialism* (New York: Routledge, 2008), chap. 5.

As we ponder the shape of created reality, we are immediately struck by the fact that creaturely beings are capable of being classified or sorted (even just in principle) in a variety of ways. To help get a grasp on the type of classification that is relevant to the task of metaphysics in particular, let's begin by distinguishing between classifications of created reality that are metaphysically "shallow" and classifications that are metaphysically "deep." Some classifications of reality—call them metaphysically shallow classifications—are human-dependent in the sense that the classification in question does not hook on to the way reality is in its own right, that is, apart from how we think about, believe, or desire reality to be. Simply put: If there were no human beings, then there would be no metaphysically shallow classifications (since there would be no humans to carve up reality).

As an example of a metaphysically shallow classification, consider the good ol' fashioned sport of baseball. The game of baseball—including its accompanying rules, customs, and traditions, etc.—is entirely the product of collective human ingenuity. If there were no human beings, there would be no sport we call baseball. And if there were ever wide enough social agreement to change the rules and customs of the game of baseball (heaven forbid!), then the very nature of the thing we call "baseball" would be different. Thus, while baseball games certainly exist, the classification *being a baseball game* is metaphysically shallow, insofar as that way of classifying reality is entirely human-dependent.

It is vitally important to grasp—important for metaphysics but, more importantly, for the sake of living in tune with God's creational design plan—the fact that not all classifications are metaphysically shallow: some are metaphysically deep or fundamental. In contrast to metaphysically shallow classifications, metaphysically deep classifications are deep in the sense that they are not dependent on how we think about, believe, or desire reality to be, whether individually or collectively. In sharp contrast to shallow classifications, deep classifications carve reality at its human-independent joints, joints that are discovered and not created and exist whether or not we think, believe, or desire differently.

Consider the classification *electron* as an example of a metaphysically deep classification. Subatomic particles that belong to the category *electron* have a unit of negative charge. That is their nature. It is one of the characteristics that ontologically delineates electrons from other existing things, including other subatomic particles such as protons and neutrons. When the scientific community gradually discovered this deep truth about the nature of electrons, it did not confer on electrons their essential nature or deep metaphysical classification; electrons would be negatively charged even if they forever remained hidden from human discovery.[10] Metaphysically deep classifications are not subject to change by committee or the collective will of society; they are not even in principle up for revision. The reason being that deep classifications are ultimately grounded in the mind-independent natures of things (i.e., what they are essentially, apart from how we think or talk about them)—*everything is what it is and not something else.*

Closely tied to this distinction between metaphysically shallow and metaphysically deep classifications is the idea that some groupings or collections of things can be deep (natural), and others shallow (nonnatural, social). This distinction pertains to whether all groupings in reality are socially constructed by humans, or whether some groupings are genuinely discovered and are not the result of human beliefs, attitudes, or social agreement.

Some ways of grouping reality are metaphysically shallow and are purely the result of human thought and action (nonnatural, social), and some groupings are metaphysically deep and have a firm basis in the objective natures of things, apart from human thought and action (natural). To see the difference between these two kinds of groupings—shallow and deep—let's compare the following four groups (see fig. 5.1).[11]

It should be fairly clear that these two sets of groupings, Groups 1–2 and Groups 3–4, are radically different in terms of how deeply they are anchored in reality. Group 1 and Group 2 are purely social groupings that fail to map onto the deep way the world is, apart from my desire to group their members together for the sake of illustration. The members of Group 1—which likely include random items like money, a phone, car keys, and the like (picture me checking my pockets as I write this!)—are in and of themselves unrelated in that they do not share any human-independent similarities or features that would naturally tie them together into a single, tight-knit group. The same applies to

---

[10]Note well: I'm not talking about the English word "electron" or the English words "unit negative charge." Words are bits of human language and thus are purely human constructs. I am talking about what the words refer to, namely, the very *being* of electrons, what they *are* and what they can *do*, by nature.

[11]I borrow Group 4 from Alyssa Ney, *Metaphysics: An Introduction* (New York: Routledge, 2014), 261.

GROUP 1:
The current contents of the pockets of the average middle-aged man in the United States.

GROUP 2:
Aristotle's household pets

GROUP 3:
The members of the taxonomic family *Canidae* (canines)

GROUP 4:
The chemical elements of the periodic table (gold, hydrogen, carbon, etc.)

Figure 5.1. Metaphysically deep versus shallow groupings

Group 2, since the grouping is solely based on animals Aristotle might have chosen as pets (if any). As such, Groups 1 and 2 are shallow and thus purely social ways of classifying reality; they don't carve reality at its deep joints.

Groups 3 and 4, by contrast, track deep, objective similarities between their members, in this case similarities at the biological (Group 3) and elemental (Group 4) levels. While the bits of language we use to label biological and elemental realities are indeed socially constructed (after all, it's mere linguistic convention that we call canines "canines" and not "tenines"), the real, existing things and objective similarities that are labeled are not. Biologically, we classify members of the *Canidae* family (domestic dogs, wolves, coyotes, etc.) the way we do precisely because of what appear to be numerically the same or similar biological features or traits shared among them (or perhaps ancestral lineage). Biologists discover natural groupings like these and develop a taxonomy accordingly. They do not create or construct such natural groupings by sheer thought, willpower, or scholarly agreement. Deep or natural groupings, and the objective natures and classifications they track in reality, are in some form or other the result of the skillful and wise craftsmanship of God (Proverbs 8:22-36), primed to be discovered in all of their richness and wonder.

Getting Theological: Is the Nature of Marriage Metaphysically Shallow or Deep?

Consider the following remarks by philosopher Alyssa Ney in her book *Metaphysics: An Introduction* about the nature and classification of the institution of marriage:

> Consider marriages. To which category do they belong? On the one hand, it seems like a mistake to say that marriages don't exist, in the manner of Pegasus. Marriage is a real phenomenon, not a mere fiction like Pegasus. But, on the other hand, it seems like a mistake to say that marriages exist, in the manner of horses. Marriages do not exist independently of our social practices, institutions, and conventions—as John Searle puts it, marriages seem to exist only because we believe them to exist. So what sort of entities are marriages then?[a]

How should a Christian metaphysician who takes the nature of marriage to be a real, divinely ordained relation between a man and a woman that is part of the deep structure of reality, understand the ontology of marriage? Are Ney and Searle right in suggesting that marriage is a purely metaphysically shallow kind of relation?

I don't think so. Biblically speaking (Genesis 2:24; Matthew 19:3-9), marriage is the kind of relation that is what it is—its very essence— independently of human social practices, institutions, and conventions. While there would be no actual *individual marriages* (marriage tokens, we might say) were there no existing human beings, this doesn't at all suggest that marriage itself is the *type* of relation it is because of human social convention. As a metaphysically deep aspect of reality, the nature of marriage is what it is apart from what humans believe or say about it.

[a]Alyssa Ney, *Metaphysics: An Introduction* (New York: Routledge, 2014), 259.

CARVING REALITY AT ITS DEEPEST JOINTS: THE ONTOLOGICAL CATEGORIES

Yet it is vitally important for the task of traditional metaphysics to point out that not all metaphysically deep classifications and groupings depend on features that are discoverable by the natural sciences (as with Group 3 and Group 4 in figure 5.1). In fact, the deepest level of classification in reality is found in what metaphysicians have traditionally called the "ontological categories," the most general kinds of created being that exist.

The ontological categories of created being constitute the most fundamental level of ontological classification, deeper than even the classification afforded by the hard sciences such as physics, biology, and chemistry.[12] As such, the ontological categories cut the deepest when it comes to classifying created reality. A categorial ontology—a system of ontological categories—aims to catalog and classify the most general kinds or sorts of existing entities. As such, a system of ontological categories will aim to be exhaustive. Every existing created being will fall within one of the categories; whether material or immaterial, scientifically detectable or not, each created being is ontologically classifiable as an entity of some general kind or other. This is precisely because all created beings have a general nature, essence, or ontological form, which specifies, in the most broad sense, what it is or what it is to be an entity of that general kind or type.[13] In short: To specify the most basic category of

---

[12]More specifically, everything that can be scientifically classified can be ontologically classified, but not everything that can be ontologically classified can be scientifically classified. There are some creaturely beings whose natures are not constituted by physical stuff and governed by physical laws (human souls, angels) and thus not classifiable by empirical means but by pure rational insight (see chap. 2).

[13]See E. J. Lowe, "The Rationality of Metaphysics," *Synthese* 178 (2011): 99-109. Recall my earlier claim that numerical identity is anchored in the more bedrock law of reality that everything *is what it is and is not something else*, that everything has a nature or essence. This is precisely what I mean here when I say that every created being is classifiable along the lines of its general nature,

being an entity belongs to is to specify its general nature and thus answer the question "What *is* it?" in the broadest sense.[14] At root, the categories get at the deep insight that all of created reality is intelligible, ultimately because it is the creative product of the skillful work of Supreme Wisdom itself (Proverbs 8:22-31; Colossians 1:15-17).

DIVERGING VIEWS OF THE ONTOLOGICAL CATEGORIES: ARISTOTLE AND KANT

Historically, there have been two very broad, overarching views regarding the nature of the ontological categories themselves, and both are in sharp contrast to one another. The first general view of the categories is Aristotle's own account, put forward in various places throughout his own work and throughout Aristotelian tradition that followed, but principally in his work *Categories*. Aristotle held to what we can call a "realist" construal of the ontological categories, that the categories are objectively existing kinds of being that structure the way the world is in itself, apart from how we conceptualize and think about the world; they are metaphysically deep classifications. As we've already seen in chapter one, Aristotle put forward ten categories of being: *Substance, Quantity, Quality, Relation, Action, Passion, Place, Time, Position*, and *Habit*. The most basic ontological category for Aristotle was that of *Substance*, with the rest of the categories depending on the category of *Substance* in various ways. As Aristotle puts it, "if the primary substances did not exist it would be impossible for any of the other things to exist."[15] For example, qualities (i.e., properties) such as *being furry* and *being stubborn* depend on there being a thing that has or stands under the qualities, namely a substance, like a cat. Qualities such as *being furry* and relations like *being loved by countless old ladies* are predicated of cats as substances, that is, they are ways cats are. Ontology, traditionally conceived, aims at exploring the shape and structure of created being by way of the ontological categories,

essence, or ontological category. For a helpful discussion of this point in particular, see Oderberg, *Real Essentialism*, chap. 5.

[14]Traditionally, something's specific essence or nature will be captured by its lowest level ontological category, or "infima species" as some medieval philosophers put it. So, a horse is, going from general to specific, first and foremost an entity, an object, a substance, a living organism, a certain kind of living organism (*mammal*), a certain kind of mammal (member of the family *Equidae*), etc.

[15]Aristotle, *The Complete Works of Aristotle*, vol. 1, ed. Jonathan Barnes (Princeton, NJ: Princeton University Press, 1984), *Categories* 5; 2b 6–7, p. 1609; *Metaphysics* 1019a 2–4.

most notably the category of *Substance* and how all other created beings relate to it.

Another historically influential view of the ontological categories, one that sharply contrasts with the Aristotelian-realist one I've laid out above, is that of the German philosopher Immanuel Kant (1724–1804). Kant famously believed that the categories were something like forms of thought (or what he called "pure concepts of understanding") and not inherent in the way reality is structured in itself, apart from the way that we think about or conceptualize it.[16] In this way, Kant's view of the categories can be thought of along "anti-realist" lines, in contrast to the realist position defended by Aristotle and others. According to one influential way of reading Kant, the deepest joints of reality are ultimately themselves carved out by the human mind; they are not out there, so to speak, waiting to be discovered by the human mind.[17]

At the risk of misrepresenting Kant's highly nuanced and complex understanding of the categories, let me offer a simple (no doubt overly simplistic) illustration that might help here. When you feed a new lump of Play-Doh through a star-shaped plastic mold, the Play-Doh takes on the form of a star; feed the Play-Doh through a square-shaped plastic mold, it will take on the form of a square, and so on. The amorphous lump of Play-Doh comes to the plastic mold in a formless state, and it is the job of the mold to carve up the Play-Doh into its various forms. The Play-Doh *itself* is unformed and only receives its form when it passes through the respective plastic mold.

Very roughly, for Kant, reality apart from how we think or conceptualize it is without intrinsic form, just like the Play-Doh; there are no categories of being that exist out there, waiting to be discovered. The raw data of our sensory experience of the world is organized and made intelligible by the twelve concepts of human thought—unity, plurality, cause and effect,

---

[16]Immanuel Kant, *Prolegomena to Any Future Based Metaphysics*, trans. James W. Ellington (Indianapolis: Hackett, 1977), Second Part. There are various interpretations of Kant's view of these matters, of course. I would recommend those reading Kant for the first time to start with his *Prolegomena to Any Future Based Metaphysics*.

[17]For more on Kant's thought here and how it relates to more contemporary discussions of realism and anti-realism about the structure of reality independently of the human mind, see Alvin Plantinga, "How to Be an Anti-Realist," *Proceedings and Addresses of the American Philosophical Association* 56, no. 1 (1982): 47-70. For more on how a theistic philosopher might sympathetically appropriate a version of Kant's view of the categories, I'd recommend reading Christian philosopher Merold Westphal's essay "Christian Philosophers and the Copernican Revolution," in *Christian Perspectives on Religious Knowledge*, eds. C. Stephen Evans and Merold Westphal (Grand Rapids, MI: Eerdmans, 1993), and comparing it with Plantinga's essay above.

substance, accident, to name just a few—concepts that are themselves built into the human mind, akin to the star- and square-shaped plastic molds of our Play-Doh illustration. Thus, any ontological form or classification in the world is due solely to human conceptual activity, and sensory experience would be an unintelligible jumble apart from the human mind's carving up reality in terms of these concepts of understanding.[18]

I have neither the space, the time, nor the expertise to delve any deeper into Kant's anti-realist understanding of the categories. Suffice it to say that most contemporary metaphysicians lean heavily toward some version of a realist view of the ontological categories, and for good reason.[19] If Kant is right, then the study of metaphysics or ontology as a quest to discover the deepest categorial structure of the world is deeply misguided from the very start. If Kant wins the day, metaphysical reflection is ultimately the study of how we think about or conceive of reality, nothing more.[20]

A CLOSER LOOK AT SOME ONTOLOGICAL CATEGORIES

Many in the history of metaphysics have considered the ontological categories to be hierarchically organized, with the most general (topmost) level of classification consisting of the category *Entity* (or *Being*); every created being that exists is an entity in this broad sense, with more specific categories of being descending from this most general ontological category.

To help get a broad handle on some more specific kinds of being or ontological categories, let's carefully consider additional groupings of created beings:

Group 5 *Objects*: bouncy balls, human beings, apples, tigers, water molecules, electrons, horses

Group 6 *Kinds*: Ball, Humanity, Apple, Tiger, Water, Electron, Equinity

Group 7 *Properties*: sphericity, rationality, sweetness, being carnivorous, wetness, negative charge, being powerful

---

[18]Kant, *Prolegomena to Any Future Based Metaphysics*, I:283, 284-86; II.

[19]Metaphysicians have defended a variety of realist or realist-like views of the ontological categories. On the contemporary scene, there have been a variety of different realist views defended by the likes of E. J. Lowe, Roderick Chisholm, and Gary Rosenkrantz and Joshua Hoffman. A very helpful, but intermediate next step is Jan Westerhoff's book *Ontological Categories: Their Nature and Significance* (New York: Oxford University Press, 2005).

[20]For a concise and somewhat accessible critique of a Kantian approach to metaphysics, see the introduction to E. J. Lowe, *A Survey of Metaphysics* (New York: Oxford University Press, 2002), 7-9.

Group 8 *Relations*: parenthood, marriage, betweenness, being five miles away from

Group 9 *Events*: the Civil War, the sinking of the Titanic, the presidential inauguration of Joe Biden

Group 10 *Objects (Substances)*: hamsters, tarantulas, cats, frogs, oak trees, human beings

Group 11 *Objects (Aggregates)*: pool tables, automobiles, espresso makers, bicycles

Groups 5–11 all aim to capture the fact that the members of each individual group are all the same kinds of beings, and thus naturally belong to the same general ontological category. Let's take a closer look at each group.

Each member of Group 5 belongs to the category of *Object*. Roughly, objects are the kinds of being that possess or bear properties and are not themselves possessed or had by anything else (apples are red and sweet, not vice versa). As we will see shortly, on some ontological systems there are further subcategories of *Object*, such as *Substance* and *Artifact/Aggregate*.

The members of Group 6 are what philosophers have traditionally called "kinds."[21] For many metaphysicians past and present, individual objects are commonly thought to "instantiate," "belong to," or "fall under" particular kinds. So, tigers are individual objects that are instances of (or belong to) the kind Tiger. Individual tigers are all mammals, carnivores, and so on, because they are all the same or similar type of being (they all have the same or similar ontological form, we might say) and thus belong to the same or similar kind.[22] In general, kinds specify what an individual object is, whether a tulip, tiger, or a tadpole (think of how a cookie-cutter stamps out a particular form of cookie into the dough).

The kinds of being in Group 7 belong to the category of *Properties* (a.k.a. *Feature* or *Characteristic*).[23] Properties "characterize" individual objects, that is, they describe *how* (not *what*) individual objects are or what they are like. So, *sweetness* and *redness* characterize how some individual objects are and

---

[21]Aristotle calls them "secondary substances" in *Categories* 5.
[22]We will see in chap. 7 that not all philosophers agree that kinds (human, canine, electron, etc.) are strictly numerically the same in each of their instances.
[23]Remember that I'm talking about the features themselves, not the English words we use to refer to those entities, e.g., "redness."

what they are like, such as apples and Turkish delight. We will explore the existence and nature of properties in detail in chapter seven.

Group 8 consists of the kinds of being philosophers call "relations." As we have seen earlier in the chapter, relations hold between individual objects; relations relate or link individual objects to each other in particular ways (causally, spatially, explanatorily, logically, etc.).

Group 9 consists of events that happen to objects at or over an extended period of time. Entities in the category of *Events* are the sort of beings that occur in time and, at least according to one influential view of the nature of events, involve an object's (Titanic) having a property (*sinking*) at a particular time (April 14-15, 1912).[24]

Finally, let's take Group 10 and Group 11 together. The members of both of these groups are all further subcategories of the category *Objects* (Group 5*).* Group 10 consists of objects belonging to the category of *Substances*, in particular, living organisms, while Group 11 consists of objects belonging to the subcategory of *Aggregates* (or *Artifacts*). Let me briefly say something about the difference between these two types of object.

One thing you might have noticed in my unpacking of the kinds of being listed in Groups 5–11 is that they all, in some way or other, revolve around the category of *Objects*. But for Aristotle and the medieval Aristotelian tradition, objects belonging to the category of *Substances* (what Aristotle called "primary substance") have a metaphysical pride of place, both with respect to other types of objects (such as aggregates or nonsubstances) as well as all other kinds of being in general (i.e., the entire system of ontological categories at large). In the Aristotelian tradition, substantial objects, living organisms in particular, are more ontologically ultimate than nonsubstantial objects such as pool tables, espresso makers, or even something like a bundle of sticks (if bundles are one thing at all).

The reason for this deep ontological divide between the types of objects is that substances do not depend for their existence or their nature on any other kind of being, while aggregates do radically depend on substances for their

---

[24]For a helpful overview of the contemporary literature on the nature of events, see Roberto Casati and Achille Varzi, "Events," in Stanford Encyclopedia of Philosophy, Fall 2023 ed., eds. Edward N. Zalta and Uri Nodelman, https://plato.stanford.edu/archives/fall2023/entries/events/. The influential view of events noted here has been developed by Jaegwon Kim, "Events as Property Exemplifications," in *Action Theory*, eds. M. Brand and D. Walton (Dordrecht: Reidel, 1976), 159-77.

existence and nature. There are rather complex reasons for this, but such reasons will need to wait until chapter eight when we get to the nature of substance in general.

Getting Theological: The Transcendentals

There is a venerable tradition in the history of Christian metaphysics, stemming from Saint Augustine and developed most fully in the thirteenth century, which maintains that there are some aspects of reality—*the transcendentals*—that are common to all created beings *as such* and apply to each and every created being *whatsoever*, no matter the ontological category. The transcendentals are said to "transcend" the categories not because they map onto some existing realm beyond the categories, but in that they are cross-categorical and apply to each and every category of created being.

According to Thomas Aquinas, one of the Christian tradition's most eminent metaphysicians, in his work *De Veritate* [*On Truth*] 1.1, the transcendentals include the following: *being, thing, one, something, true,* and *good*. For Aquinas, the transcendentals are all "convertible" in that they each uniquely convey a different aspect of the shape of created being under a different description. The transcendentals each uniquely illumine the specific contour of created reality in a way that that the general term "being," on its own, does not.

So, to say that everything created is a *thing*, in this sense, is to say that everything is a being of some kind or other. To say that everything is a *something* is to say that every being is and is not nothing. To say that everything is *one* is to say that every being is numerically distinct from other beings. To say that everything is *true* is to say that every being is intelligible and to some degree or other conforms to the kind of being it is (e.g., a *true* word spoken is a word that accurately represents the way the world is), ultimately with reference to its truest exemplar existing in God's own mind. To say that everything is *good* is to say that everything has being as a particular kind of entity and, by simply existing, conforms (to some degree or other) to the kind of being it is and ought to be by nature (again, ultimately in reference to its perfect exemplar in God's mind). Photons, pebbles, and pens are good simply by virtue of existing (thus the type of goodness at play here is much broader than moral goodness). While a pen can be a more or less good instance of its kind, it is "good" in this broad sense simply in virtue of the fact that it exists and is a pen. A truly excellent pen—one that fully embodies all that a pen is and ought to be—is one that properly realizes what it is and what it is for by nature, a writing instrument designed for the purpose of writing well.

For Aquinas and other classical Christian thinkers, there is an astonishing (though in no way coincidental) metaphysical fit between human beings and all other created reality. We are both divinely created with a deep hunger for being as well as divinely endowed with the needed capacities to satisfy that deep hunger for being. In particular, humans are the kinds of created beings that both hunger for the *true* and the *good* and have been endowed with needed intellectual and volitional capacities adequate to satisfy that hunger. The human intellect hungers for being under the aspect of the *true*, it craves intelligibility and understanding. As meaning-seeking animals, human beings have a deep hunger to know, as Aristotle identified so many years ago. Humans also have a deep, metaphysical hunger for the *good*, to lay hold of and conform to the way things ought to be. These two astonishing facts—our deep hunger for being under the guise of the *true* and the *good* as well as our being uniquely endowed with the ability to satisfy these hungers—are ultimately rooted in a deep metaphysical truth about human nature (consider the fact that you do not share this deep hunger for truth with squirrels or iPhones). Like a key fit for a specific lock, the human being has been divinely endowed with two faculties—the intellect and the will—that were made to feed on reality. Consequently, when we are deprived of truth and goodness, the human being will starve in the worst possible way.

GOING DEEPER: CLASSIFYING CREATURELY REALITY

Key Concepts in Metaphysics

- identity
- indiscernibility of identicals
- identity of indiscernibles

- Leibniz's Law
- synchronic identity
- diachronic identity
- events
- carving reality at the joints
- relata
- postmodernism
- realism versus anti-realism (global)

Historical

- Aristotle, *Categories; Topics* I, chap. 7, "Senses of 'Same'"
- Medieval Philosophers on the Ontological Categories: Robert Pasnau, chapter 12 of *Metaphysical Themes 1274–1671*
- John Duns Scotus, "Qualified and Unqualified Distinctions," 5.4 in *Basic Issues in Medieval Philosophy*
- Francisco Suarez, *On the Various Kinds of Distinction*
- Immanuel Kant, *Prolegomena to Any Future Metaphysics*, parts I-II
- Peter Coffey, *Ontology or the Theory of Being: An Introduction to General Metaphysics*, chaps. 3-4, 8, 10, 12

Contemporary

- Reinhardt Grossman, *The Existence of the World: An Introduction to Ontology*
- Alvin Plantinga, "How to Be an Anti-Realist," in *Proceedings and Addresses of the American Philosophical Association*
- David Oderberg, *Real Essentialism*, chap. 5
- E. J. Lowe, *The Four-Category Ontology*, chaps. 1-2
- Michael Rea, "Social Metaphysics—Gender," in *Metaphysics: The Basics*, 2nd ed.
- Alyssa Ney and Allan Hazlett, "The Metaphysics of Race," in *Metaphysics: An Introduction*
- Jan Westerhoff, *Ontological Categories: Their Nature and Significance*

6

CREATURELY NATURES

ESSENCE AND MODALITY

THE WONDER OF WHAT COULD BE AND WHAT MUST BE

I have three wonderful children, each of whom is precious and life-giving to me and my wife. While my children are one of my greatest treasures in life, the fact remains that I could have failed to be a dad. There is nothing about what I am essentially that makes it the case that I *must* be a father. Likewise, while I am a teacher, I could have been a world-renowned yodeler. I am also a human being, of course. But could I have failed to be a human being? *Could* I have been anything other than a human being? If I exist at all, must I be a human being or could I have been a turnip or an overdue library book?

Claims about what could be and what must be are claims about what is *possible* and what is *necessary*, or what philosophers call claims about "modality" (relating to the mode or manner in which statements or things are). Claims about what is possible and necessary are ordinary and commonplace, really. We frequently make decisions on the basis of what could and could not be in various ways. The topic of the nature of possibility and necessity has been central to metaphysical reflection in the history of Western philosophy. What exactly accounts for how things could have been, and how things must be? What basis in reality is there for the clear truth of claims of possibility and necessity? What are essences and natures, and how do "possible worlds" factor in this question? This chapter serves as an introductory guide to some of the most important concepts and topics in the metaphysics of modality.

DISENTANGLING VARIETIES OF POSSIBILITY AND NECESSITY

In ordinary life and discourse, we frequently make various types of claims that refer to what is possible and what is necessary. However, it is important to carefully reflect on the different kinds of possibility and necessity, in order to get clear on what kind of possibility and necessity metaphysicians principally have in mind when they discuss the metaphysics of modality.

To help set the table, consider the following modal claims of possibility (and impossibility) and necessity:

1. I can't yodel, but I'm sure I could if I had an expert yodeling teacher.

2. No triangle can have four interior angles.

3. While nothing can travel faster than the speed of light (186,000 miles per second), it is possible that a future human civilization builds a vehicle that travels at a slightly slower speed.

4. The speed of light could have been different from what it is (186,000 miles per second).

Let's start by focusing on statement 1. To say that I could learn to yodel is to say that it is currently possible for me to acquire the ability to do so, but only in the sense that I actually have the ability or power to learn to yodel. Put it this way: If I were to undergo a strict training regimen with a skilled yodeling master, I would acquire the ability to yodel. This is what we might call "power possibility," since it is the kind of possibility that is anchored in the actual power or ability a thing has to bring about a particular scenario (my learning to yodel). So, power possibility is what *could* be given the powers of things, and "power necessity" is what *must* be given the powers (or lack of powers) of things. Power possibility and necessity are rather mundane insofar as they root what is possible and necessary in the way the world actually is, in terms of the existing causal powers of things (or their lack).

Statement 2—that no triangle can have four interior angles—seems to be a modal statement of a very different kind than statement 1. In contrast to statement 1, statement 2 is a claim about impossibility, that it is straightforwardly impossible for triangles to have four interior angles. Why, exactly? Well, it belongs to the very nature of *tri*angles to have three and only three interior angles. And to say that a geometric shape can have only three interior angles *and* four interior angles (at the same time and in the same sense) would be to cut against a law of reality known as the law of noncontradiction. On this understanding, some statement P, say, "triangles have four interior angles," is logically impossible if P entails a logical contradiction, that is, if it runs contrary to a rule of logic. So, what we'll call "logical possibility" (sometimes "narrow logical possibility") is simply what *could* be given the laws of logic, and "logical necessity" is what *must* be given the laws of logic. Since P entails a logical contradiction, P is not logically possible, which is precisely what statement 2 communicates; under no circumstances could P be true, given the laws of logic (i.e., statement P *must* be false, given the laws of logic).

Statement 3 pertains to what could and could not be given the laws of nature in particular. We can, roughly, think of a law of nature as simply an orderly way that objects in the natural world tend to behave in normal circumstances. Since the speed of light (186,000 miles per second) is a physical constant of nature, it is physically impossible to travel faster than the speed of light. However, it is possible, given the laws of nature, to build a vehicle that can travel at a slightly slower speed, say 185,000 miles per second. There is no known law of nature that precludes this possibility, even if human technology precludes this possibility from ever being realized. Note that the impossibility and possibility at play in statement 3 don't stem from the rules of logic or anything of the sort. Rather, the impossibility and possibility here derive from the actual structure and contour of the physical universe. So, what philosophers call "physical possibility" is what could be given the laws of nature (and likewise physical impossibility of what could not be given said laws), and "physical necessity" is what must be given the laws of nature.

Last, consider statement 4 as a statement about what could be *come what may*. Notice that in 4 all previous qualifications have been removed from what could be the case (e.g., given the laws of logic or of nature). There seem to be some scenarios that are possible and impossible that fail to correspond to what is logically and physically possible and impossible. For instance, while my jumping over the moon unaided is physically impossible (as it is ruled out by the current laws of nature), nevertheless such a scenario is metaphysically possible (as God could have arranged the natural world in such a way as to behave in accordance with different laws of nature). Likewise, while "the American president's being identical to a prime number" is logically possible (as it does not entail a logical contradiction), this scenario is nevertheless metaphysically impossible (as human beings and numbers are just fundamentally different kinds of things, and necessarily so). So, this last variety of possibility diverges in important ways from (narrow) logical and physical possibility (and impossibility). This final sense of possibility is what philosophers call absolute, broad logical possibility, or simply, "metaphysical possibility."[1]

While our current physical laws make it impossible for light to travel faster than 186,000 miles per second, such a voyage certainly *seems* possible in a wider, philosophical sense. Why think this? Well, it strikes many philosophers as reasonable to think that reality could have included a speed of light constant with a different value than the one it, in fact, has.[2] Isn't it possible that the speed of light be 187,000 miles per second, instead? At the very least, it sure *seems* to be possible for reality to have been that way, doesn't it? To put it differently: Couldn't God have created the universe in such a way that the speed of light constant was faster than what it actually is? (Just imagine God saying: "Let the speed of light constant be X" where X is some value greater than what it actually is). If so, then it seems to be metaphysically possible in this wider sense that light travel faster than the current speed of light, even if this possibility is precluded by the current laws of nature. "Metaphysical possibility," then, is what *could* be, come what may, and "metaphysical necessity" is what *must* be, come what may.

A CLOSER LOOK AT METAPHYSICAL NECESSITY: *DE DICTO* AND *DE RE*

When it comes to distinctively metaphysical possibility and necessity, metaphysicians have traditionally distinguished between modality *de dicto* (Latin: "of the saying") and modality *de re* (Latin: "of the thing"). Modality *de dicto* pertains to the modal status—whether metaphysical possibility or necessity—of a statement, proposition, or fact. By contrast, modality *de re* pertains to the modal status of things, how individual things in particular could or must be.[3]

---

[1]For a helpful overview of the varieties of modality, see Boris Kment, "Varieties of Modality," *Stanford Encyclopedia of Philosophy*, March 2021, https://plato.stanford.edu/archives/spr2021/entries/modality-varieties/. For a more challenging treatment of the nature of metaphysical necessity and how it differs from other varieties of necessity, see chap. 1 of Alvin Plantinga, *The Nature of Necessity* (Oxford: Clarendon, 1974).

[2]Note, not all metaphysicians agree with this. Many, myself included, think that the laws of nature are really just the laws of *natures* and thus (hypothetically) metaphysically necessary. The only way for the laws of nature to be different is if God were to embed different natures/essences into the natural world.

[3]It is important to point out that in the history of Western philosophy, the very concept of metaphysical necessity has come under attack by David Hume and "neo-Humeans" who follow closely in his wake in the twentieth century (especially W. V. Quine and his disciples). These

When doing theology and developing a Christian worldview, it is vitally important to be aware of and to heed the distinction between modality *de dicto* and modality *de re*. So, consider the following examples of *de dicto* and *de re* modal statements, all involving distinctively metaphysical possibility/necessity:

(a) Possibly, there are purple polka-dotted donkeys.

(b) Necessarily, no contradiction is true.

(c) Human beings are necessarily rational.

(d) Water is necessarily H_2O.

(e) Ross is possibly six feet five inches.

Statements (a) and (b) are both *de dicto* modal statements as they each assign a different modal status to statements or propositions (*possible* is attributed to the statement "there are purple polka-dotted donkeys" and *necessary* to the statement "no contradiction is true").

By contrast, statements (c)-(e) are all *de re* modal statements as they assign different modal statuses to various things (human beings, water, myself). Note that (c) and (d) state that rationality and being H_2O are necessary in order to be human and water, respectively; human beings and water *must* be rational and made up of hydrogen and oxygen in order to be human and water, respectively. Statements like (c) and (d) capture what is part of the essence of human beings and water, respectively (more on this below).

There is great conceptual trouble that awaits if we fail to heed the age-old difference between *de dicto* and *de re* modality. On the surface, our language about what is metaphysically possible and necessary can be ambiguous as to whether a statement should be read along the lines of a *de dicto* or a *de re* modal claim. Consider the following example, and see if you can spot the modal ambiguity:

S1: The number of apostles is necessarily even.[4]

The ambiguity of S1 lies in the fact that it is not clear on its surface whether it intends to ascribe metaphysical necessity to a *statement*, in this case "the

---

philosophers deny that there are *de re* metaphysical necessities in the real world, how things *must* be and are interrelated (no "necessary connections" between things), apart from how we *talk* about the world.

[4]Plantinga, *Nature of Necessity*, chap. 2, section 3.

number of apostles is even," or to a *thing*, the number 12 (the number that numbers the apostles). These two different readings of S1 can be stated as follows:

> *De Dicto*: Necessarily, the number of apostles is even.

> *De Re*: The number 12 is *necessarily* even.

Don't miss this important point: whether S1 is true or false depends on how one reads S1, whether in terms of a *de dicto* or a *de re* reading above. If read as a *de dicto* claim of metaphysical necessity, S1 is emphatically false since it implies that it is metaphysically necessary that an even number of apostles were chosen; but that can't be right. Surely, it was metaphysically possible for Jesus to have picked an odd number of apostles! But if read as a *de re* claim— that is, as a claim about the number 12 *itself* (the number that numbers the apostles)—then S1 is true since it is part of the nature of the number 12 that it is an even number; it's not possible for the number 12 to be an odd number.

Getting Theological: Divine Foreknowledge and *De Dicto/De Re* Necessity

Let's quickly apply the *de dicto/de re* distinction to a substantive, theological topic: the seeming incompatibility of human freedom and divine foreknowledge. Consider the statement:

> S2: Whatever God foreknows *necessarily* comes to pass.

This statement is ambiguous on its face and can be read along either *de dicto* or *de re* lines:

> *De Dicto*: Necessarily, if God foreknows something, then it will come to pass.

> *De Re*: If God foreknows something, then *necessarily* it will come to pass.

Again, as metaphysically trained classical Christian theologians have spotted, how one interprets statements like S2 have significant theological implications. Thomas Aquinas, for instance, referred to the *de dicto* reading of S2 (De Dicto) as "the necessity of the consequence" since the necessity is assigned to the whole conditional statement (if . . . then). By contrast, Aquinas referred to the *de re* reading (De Re) as "the necessity of the consequent" since the necessity is attributed to the consequent alone (the consequent here being the phrase "it will come to pass"). One of these readings entails the theologically contentious view that God's foreknowledge eliminates all creaturely contingency in the world (everything creatures do, they do of necessity). I'll leave it as an exercise to you the reader to find which reading entails the theologically contentious view and which does not.

METAPHYSICAL TARGET PRACTICE: ACCIDENTAL AND NONACCIDENTAL TRUTHS

Traditionally, when it comes to *de re* (metaphysical) modality—what could and must be as it pertains to things—philosophers have distinguished between two different types of *de re* modal truths, "accidental" and "nonaccidental." Let's start with accidental, *de re* modal truths. There are various truths about you, for example, that could have failed to be true and you still exist all the same. Truths about how tall you are, how much you weigh, your specific hair color, your current profession, and your being a student of metaphysics are all truths about you that could have been false and you still exist. Philosophers call these truths "accidental truths."

Here is a very important metaphysical point about the structure of reality: Not all *de re* modal truths are accidental. Some *de re* modal truths about you (and every other created being) are such that it is not possible for you to exist and these sorts of truths about you be false. Metaphysicians call these sorts of *de re* modal truths, "nonaccidental" or "necessary truths" (sometimes "essential truths").[5]

Nonaccidental truths about you must be true of you in order for you to exist. So, for example, "_____ is human" (where you can fill in the blank with your own name) is true of you and arguably must be true of you; it is impossible for you to exist without being human.

In this way, nonaccidental truths are indicative of what you are in a deeper, ontological sense than accidental truths. Your current job and hair color are

---

[5]For reasons that will become clear soon, I am deliberately avoiding using the language of "essential" here. Historically, the class of nonaccidental truths is much broader than essential truths and includes all necessary truths about a thing that do not belong to its essence, strictly speaking.

not as central to your core metaphysical identity in this sense. But the facts that you are human, that you are created by God, and that you are the kind of being that is capable of laughter ("risible," a fun and much older word for this), cut more to the core of what is definitive of the kind of being you are.

Historically, metaphysicians have identified two sorts of nonaccidental truths about things, both of which are more definitive to a thing's identity or nature (recall: "everything is what it is and not anything else") than accidental truths about your hair color, height, and current job. Let's distinguish between the following types of nonaccidental truths about things:

> NA1: *Necessary Truth*: a truth about a thing that couldn't fail to be true of it and that thing still exist.

> NA2: *Essential Truth*: (a) a truth about a thing that couldn't fail to be true of it and that thing still exist, and (b) a truth that defines what that thing is in the most basic sense in terms of its essence or nature.

Notice that NA2 encompasses NA1 in clause (a) but is more specific in that it adds clause (b). As such, while NA1 and NA2 are both nonaccidental truths, essential truths are more fine-grained and specific than mere necessary truths. Both species of nonaccidental truths illumine, to some degree or other, what a thing is in the most basic, ontological sense.

To illustrate, imagine that all the truths about you could be mapped onto an archery target with concentric circles centering on a bullseye in the middle (see fig. 6.1). We might say that accidental truths, like truths about your height, hair color, and profession, hit the outer circles of the target. Nonaccidental truths, by contrast, both in terms of necessary (NA1) and essential truths (NA2), hit much closer to the center of the target. Essential truths about you hit right smack in the center of the bullseye. These truths, such as your being human and your being created by God, constitute your nature or essence. Not only must they be true of you in order for you to exist, they are *definitive* of what you are essentially. Necessary truths about you, by contrast, hit just outside of the bullseye, yet closer to the center of the target than mere accidental truths. Necessary truths involving you, we might say, follow immediately on the heels of essential truths about you. But—and here's the key takeaway from this discussion—necessary truths and essential truths are not the same. Essential truths directly track your identity or essence; necessary truths do not.

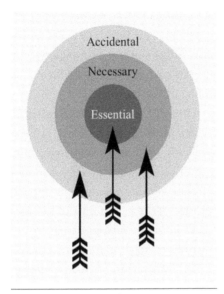

Figure 6.1. Metaphysical target practice:
Accidental and nonaccidental truths

From a more classical, Aristotelian understanding of the relationship between these two types of nonaccidental truths, necessary truths flow out of the essential truths. Necessary truths are nonaccidental in that they are true of you and they must be true of you if you are to exist. However, necessary truths do not indicate what you are in the most basic sense, your essence or identity—what kind of being you are most fundamentally. Rather, necessary truths are themselves explained by the essential truths. The concentric circles on a target center around the innermost circle as the focal point, the bullseye. The bullseye centers and grounds, in some way or other, all other outer rings on the target. This is a bit like how the essential truths about you—and the human essence to which they point—ultimately explain all other truths about you, the necessary and accidental truths.

It should be pointed out that in contrast to this classical, Aristotelian understanding of nonaccidental truths, NA1 and NA2, a good number of contemporary metaphysicians think that necessary truths just *are* essential truths, that what is true of you *necessarily* is what is true of you *essentially* (as we will see below, this is due to the influence of what is often called "modal essentialism"). Suffice it to say that, historically, the class of nonaccidental truths was thought to be much broader than this and included both necessary and essential nonaccidental truths.[6]

MODAL ESSENTIALISM AND THE METAPHYSICS OF POSSIBLE WORLDS

As I mentioned in the first chapter, metaphysical reflection (as least traditionally conceived as it is practiced in this book) was in dire straits at the dawn

---

[6]To use more historic terminology here, there are truths about the essence proper (essential, nonaccidental truths) and truths about what necessarily follows from the essence, or "propria" (necessary, nonaccidental truths).

of the twentieth century, buried as it was underneath the ruins brought on by the wrecking ball of logical positivism (see chap. 2). Yet, due in part to the influential work of philosophers like Saul Kripke, Alvin Plantinga, David Armstrong, and others, metaphysics began to emerge from the rubble in the wake of the demise of logical positivism.

One of the first areas of metaphysical inquiry to rise again was that of the nature of metaphysical necessity and possibility. The story is very complex, and I don't have the space to tell it here.[7] But it is very important to point out that the initial resurgence of thinking about metaphysical modality was largely on the coattails of important developments in modal logic in the mid-twentieth century, the logic of the necessary and the possible. While many philosophers during this time remained suspicious of heavyweight metaphysical notions for various reasons (some of which have to do with the reasons laid out in chap. 2), others remained convinced that such notions like necessity and possibility were indispensable to our best formal-logical systems.[8]

One of the leading early thinkers to reinvigorate the area of modal metaphysics in the mid-to-late-twentieth century was Saul Kripke (1940–2022). Kripke had an eye on developing a framework to account for the truth of modal statements, statements that many believed were indispensable to our best modal logic. In doing so, Kripke was one of the first to breathe new life into the old notion of a "possible world"—a complete, alternative way things could have been—as a useful concept to help account for the truth of modal statements.[9] For Kripke and others who followed suit in utilizing the framework of possible worlds to ground the truth of modal statements, a *de dicto* modal statement like "Necessarily, 2+2=4" is true if and only if "2+2=4" is true in every possible world; that is, in every way things could have been, it is true that 2+2=4. Alternatively, a *de re* modal statement like "LeBron James could have been a professional golfer" is true if and only if in at least one

---

[7]For an extremely insightful, though challenging, discussion of this story, see Michael Loux's introduction to the book he edited titled *The Possible and the Actual: Readings in the Metaphysics of Modality* (Ithaca, NY: Cornell University Press, 1979).

[8]The very notion of logical consequence and soundness, where an argument is sound if and only if the truth of the conclusion follows necessarily—i.e., couldn't fail to follow—from the truth of the premises, employs distinctively modal notions.

[9]The formal concept of a possible world originated first in the work of medieval philosopher John Duns Scotus and can be found in the work of German Christian philosopher Gottfried Wilhelm Leibniz.

possible world LeBron is a professional golfer; that is, according to at least one way things could have been, it is true that LeBron James is a professional golfer.

Call "modal essentialism" the view that the framework of possible worlds is entirely sufficient to account for the truth of modal claims, both *de dicto* and *de re* (including truths about the essences or natures of things).[10]

But what are possible worlds, metaphysically speaking? How exactly do they help explain and ground truths about modality? There are two over-arching questions that will guide us in the remainder of the chapter:

1. What are some prominent modal essentialist views concerning both the nature of possible worlds and the role possible worlds play in explaining the truth of modal claims?

2. Is modal essentialism itself sufficient to account for a thing's essence (*de re* necessity)?

So, let's get metaphysical![11]

MODAL CONCRETISM: DAVID LEWIS'S EXTREME MODAL REALISM

Let's turn to exploring question 1 first. There are two broad versions of modal essentialism. Both versions have radically different views as to the precise nature of possible worlds, and both have been immensely influential in con-temporary metaphysics.

Let's start by taking a look at perhaps the most extreme variety of modal essentialism on the market today, what has been called "extreme modal re-alism" and eloquently defended by David Lewis in his 1986 book *On the Plurality of Worlds*.[12] According to Lewis, possible worlds really do exist. They

---

[10]It should be pointed out for reference that not all contemporary accounts of modality accept that a realist construal of possible worlds is needed in order to account for modal statements. The view known as "modal fictionalism," defended most notably by philosopher Gideon Rosen, holds that true modal claims are true according to the *fiction* of possible worlds. Fictions in this sense are like stories and are not *literally* true (just like it is true according to the fiction of Harry Potter that Harry is a wizard, but not literally true per se). This is one way to utilize possible worlds discourse without being ontologically committed to an ontology of possible worlds as with modal essentialism.

[11]I owe this phrase, which is a play off Olivia Newton-John's 1981 song "Physical," to J. P. Moreland.

[12]David Lewis, *On the Plurality of Worlds* (Malden, MA: Wiley-Blackwell, 1986). An important selection from this book can be found in chap. 16, "A Philosopher's Paradise," in *Metaphysics: An Anthology*, 2nd ed., eds. Jaegwon Kim, Daniel Z. Korman, and Ernest Sosa (Malden, MA: Wiley-Blackwell, 2012).

are not simply ways of thinking about or formally representing reality; they are themselves genuine pieces of the furniture of reality. In fact, possible worlds exist in precisely the same way that tables, chairs, tulips, and fire engines exist; they are very large spatial and temporal things. In Lewis's view of worlds, roughly, a possible world is a total, concrete way things could have been; possible worlds are large, concrete objects, all of whose parts are spatially and temporally connected to each other (and to no other objects and thus no other possible worlds). Let's call Lewis's view of possible worlds "modal concretism."[13]

So, think of Lewis's notion of a possible world along the lines of an entire, alternative physical universe, one that is completely disconnected—spatially, temporal, and causally—from our own world. Our world—the "actual" world—is just one of the infinitely many total, concrete ways things could have been, and other possible worlds are just "more things of that sort, differing not in kind but only in what goes on at them."[14] The actual world is only actual insofar as it is the large, concrete object of which you and I are parts; being actual is a bit like being "here"; it depends on where you are standing. Other possible worlds and their inhabitants—possible objects like golden mountains, flying pigs, unicorns, Middle-earth, and so on—genuinely exist; they just aren't actual, since they are not parts of the same large, concrete object that we are a part of. This aspect of Lewis's view is known as "possibilism," that there genuinely exist possible but nonactual concrete objects.

According to Lewis's own concretist version of modal essentialism, *every way that the world could be is a way that some world is.* Read that statement again, slowly, and let it sink in for a moment. As a proponent of modal essentialism, Lewis appeals to possible worlds to explain modal truth. Thus, the possibility claim "possibly, pigs can fly" (*de dicto*) is true if and only if there is at least one total, concrete world that exists that includes flying pigs. Yes, you heard that right, if and only if there really are flying pigs that are parts of at least one other alternative, isolated physical universe. Claims of necessity, such as "Necessarily, triangles have three sides" (*de dicto*), are true if and only if in every total, concrete possible world it is true that triangles have three sides.

---

[13]I borrow the labels "modal concretism" and "modal abstractionism" from Peter van Inwagen's paper "Two Concepts of Possible Worlds," in *Ontology, Identity, and Modality* (Cambridge: Cambridge University Press, 2001).
[14]David Lewis, *Counterfactuals* (Cambridge, MA: Harvard University Press, 1973), 84-85.

When it comes to truths about the essences or natures of things (*de re* necessities), things get even weirder in Lewis's view. Again, along the lines of modal essentialism, Lewis thinks that something's being essentially F (a dog's being essentially canine) has something to do with its being F in every concrete world in which it exists. But here there is a crucial twist on Lewis's view. Lewis does not believe that things exist in more than one world; things are what he calls "worldbound." His reason for thinking this stems from the following line of reasoning based on Leibniz's Law of Identity (see chap. 5): Suppose we say that one and the same apple could be green all over and it could be red all over; thus, there is a possible world where one and the same apple is red all over, and a possible world where the apple is green all over; if so, then one and the same apple can have incompatible properties (*being red all over* and *being green all over*), which is impossible given Leibniz's Law. So, according to Lewis, nothing exists in more than one possible world.

But how does Lewis make sense of *de re* modal truths, if things are worldbound and only exist in a single world? Here Lewis introduces the idea of a counterpart. A "counterpart" of you, for Lewis, is an existing thing that is a lot like you, but is strictly not identical to you (it is not strictly one and the same thing as you).[15] For Lewis, for any way that you could be, say badly sunburned, there is an existing counterpart of yours in another concrete world that is that way, in this case, badly sunburned. In fact, and this is vitally important, it is precisely *because* you have at least one sunburned counterpart in another concrete possible world that it is possible for you to be sunburned.

How about essential truths about a thing's essence or nature? The *de re* modal claim "LeBron James is essentially human" is true if and only if all of Lebron's counterparts are human. As Lewis puts it, "an essential attribute of something is an attribute it shares with all its counterparts. All your counterparts are probably human; if so, you are essentially human."[16] For Lewis, then, it is not strictly LeBron, or you for that matter, but LeBron's modal counterparts that explain essential truths about LeBron. In sum, it is your modal counterparts—inhabitants of other worlds that are not strictly you but are

---

[15]The precise details of Lewis's counterpart theory, of course, outstrip my presentation of his view here. For Lewis's own discussion and defense of counterpart theory, read chap. 4, titled "Counterparts or Double Lives?," in his book *On the Plurality of Worlds*.

[16]David Lewis, "Counterpart Quantified Modal Logic," *The Journal of Philosophy* 65, no. 5 (1968): 122.

sufficiently similar to you—that ultimately explain *de re* modal truths about you, whether of possibility or necessity.

You might be surprised to learn (you shouldn't be since Lewis was "wicked smart," as they say) that Lewis marshaled some powerful philosophical arguments in favor of his extreme modal realism. Let me mention a few here, before we turn to some important objections to the view.

First, Lewis's concretism has the virtue of being able to explain modal notions like necessity and possibility in terms of nonmodal notions (terms that don't rely on the concepts of necessity and possibility). What do I mean? Well, it seems pretty clear that any good, noncircular analysis of a concept— say, the concept of *color*—can't appeal to the thing that it seeks to analyze, namely color (here's an example of a doubly circular analysis: something is a color if and only if it is a color that can be located somewhere on the color spectrum). Lewis argues that his view—which analyzes modal concepts like possibility and necessity strictly in terms of nonmodal concepts, namely, goings-on at other isolated spatiotemporal universes like our own—is the only view that can do so on the market. And, by golly, he's right! Whether this tips the scales in favor of Lewis's extreme modal realism is, however, another matter altogether.

Second, Lewis argues that since his view can do a lot of explanatory work— and indeed it can—it should be accepted on that basis. Concretism about possible worlds can be used to explain a host of very difficult metaphysical notions like properties, counterfactuals, and so on, in a nominalist-friendly way that doesn't appeal at all to abstract objects (see chap. 7 on properties and universals). For example, properties, say *redness*, in general can be analyzed as the set of all red things, throughout all possible worlds (that is, gather together all the red things throughout all possible worlds and the set of those things is the property *redness*).

But, of course, Lewis's extreme modal realism suffers from significant objections, both philosophical and theological. First, and perhaps most obvious, is that the view is downright bizarre; as Lewis himself recognizes, it evokes the infamous "incredulous stare."[17] Lewis's extreme form of modal realism requires us to say that there really are concrete things such as flying pigs, witches, unicorns, Harry Potter, the Fountain of Youth, and philosophers who

---

[17]Lewis, *On the Plurality of Worlds*, 133-35.

are rich and famous. And, to many, it doesn't put to rest the worry in the least to say that while these things exist, they just don't exist here in our world, the actual world.

Second, one of the most powerful objections to Lewis's modal counterpart theory was originally pressed by Saul Kripke in his important book *Naming and Necessity* and is now referred to as the "Humphrey Objection."[18] The name of the objection is taken from the following passage from Kripke's book:

> The counterpart of something in another possible world is never identical with the thing itself. Thus if we say "Humphrey might have won the election (if only he had done such-and-such)," we are not talking about something that might have happened to Humphrey but to someone else, a "counterpart." Probably, however, Humphrey could not care less whether someone else, no matter how much resembling him, would have been victorious in another possible world.

At bottom, the worry at the heart of the Humphrey Objection is simple: How can facts about people that are strictly *not me* explain modal truths about *me*? How can a numerically distinct person's being a truck driver in another world ground the truth of my possibly being a truck driver in this, the actual, world?[19]

Third and finally, consider the following theological worry with counterpart theory. Clearly, there are *de re* modal truths about God, since there are truths about what God's nature or essence is like as revealed by the light of Scripture and the light of nature. God is essentially morally perfect, for example. According to Lewis's counterpart theory, the statement "God is essentially morally perfect" is presumably true in the same way in which any essential truth is: Each of God's modal counterparts—beings that highly resemble God that populate each and every possible world (since God exists of necessity)—are morally perfect. But the idea that there exist an infinitely many other-worldly God-counterparts, all of which are supremely morally perfect (perhaps, for this reason, even worthy of worship), yet are not strictly identical

---

[18]See Saul Kripke, *Naming and Necessity* (Cambridge, MA: Harvard University Press, 1972), 45n13. The Humphrey Objection is also forcefully pressed by Plantinga, *Nature of Necessity*, 102-7; and Trenton Merricks, "The End of Counterpart Theory," *The Journal of Philosophy* 100, no. 10 (2003): 521-49.

[19]The bold and courageous reader will also want to check out the interesting and powerful ethical arguments against counterpart theory outlined in Alexander Pruss in part III of his book *Actuality, Possibility, and Worlds* (New York: Bloomsbury, 2011).

to God (but are highly similar to God) will give any proponent of a robust view of divine aseity serious pause.

MODAL ABSTRACTIONISM: PLANTINGA'S MODAL REALISM

Let's turn to the second monumentally influential view of possible worlds in contemporary metaphysics, using the work of Christian philosopher Alvin Plantinga as our guide.[20] In sharp contrast to Lewis's concretist conception of possible worlds, Plantinga is one of several metaphysicians who think that possible worlds are not concrete at all but are abstract, hence the label "modal abstractionism."[21]

Worlds, for Plantinga and others, are not large spatiotemporal and concrete things akin to parallel universes; rather, they are the sort of things that somehow represent comprehensive ways things could have been. More specifically, Plantinga thinks that possible worlds are certain kinds of abstract objects, namely, "states of affairs." Hang on, this next bit is going to be challenging! Roughly, a state of affairs is a bit like a situation involving a particular thing, a *thing's being such-and-such*. I know, I know, that's about as clear as mud, isn't it? Let's try some examples, to see whether it helps. Examples of states of affairs include *Ross's being a teacher at Southeastern Seminary, Jane Austin's being the author of Pride and Prejudice, Paul Gould's being a dazzling Broadway showman*, and *Plantinga's being an ardent defender of naturalism*. States of affairs either obtain or fail to obtain. So, the state of affairs of *my being a teacher at Southeastern Seminary* obtains (I do, in fact, teach there), while the states of affairs *Plantinga's being an ardent defender of naturalism* and *Paul Gould's being a dazzling Broadway showman* do not obtain.

It is important to point out that Plantinga endorses a certain form of Platonism about abstract objects. For our purposes here, Platonism about abstract objects like properties (*being even, being red*, etc.) and mathematical entities (the number 2) claims that such objects exist necessarily, are causally

---

[20]Plantinga's most extensive single-volume treatment of the metaphysics of modality is his book *The Nature of Necessity*. But be warned that the book is challenging and requires the development of prior philosophical and logical muscles to properly engage. As a first step, readers who are those who want to read Plantinga himself on this topic may want to start with chap. 14 of *Metaphysics: An Anthology*. For a collection of some of Plantinga's most important articles on modality, see Alvin Plantinga, *Essays in the Metaphysics of Modality*, ed. Matthew Davidson (New York: Oxford University Press, 2003).

[21]Other contemporary analytic philosophers who endorse something along the lines of modal abstractionism include Robert Stalnaker, Robert Adams, Roderick Chisholm, and Saul Kripke.

inert, and are transcendent in that they do not exist in space and time. For the Platonist, states of affairs are a certain kind of abstract object. As such, states of affairs exist necessarily (dependent on the divine mind in some sense, for Plantinga), are causally inert, and are strictly nowhere in space and time (no temporal or spatial location). So, for Plantinga, all states of affairs necessarily *exist* (indeed, they couldn't fail to exist), but not all *obtain*. So, the state of affairs *Plantinga's being an ardent defender of naturalism* exists; it just does not obtain. Also, I should clarify, not just any old states of affairs *can* obtain. Consider the state of affairs *Chris Lee's being a married bachelor*. While this state of affairs *exists*, for Plantinga, it is an impossible state of affairs in that it cannot obtain. Since no one thing can have contradictory properties (*being unmarried* and *being married*), no state of affairs involving this situation can possibly obtain.

Plantinga builds possible worlds out of possible states of affairs. In particular, possible worlds are comprehensive, possible states of affairs in that they include every possible state of affairs and leave out none. That is, possible worlds are thought to represent not just a slice of the ways things could be, but a total way things could be. The *actual* world—our world—is the one possible world among all existing possible worlds that obtains.

This is really dense stuff, no doubt. But let me try to head off at the pass a potential confusion at this point (or at least one that arises often when I teach this subject). Let me reiterate: There's an important difference between saying that all possible worlds *exist* (and thus are part of the actual world) and saying that all possible worlds *obtain* or are *actual* (just like all states of affairs exist in the actual world, but not all of them obtain). As odd as it sounds, all possible worlds exist in the actual world; they are part of the contents of the actual world. Think of a row of five houses and only one of them is illumined by a police helicopter searchlight; all the houses are real, but just one of them is illumined by the searchlight. In a roughly similar sort of way, for Plantinga, while all possible worlds exist in the actual world (our world), only one such world has the metaphysical privilege of *obtaining*, or *being actual*.

In contrast to Lewis, Plantinga thinks that things can exist and have properties in more than one possible world; he rejects Lewis's idea of worldbound individuals and defends what is known as "transworld identity."[22] After all,

---

[22]See chap. 4 of Plantinga's *The Nature of Necessity* for his defense of transworld identity over against Lewis's worldbound individuals.

when you think that things could have been different for you, it's quite natural to think that this has something to do with how things go in another possible world with *you*, and not someone else, strictly speaking. But don't be dismayed, Plantinga does not mean that you or one of your otherworldly counterparts exist and have properties in some far-off alternative physical universe, à la Lewis. Rather, you exist in a different possible world, call it *w*, in the sense that *had w* obtained (or been actual), you *would* have existed. And your being a professional daredevil in *w* amounts to the idea that *had w* obtained (or been actual), you *would* have been a professional daredevil, nothing more.

In fact, Plantinga thinks that the entire distinction between accidental and nonaccidental truths (and properties) completely falls apart without a commitment to transworld identity. If things are truly worldbound and this is the only world in which you exist, then *all* of your this-worldly properties are essential to you, since what is true of you in every possible world in which you exist is what is essentially true of you. In response to Lewis's Leibniz's Law–style argument in favor of worldbound individuals (see above), Plantinga counters that we can understand properties as being tied to or indexed to worlds. So, in our world, call it w_1, I am a father of three. But in another possible world, w_2, I am a father of eight (since this is a real possibility). This in no way violates Leibniz's Law, Plantinga argues, if we construe the respective properties as being tethered to worlds or "world-indexed" as he puts it. So, *being a father of three in w_1* and *being a father of eight in w_2* are world-indexed properties, the former indexed to w_1 and the latter to w_2. Since these are not contradictory properties (like P and not-P would be), one and the same person can have them in different possible worlds.

According to Plantinga's abstractionist view of possible worlds, modal claims of necessity and possibility are understood in terms of what is (and is not) the case in various possible worlds (as in line with modal essentialism generally). So, the *de dicto* possibility "possibly, pigs can fly" is true if and only if there is at least one possible world in which it is true that pigs fly. Likewise, the *de dicto* necessity "necessarily, 2+2=4" is true if and only if 2+2=4 is true in every possible world.

Moreover, *de re* modal truths, including what belongs to the essence or nature of things, are understood along similar lines. For Plantinga, "LeBron James could have been a professional golfer" (being a professional golfer is an *accidental* feature of LeBron) is true if and only if there is at least one possible world in which LeBron James has the property of *being a professional golfer*. Likewise, "LeBron James is essentially human" is true—being human is part of LeBron's essence—if and only if LeBron has the property of *being human* in every possible world in which he exists.[23]

Getting Theological: The Modal Ontological Argument

With the return to serious modal metaphysics in contemporary analytic philosophy, Christian philosopher Alvin Plantinga, true to form, helped draw attention to the theistic implications of endorsing a standard possible worlds semantics by reinvigorating the age-old ontological argument for the existence of God. Plantinga's modal ontological argument relies heavily on the standard concept of God as maximally excellent, having maximal knowledge, power, and moral perfection in every possible world. God, if he existed, would be maximally great in the sense of being that which none greater can be conceived, and thus maximally excellent according to each and every way things could have been, i.e., every possible world. If God existed, He would be a necessary being, which Plantinga defines using standard possible world semantics as a being that exists in every possible world.

Moreover, Plantinga wielded the very plausible logical principle, referred to as S5 in contemporary modal logic, that if it is *possible* that something exists necessarily, then it exists necessarily. That is, if a necessary being exists in at least *one* possible world, then it will exist in *every* possible world. Here's why: If you say that it's possible for a *necessary* being to exist, you are saying that such a being exists in at least one possible world. And if it exists in at least *one* possible world, then such a being will exist in *every* possible world since it, by nature, exists of necessity. Informally: If you give a necessary being an existential foot in the door of one possible world, then it will, by virtue of what it is by

---

[23]A thing's general essence, like *being human* for LeBron James, is how it is in every possible world in which it exists but can be shared in common with others, like Michael Jordan. Plantinga also thinks there are individual essences that mark out how LeBron and only LeBron is in every possible world—what is ontologically specific and unique to LeBron that sets him apart from other humans. So, the property *being identical to LeBron James* is both essential to LeBron and one of LeBron's many individual essences (of which he has countless many, for Plantinga).

nature, get an existential foot in every possible world, including our own (actual) world. Conclusion: A being with maximal knowledge, goodness, and moral perfection exists in the actual world, and this unsurpassable being we call God. The argument can be succinctly stated like this:

1. God, if he exists, is a necessary being, B.

2. If it's possible for B to exist, then B exists. (S5 logical principle)

3. It's possible for a necessary being, B, to exist. (Possibility Premise)

4. Therefore, B exists.

The primary challenge to Plantinga's modal ontological argument has been to the premise known as the Possibility Premise, premise 3. The linchpin of the argument is the claim that it's metaphysically possible for a necessary being—a being that exists in every possible world—to exist. The difficulty in challenging the possibility premise is twofold. First, there are remarkably compelling philosophical-theological considerations in favor of both the *possibility* and the *actuality* of a necessary being, including a host of variations of what is known as the argument from contingency or the Leibnizian cosmological argument (see the Mystery of Creaturely Being callout in chap. 4). Second, there are few if any (non-question-begging) positive reasons to think that a necessary being is metaphysically impossible. Establishing this is a tall task indeed!

All in all, while the two views depart significantly on the nature of possible worlds and whether individuals are worldbound, Plantinga's abstractionism shares in common with Lewis's concretism the assumption that what is possible and what is necessary are explained by what is the case in some or all possible worlds.[24]

Plantinga argues for his conception of modality on a variety of grounds, two of which I'll very quickly mention here. First, since Plantinga contends

---

[24]The careful reader will note that Plantinga has constructed possible worlds from ontological items that themselves rely on modal notions, in this case, possible states of affairs. Plantinga admits that on his account, modality is rock bottom and unanalyzable.

that there are good, independent reasons for believing in Platonic abstract objects, an abstractionist view of modality fits nicely with what one already has good reason to believe exists.

Second, Plantinga thinks that his actualist view avoids the incredulous stare of Lewis's possibilism, the view that there really are things (flying pigs, unicorns, etc.) that do not exist in the actual world. For Plantinga, only things that exist in the actual world exist *full stop* (remember: this is not to say that the only things that exist are those that obtain). While flying pigs *would* have existed had worlds that represent there being flying pigs been actual, for Plantinga, there are no flying pigs that are part of the actual world. And this fits better with our intuitive understanding of existence, he argues.

Yet many critics of Plantinga's version of abstractionism (and abstractionism in general) point out that the alleged virtue of explaining modal notions in terms of abstract objects of any sort is also one of its chief costs. Plantinga's view *requires* a commitment to abstract objects, indeed, a Platonic conception of abstract objects as necessarily existing beings. As such, many metaphysicians who gravitate toward a leaner ontology of properties will balk at what they perceive to be the bloated ontology required by an abstractionist view of modality (see chap. 7 for more on the ontology of properties).

But it's not just those with leaner ontological sympathies that might balk at the existence of Platonic abstract objects and Plantinga's abstractionist account of possible worlds. Christian theists who affirm a robust view of divine aseity (see chap. 3) may well think that Plantinga's view of abstract objects as necessary beings conflicts with the view that God is the sole, ultimate reality (see chap. 7). Even if we were to root necessarily existing abstract objects within the divine mind, as Plantinga does in the end, we are still left with the fact that there are infinitely many, necessarily existing beings that are *not identical to God*. Though these beings are somehow the products of God's mental life and closely depend on him, they are strictly speaking not God. Unless one is willing to collapse these necessarily existing beings into the divine nature itself and *identify* the realm of abstract objects with God by way of divine simplicity, then Plantinga's commitment to a plenitude of necessarily existing beings that are not God will be in tension with a strong view of divine aseity.[25]

---

[25]The widespread historic view on this has been a form of divine conceptualism, the view that items normally thought to be independently existing abstract objects—properties, universals, numbers, propositions, and the like—are nothing more than aspects of God's mental life.

SERIOUS ESSENTIALISM: KIT FINE'S CRITIQUE
OF MODAL ESSENTIALISM

Up to this point we've explored two prominent views concerning the metaphysics of modality, in particular Lewis's concretism and Plantinga's abstractionism. Both views fall under the umbrella of modal essentialism in that they appeal to the utility of possible worlds to ground truths of possibility and necessity. This brings us to our second guiding question concerning the entire framework of modal essentialism, in particular, whether it can adequately capture the notion of *essence* or *de re* necessity in the first place (question 2 above).

There are an increasing number of contemporary metaphysicians who have grown dissatisfied with the framework of possible worlds and its ability to fully capture the notion of essence in particular. Several notable philosophers such as Kit Fine, E. J. Lowe, and David Oderberg have argued that modal essentialism is on shaky ground, precisely because it is insufficient to capture a robust and intuitive notion of essence. In its place, these metaphysicians have recommended a return to a more Aristotelian conception of essence in terms of real definition.

Kit Fine has been the most influential contemporary critic of modal essentialism.[26] Fine has argued that an account of essence in terms of necessity, namely what is true of a thing in every possible world in which it exists, is in no way sufficient to account for the notion of a thing's essence. That is, Fine has powerfully—and convincingly in the eyes of many—challenged modal essentialism's claim that a possible worlds framework is sufficient to shed light on a thing's essence. The reason is that, intuitively, there are many things that are true of Fido in every possible world in which he exists, but that do not *define* what Fido our beloved dog is in terms of his essence, what he is in the most explanatorily basic, ultimate sense.

Historically, and in contrast to many defenses of the view today, divine conceptualism was traditionally affirmed in conjunction with (and not seen to be in tension with) some form of the doctrine of divine simplicity. See Lindsay K. Cleveland, "Divine Aseity and Abstract Objects," in *T&T Clark Handbook of Analytic Theology*, eds. James M. Arcadi and James T. Turner Jr. (New York: Bloomsbury, 2021). See also Thomas Ward, *Divine Ideas* (New York: Cambridge University Press, 2020).

[26]Here I recommend the reader consult Fine's influential article "Essence and Modality," *Philosophical Perspectives* 8 (1994): 1-16. Fine's influential article can be found as chap. 19 in *Metaphysics: An Anthology*.

Consider the following adaptation of an example, used by Fine, of Fido the dog and the set whose sole member is Fido, {F}. Now, {F}, the set, exists by virtue of Fido's existing; if there were no Fido, then there would be no set having Fido as its sole member. Yet Fido is arguably a member of {F} in every possible world in which Fido exists; many philosophers think that if Fido exists, then you automatically get the set containing Fido as its sole member for free. On modal essentialism, then, since Fido belongs to {F} in every world in which he exists, *being a member of {F}* is part of the essence of Fido; it is one of Fido's essential properties (properties that he could not fail to have and still exist) and thus definitive of the very being of Fido.

But herein lies the worry. Traditionally, a thing's essence is supposed to be definitive of the thing in some deep and metaphysically substantive sense. The essence of Fido should tell you what sort of thing Fido *is* at his metaphysical core; essential truths, if you recall from our earlier illustration, should hit directly in the center of the metaphysical bullseye regarding what a thing *is*. But *being a member of a set* conveys no such thing; or so it seems.[27] How does being a member of a set (in this case {F}) tell me what Fido is in the most fundamental sense? In short, so-called serious essentialists have argued that a modal essentialist account of essence is much too coarse-grained to account for creaturely essences, what a thing is fundamentally. An account of essence solely in terms of what is true of Fido necessarily (i.e., what is true of Fido in every world in which he exists) lets in far too many features of Fido—features that Fido has in every possible world in which he exists—that arguably are not definitive of what Fido is in a metaphysically bedrock sense. According to Fine and company, any attempt to adequately explain or analyze a thing's essence in terms of how it is in every possible world in which it exists is conceptually misguided.

In its place, Fine, Lowe, and Oderberg recommend moving away from the framework of possible worlds and modal essentialism altogether as a way of explaining the truths of possibility and necessity, and moving to a deeper, more ancient understanding of essence in terms of Aristotelian real definition. As noted in chapter one, by "definition" here philosophers most certainly do not mean a linguistic or dictionary definition, that is, the kind of definition you'd find in the *Oxford English Dictionary* or a *Webster's*

---

[27] For a contrary opinion by someone who is sympathetic to serious essentialism, see David Oderberg, *Real Essentialism* (New York: Routledge, 2008), chap. 1.

pocket dictionary. Rather, for Aristotle and other philosophers who followed in his wake, entities can be defined just as much as bits of language like words. To define an entity or thing in this classical sense is to specify *what that entity is*, or *what it is to be an entity of that kind*. The real definition of the element gold, for example, captures what it is to be gold, specifically to be a metal whose atomic constituents have the atomic number 79. *Being a metal* and *having atomic constituents* tell us something ontologically basic and essential to what gold *is*, its identity. Notice that there is no mention of possible worlds in this understanding of essences or natures. According to Fine and others in the serious essentialist camp, the notion of essence is incapable of being further explained in terms of anything else; it is a primitive and ultimately bedrock notion. Even more, what a thing is by way of its real definition or essence explains the way it is in every possible world in which it exists (e.g., essential truths about gold explain what is necessarily true of it). According to the serious essentialist view, the notions of metaphysical necessity and possibility are explained in terms of essence, *and not vice versa* (the shoe, in contrast to modal essentialism, is precisely on the other foot).

POWERS, MODALITY, AND GOD: A THEISTIC PROPOSAL

Recall our earlier discussion of the various kinds of modality. We distinguished between power possibility/necessity, logical possibility/necessity, physical possibility/necessity, and metaphysical possibility/necessity. Interestingly enough, there has been a recent rise among Aristotelian-minded metaphysicians as to the prospects of grounding truths of metaphysical possibility and necessity in the powers or abilities of existing things. In this view, power possibility/necessity and metaphysical possibility/necessity are not distinct forms of modality, as we originally assumed. Rather, metaphysical possibility just *is* power possibility (and similarly for necessity). This is an interesting development that aims to identify the grounds for true modal statements in the properties and powers of actually existing things, and not outsource the truth-explainers for modality to other possible worlds.

Contemporary defenders of a powers ontology of modality include thinkers like Jonathan Jacobs, Stephen Mumford, Rani Lill Anjum, Alexander Pruss, Barbara Vetter, Brian Leftow, and Timothy Pawl (at least four of whom are Christian philosophers, I might add).[28] A version of the view has also been attributed to Thomas Aquinas.[29] Proponents of a powers-based account of modality generally begin with the Aristotelian intuition that *actuality is prior to possibility*; that is, what is actual (this-worldly) determines or fixes what could be (what is other-worldly), rather than vice versa. So, the thought here is that the actual powers or abilities of actual, existing things can serve to explain truths of necessity and possibility, whether *de dicto* or *de re*.

On a powers-based account of modality, a *de dicto* metaphysical possibility like "possibly, I am a truck driver" is true if and only if *there was, is, or will be something that has the power to bring it about that I am a truck driver*. Thus, what is genuinely possible is explained in terms of what powers there were, are, or will be in the actual world.

However, things aren't as simple for metaphysical necessity, both of the *de dicto* and *de re* variety. So, consider the following necessary truth, "Necessarily, 2+2=4" along with its logical complement, "Possibly, not (2+2=4)." According to one powers proposal, "Necessarily, 2+2=4" is true precisely because "nothing had, has, or will have a power to bring about the truth of the claim 'Possibly, not (2+2=4).'"[30] In other words, "necessary truths are true by virtue of their complements' lacking truthmakers."[31] So, *de dicto* necessary truths are true by virtue of the absence of powers to bring about the truth of their complements. Since there was, is, or will be no powers to do so, 2+2=4 *must* be true.

How might a powers-based account ground truths about *de re* necessities? Well, there are various ways to go here, but one way would be to say that "*x is essentially F*"—say, "LeBron James is essentially human"—if and only if nothing had, has, or will have a power to bring about the possibility of

---

[28]In particular, see Jonathan Jacobs, "A Powers Theory of Modality: or, How I Learned to Stop Worrying and Reject Possible Worlds," *Philosophical Studies* 151, no. 2 (2010): 227-48; Timothy Pawl, "Nine Problems (and Even More Solutions) for Powers Accounts of Possibility," in *Causal Powers*, ed. Jonathan Jacobs (New York: Oxford University Press, 2017); Brian Leftow, "The Nature of Necessity," *Res Philosophica* 94, no. 3 (2017): 359-83; and Alexander Pruss, "The Actual and the Possible," in *The Blackwell Guide to Metaphysics*, ed. Richard Gale (Malden, MA: Blackwell, 2002), 317-33.

[29]See the important exchange between Brian Leftow, "Aquinas on God and Modal Truth," and Jeffrey Brower, "Aquinas's Metaphysics of Modality: A Reply to Leftow," *Modern Schoolman* 82, no 3 (2005): 171-212.

[30]Pawl, "Nine Problems," 110.

[31]Pawl, "Nine Problems," 110.

LeBron's not being human (i.e., not-F). So, ultimately, *de re* necessities can be grounded in the absence of absolute possibilities. Since no powers exist to make it the case that Lebron could fail to be human, LeBron is essentially (i.e., necessarily) human.

Proponents of a powers-based view of modality grant that at metaphysical rock bottom, modality is incapable of being analyzed in nonmodal terms, terms that don't already appeal to basic notions of power, ability, or possibility. However, defenders of the view such as Jacobs have powerfully argued that all brands of modal essentialism suffer from what we can call the "Irrelevance Objection."[32] The Irrelevance Objection is a spin-off of the previous objection we explored to Lewis's counterpart theory, the Humphrey Objection. Jacobs, using the *de re* possibility "I could have been a truck driver," puts the worry as follows:

> Suppose you were told that somewhere deep in the rainforest is a book that includes a story about you and your truck-driving ways. I doubt that you would be inclined to think that that story, that book, is the reason you could have been a truck driver. You would rightfully respond to such a theory with an incredulous stare. But being informed that it's not literally a story, and that it's not actually written in a concrete book, and that it's not located in the rainforest (or anywhere else, for that matter)—that is, being informed that the story is instead an abstract object—should serve only to make you more, not less, incredulous.[33]

The nub of the worry is that possible worlds themselves—whether understood in terms of other concrete isolated universes (à la Lewis) or abstract states of affairs (à la Plantinga)—are just not the right sort of things to ground the truth of ordinary modal statements about ordinary objects. The existing things that make it possible for me to be a truck driver and for you to exist without a body in the intermediate state—the "possibilifiers," we might call them—seem to be intrinsic features, powers, or capacities of ordinary objects like you and me. Possible worlds just seem irrelevant to play the role of possibilifiers in one's modal metaphysics.

But a significant problem for the powers view lurks in the neighborhood here, one that threatens to undermine the entire framework from the start.

---

[32]For another discussion of the *Irrelevance Objection* as a critique of modal essentialism, see David Oderberg, *Real Essentialism* (New York: Routledge, 2007), chap. 1.
[33]Jacobs, "Powers Theory of Modality," 232.

What about genuine, metaphysical possibilities that seem to outstrip the causal powers of any past, present, or future created being (whether individually or collectively)? Doesn't the powers-based view drastically diminish the range of what is possible? Are there not possibilities concerning ways that things could be that fall outside the power of any created being or beings? To illustrate, consider the following two possibility statements:

A: Possibly, the laws of nature could have been different.

B: There could have been none of the contingent beings that actually exist.

Statements A and B pertain to what are called "global possibilities," possibilities about how things could have been with respect to entire worlds, and not just to individual, local segments of worlds (like "I could have been a Navy Seal"). A and B sure *seem* to be genuine, global metaphysical possibilities. If so, then in the powers view it must be the case that there was, is, or will be something with the power to bring them about. But what created being or combination of created beings has the power to bring about such global possibilities?

There are a few responses available to the powers theorist at this point. First, they might dig their heels in here and simply deny that A and B are genuine possibilities; while they *seem* possible, they are, in fact, not. This is because it is this-worldly powers of objects that determine the scope of what is genuinely possible and what is not. Since A and B outstrip the causal power of any actually existing created being or beings, they are actually not genuine metaphysical possibilities.

Second, powers proponents might accept that A and B are genuine metaphysical possibilities and try to identify some powers of actually existing created beings to explain their truth. But it's hard to see what actually existing created being could act to bring about the laws of nature being different or an entirely different collection of contingent beings than the ones that actually exist (or no contingent beings at all for that matter).

Last, and this is my own preferred route, a powers theorist might adopt a theistic version of a powers-based view of modality that says the truths of A and B (indeed all global possibilities) are explained by way of divine causal power: God has the causal power to bring about global possibilities. Indeed, it seems that *only* God as an all-powerful, necessarily (noncontingently) existing being could ground the truth of global possibilities.

So, in this theistic version of a powers-based account of modality, local metaphysical possibilities ("I could have been a Navy Seal instead of a philosopher") are immediately grounded in the powers and abilities of actually existing created beings, and all global possibilities (like A and B) are grounded in divine causal power. Either way, all metaphysical possibilities are grounded in actually existing causal powers, whether created or uncreated. However, we should point out that in line with our metaphysical lodestar, divine aseity, God ultimately factors into the explanation of all creaturely metaphysical possibilities at some level, whether due to his will or his nature, insofar as God is the exemplar and absolute Creator of this-worldly creatures and their respective causal powers.[34] This power-based approach to the metaphysics of modality coheres nicely with the theo-centric habit of mind I outlined earlier in chapter three: God is explanatorily relevant, in some way or other, to the nature and existence of all beings that are not God. A theistic version of a powers account of possibility and necessity, in which the triune God, in some way or other, ultimately grounds all creaturely possibilities and necessities, is also a natural fit with our metaphysical lodestar, divine aseity.

GOING DEEPER: CREATURELY NATURES

Key Concepts

- necessity
- essence
- possible worlds
- modal realism
- Humeanism
- dispositional properties
- natural necessity
- contingent truth

[34]See Brian Leftow, *God and Necessity* (New York: Oxford University Press, 2012), for a rich and technical discussion of a theistic grounding for modal truths. For the idea that God is the exemplar for all creaturely natures, see my essay "Grounding and Participation in God," *Neo-Aristotelian Metaphysics and the Theology of Nature*, eds. William M. R. Simpson, Robert C. Koons, and James Orr (New York: Routledge, 2021); Andrew Davison, *Participation in God: A Study in Christian Doctrine and Metaphysics* (Cambridge: Cambridge University Press, 2019); and Ward, *Divine Ideas*.

- logical truth
- Singleton

Historical
- Thomas Aquinas, *On Being and Essence*
- Peter Coffey, *Ontology or the Theory of Being: An Introduction to General Metaphysics*, chap. 3

Contemporary
- Kit Fine, "Essence and Modality," chap. 19 in *Metaphysics: An Anthology*
- David Lewis, "A Philosopher's Paradise," in *On the Plurality of Worlds*, chap. 16 in *Metaphysics: An Anthology*
- Alvin Plantinga, "Modalities: Basic Concepts and Distinctions," selections from *The Nature of Necessity*, chap. 14 of *Metaphysics: An Anthology*
- Peter van Inwagen, "Two Concepts of Possible Worlds," in *Ontology, Identity, and Modality*
- David Oderberg, *Real Essentialism*, chaps. 1-3
- Alexander Pruss, *Actuality, Possibility, and Worlds*; "The Actual and the Possible," in *Blackwell Guide to Metaphysics*
- Jonathan Jacobs, "A Powers Theory of Modality," *Philosophical Studies*
- Ross D. Inman, *Substance and the Fundamentality of the Familiar: A Neo-Aristotelian Mereology*, chap. 1

7

CREATURELY CHARACTERISTICS

PROPERTIES AND UNIVERSALS

THE WONDER OF OUR QUALITATIVELY RICH WORLD

We live in a world suffused with qualitative richness and complexity, a world of wonders. We are moved by the richness of the natural world, from the beauty of a setting sun over the Pacific Ocean, the towering giant sequoias of the Kings Canyon National Park, to the wild rocky peaks of the snowcapped Eastern Sierras. We are also gripped by the richness of ordinary human life, from the sweetness of a glass of Southern sweet tea, the laughter of good friends, the joy of playing fetch with a four-legged friend, to being justly treated by a superior in the workplace.

But in addition to charactered things like beautiful sunsets, tall trees, rocky peaks, sweet tea, good humans, beautiful sunsets, four-legged dogs, and just societies, are there also existing characteristics, qualities, or features like *beauty, tallness, rockiness, sweetness, goodness, humanity, four-leggedness,* and *justice*?[1] Or, in a way that is a bit more existentially relevant to your life: In addition to individual human judgments about love, beauty, goodness, and justice, are there objective, human-independent standards of love, beauty, goodness, and justice, which human judgments must reflect in order to be true to objective reality?

Many metaphysicians, past and present, have labored over the question of whether there exists a dimension to reality that orders and explains the various ways that familiar objects are and how they are similar (or dissimilar) to one

---

[1]I'll use "features," "qualities," "characteristics," and "properties" interchangeably throughout this chapter.

another in certain qualitative respects. In this chapter, my aim is to introduce you to the main contours of the contemporary discussion concerning the metaphysics of properties.

SETTING THE STAGE: SOME PRELIMINARY DISTINCTIONS

It may not surprise you (especially if you've read this far!) that philosophers in general, and metaphysicians no less, love distinctions. But metaphysicians love distinctions not simply for the sake of distinctions. Metaphysicians make conceptual distinctions when they think that doing so better captures the way the world actually is in all of its intricate detail and complexity.

So, in this spirit, let me offer some initial definitions that will help keep things clear as we move through the chapter. Take, first, the *concrete/abstract* distinction. While there is no universally agreed-upon way to cut things up here, metaphysicians tend to think that concrete entities are those that are capable of (a) bringing about causal effects in the world and (b) being somewhere in space and time (indeed, most are). Examples of concrete entities include electrons, tulips, humans, God, angels, and so on (be careful not to conflate "concrete" with "physical"). Abstract entities, by contrast, are those that are capable neither of bringing about causal effects in the world (they are causally inert) nor of being somewhere in space and time (e.g., the number 2, the set of all prime numbers). Abstract entities lack spatial and temporal location in the material world.

Second, the *object/property* distinction. Broadly, an object is a unified property-bearer, a single entity that has features or characteristics, such as you, Fido the dog, and a glass of sweet tea. A property (i.e., characteristic, feature, or attribute), by contrast, is an entity that is had or possessed by an object (*humanity* is had by you; *sweetness* is had by the tea; *furriness* is had by Fido).

Third, the *universal/particular* distinction. Again, glossing over some important debates in contemporary metaphysics, suffice it to say that a universal is an entity that is sharable and capable of being possessed by distinct entities at the same time (i.e., "multiply exemplifiable"). So, if your humanity and my humanity and Christ's humanity are all numerically one and the same *humanity*, then humanity is a universal. A particular, by contrast, is an entity that is nonsharable and incapable of being possessed by distinct entities at the same time (i.e., "not multiply exemplifiable").

Fourth and finally, let's consider the very important distinction between *quantitative* and *qualitative simplicity*. A metaphysical theory, call it T1, is more *quantitatively* simple than theory T2 if T1 appeals to fewer entities in total than theory T2. On the other hand, some metaphysical theory T1 is more *qualitatively* simple than theory T2 when T1 appeals to fewer basic or fundamental types of entities ("primitive," "rock-bottom," or "unanalyzable" entities).

Since the difference between quantitative and qualitative simplicity is vital in grasping the arguments for and against the existence of properties in this chapter, let me offer an illustration of the difference at work. Suppose T1 and T2 stand for two different color theories that are put forward to adequately capture the vividness and vibrancy of color perceived in a sunset over the Pacific Ocean. Recall from elementary school that the primary colors (red, yellow, and blue) are basic in that they are the building blocks for all other colors (and they are not themselves mixtures of other colors). Secondary colors (orange, green, purple) are what you get when you mix two primary colors together (e.g., red + yellow = orange), and tertiary colors are made from mixing equal amounts of a primary color with a secondary color (e.g., yellow + orange = yellow-orange).

Now, suppose each color theory, T1 and T2, posits a range of primary, secondary, and tertiary colors to depict the vivid colors perceived in the sunset:

Color Theory T1: red, yellow, and blue (3 primary colors) and orange (1 secondary color) [4 colors total]

Color Theory T2: red and yellow (2 primary colors), purple and green (2 secondary colors), and red-purple and yellow-green (2 tertiary colors) [6 colors total]

As you can clearly see, at 6 total colors, theory T2 posits more overall colors than theory T1 (4 total colors). In this way, color theory T1 is more *quantitatively simple* than theory T2; the fewer total colors, the more quantitatively simple the color theory. However, notice that theory T1 posits one additional primary or basic color than theory T2 (blue). In this way, color theory T1 consists of an additional basic type of color compared to T2. Even though theory T2 is not as quantitatively simple as T1, it is nevertheless more *qualitatively simple* than T1 since it posits fewer basic colors; the fewer number of basic, primary colors, the more qualitatively simple the color theory.

Which kind of simplicity—quantitative or qualitative—is more important when choosing a theory, whether about color or a metaphysical theory? In contemporary metaphysics, it is typically assumed that qualitative simplicity (positing fewer basic kinds of beings) is more important than quantitative simplicity (positing fewer beings per se) and should be weighed more heavily when deciding on a metaphysical theory. It is thought that if a theory is more qualitatively simple than another, all else being equal, then that theory should be preferred. The fewer basic or fundamental kinds of beings in one's ontology, the better.

Yet, a metaphysical theory's being qualitatively simple does not settle the score on its own. Which theory is the best overall and wins the day will largely be determined not only by considerations regarding ontological simplicity but also by the degree to which the theory explains what needs explaining about the world (hence the "all else being equal" clause). To help illustrate this important point—hang with me—compare color theories T1 and T2 about the variety of colors perceived in the sunset over the Pacific Ocean. If you've ever actually seen a sunset over the Pacific, you know well the stunning array of orange that paints the sky at dusk. Any proposed account of the colors on display in the sunset that fails to include the color orange is woefully inadequate to the reality at hand. So, even though theory T1 is not as qualitatively simple as T2 (since it posits more primary colors), theory T1 fares better overall insofar as it more adequately captures what needs capturing about the world. To sacrifice this adequacy or fit to reality at the altar of qualitative simplicity would, I think, be a grave metaphysical mistake.

With these four pairs of crucial conceptual distinctions in hand, let's consider the following four questions that will guide our metaphysical exploration about characteristics or properties in this chapter:

1. *The Property Existence Question*: Are there characteristics (properties) in addition to charactered objects?

2. *The Property Nature Question*: If there are properties, what are they like? Are properties universal (sharable), or are they particular (nonsharable)?

3. *The Property Location Question*: If properties are sharable, are they immanent (within space-time) or transcendent (outside of

space-time)? Do universals depend for their existence on particulars, or vice versa?

4. *The Property-God Question*: What role does God play, if any, in answering the above three questions?

THE PROPERTY EXISTENCE QUESTION

So, let's turn to our first question: Do properties exist? In addition to charactered objects (red apples, sweet tea, virtuous people, etc.), do characteristics or properties themselves exist (*redness, sweetness, wisdom*, etc.)? Realist views about the existence of properties hold that properties are indeed real, existent beings that mark out a distinct ontological category (and thus answer our first guiding question in the affirmative). By contrast, anti-realist views about properties hold that properties are in no sense real, existent beings in addition to charactered objects, and that there is no distinct ontological category of *Property* (and thus answer in the negative).

There are a variety of both anti-realist and realist views concerning the existence of properties. While realist views of properties differ as to the precise nature and location of properties (questions 2-4 above), they nevertheless all share the common ground that properties are real, existing beings of some sort. Any account of the nature and categorial structure of reality that left out properties would be inadequate to the way things are, or so says the realist. We can state the divide between these two answers to the Property Existence Question as follows:

(No) Anti-Realism About Properties: Properties do not exist in any sense; charactered objects exist, but not characteristics.

(Yes) Realism About Properties: Properties exist; charactered objects exist, in addition to characteristics.

THERE ARE PROPERTIES: PROPERTY-REALISM

Realists about the existence of properties—call them "property-realists"—have typically offered two general types of philosophical arguments in favor of the existence of properties (broadly conceived). There are both metaphysical and semantic arguments for property-realism. Roughly, metaphysical arguments for the existence of properties all trade on the fact that properties (however construed) best explain a host of features or phenomena about our world. Some metaphysical arguments claim that properties best explain why objects have the rich, qualitative character they do and why some of them qualitatively resemble one another. Others maintain that properties, particularly universals, provide the necessary metaphysical framework to make sense of why the natural world behaves in a regular, law-governed manner.[2] Others still claim that properties of some kind best account for the objects of scientific inquiry itself.[3] We'll look at one such metaphysical argument for property-realism (the argument from qualitative and resemblance facts below).

Semantic arguments for property-realism, by contrast, trade on the fact that properties best explain the structure of our language about the world (including the language of logic).[4] Some semantic arguments maintain that properties best make sense of the meaning of particular kinds of ordinary language statements involving singular terms, terms that have a unique referent in the world like proper names ("Verity Inman") and what philosophers call definite descriptions (e.g., "the only daughter of Ross Inman"). We will examine one such semantic argument below (the argument from abstract reference). Other semantic arguments claim that property-realism is needed to account for the truth of statements that seemingly appeal to properties or features, such as "Spiders share some of the anatomical features of insects."[5] By affirming the truth of this claim about spiders, it is argued, we thereby commit ourselves to the existence of features (properties).[6]

In the remainder of this section, I'll first briefly unpack two arguments for property-realism—the argument from qualitative and resemblance facts and the argument from abstract reference—before moving to explore property-anti-realism.

---

[2]See D. M. Armstrong, *What Is a Law of Nature?* (New York: Cambridge University Press, 1985); Alexander Bird, *Nature's Metaphysics: Laws and Properties* (New York: Oxford University Press, 2007); and E. J. Lowe, *The Four-Category Ontology: A Metaphysical Foundation for Natural Science* (New York: Oxford University Press, 2006).
[3]See Scott Bergman, *Platonism and the Objects of Science* (New York: Bloomsbury Academic, 2020).
[4]For an excellent introductory treatment of these different kinds of arguments for a realist ontology of properties, see Douglas Edwards, *Properties* (Malden, MA: Polity, 2014), chap. 1.
[5]This exact statement is taken from Peter van Inwagen, "A Theory of Properties," in *Oxford Studies in Metaphysics*, ed. Dean Zimmerman (Oxford: Oxford University Press, 2004), 1:114.
[6]This approach should bring to mind our discussion of a Quinean metaphysical method from chapter one.

A METAPHYSICAL ARGUMENT FOR PROPERTY-REALISM: THE ARGUMENT FROM QUALITATIVE AND RESEMBLANCE FACTS

One perennial, metaphysical argument for the existence of properties (however construed) is that a realist view of properties best explains certain kinds of truths or facts about the world, in contrast to anti-realist views of properties. What kinds of facts, exactly?

There are two sorts of rather mundane facts about the world that factor into this metaphysical argument, what some have called "qualitative facts" and "resemblance facts."[7] Qualitative facts are simply facts about what particular objects are like, qualitatively. Consider the following two qualitative facts:

(Q1) The apple is red.

(Q2) Electrons are negatively charged.

Q1 and Q2 are examples of ordinary, humdrum truths about the ways (red, negatively charged) various objects (apple, electrons) are with respect to their features.

Resemblance facts, on the other hand, are facts about how particular objects resemble one another in certain respects. Consider the following resemblance facts:

(R1) Hudson and Declan are both human.

(R2) Earl Grey and Lapsang Souchong are both teas.

Intuitively, qualitative and resemblance facts cry out for explanation; *why*, exactly, is it the case that the apple is indeed red (qualitative) and that Hudson and Declan are both human (resemblance)? What is it about the world by virtue of which these facts are true? It would be odd, the realist argues, to think that these facts admit of no deeper metaphysical explanation at all; that these truths are ultimately ontologically groundless.

But if qualitative and resemblance facts have explanations and thus are not ultimately groundless—as they naturally appear to be—what might that

---

[7]Here and in what follows I draw from the always clear and accessible work of two of my friends, Paul Gould and Robert Garcia. See Paul Gould, "There Are Universals," in *Problems in Epistemology and Metaphysics: An Introduction to Contemporary Debates*, ed. Steven B. Cowen (New York: Bloomsbury Academic, 2020); and Robert Garcia, "Platonism and the Haunted Universe," in *Loving God with Your Mind: Essays in Honor of J. P. Moreland*, eds. Paul M. Gould and Richard Brian Davis (Chicago: Moody, 2014).

explanation be? What is it about the apple that metaphysically explains its being red (and not green, say), or about Hudson and Declan that they are both human (and not tigers)? Realists argue that there ought to be some ontology— some objective way the world is—that grounds and metaphysically explains qualitative and resemblance facts (since what is true must be appropriately connected to what exists in the world).

Property-realists argue that realism offers the most powerful and natural explanation for both qualitative and resemblance facts: It is by virtue of the apple's having or exemplifying the property of *redness* that "the apple is red," and by virtue of Hudson and Declan both exemplifying the property of *humanity* that "Hudson and Declan are both human." According to a realist ontology, exemplification is, roughly, best thought of as a relation that links together objects and properties. So, it is because the apple exemplifies the real, existing property of *redness* (and not *greenness*, say) that it is red. Likewise, it is because Hudson and Declan both exemplify the property of *humanity* (and not *felinity*) that they are both human.

More precisely, consider the following way in which property-realists metaphysically explain the truth of qualitative and resemblance facts in terms of concrete particular objects, the relation of exemplification, and properties:

> Q1-Realism: "The apple is red" is true by virtue of the apple's exemplifying the property *redness.*

> R1-Realism: "Declan and Hudson are both human" is true by virtue of Declan and Hudson each exemplifying the property (or kind) *humanity.*

So, the realist ontologically explains the truth of qualitative and resemblance facts in terms of the following types of entities: concrete particular objects (apple, Declan, Hudson), the relation of exemplification, and properties (*redness, humanity*).[8] While putting forward the above realist ontology as the explanatory ground of qualitative and resemblance facts has its problems (as we will see shortly), the realist argues that the view has the least problems and the greatest explanatory benefits. As we will see, the force of any claim that one's view offers the best explanation of a certain range of facts depends in large part on the plausibility of rival explanations for qualitative and

---

[8]Whether the realist is committed to *two* or *three* basic types of entity here will depend on whether relations—exemplification included—are themselves understood as a certain kind of property, a polyadic or many-place property (which most realists take to be the case).

resemblance facts, and even whether such facts intuitively require a deeper explanation at all (as some forms of anti-realism contend).

A SEMANTIC ARGUMENT FOR PROPERTY-REALISM: THE ARGUMENT FROM ABSTRACT REFERENCE

Let's turn now to explore a well-known semantic argument for property-realism, often referred to as the argument from abstract reference. Consider the following simple but true sentences:

- Triangularity is a shape.
- Wisdom is a virtue.
- Redness resembles orangeness more than it resembles blueness.

Each of these true sentences employs what are called "singular terms"—triangularity, wisdom, redness—terms that play the grammatical role of subject in the above sentences that purport to pick out something about the world. Yet if statements involving these singular terms are true, which they seem to be on first pass, then the question naturally arises: What exactly do these singular terms refer to? The property-realist claims to have a ready answer: The singular terms in the above true sentences refer to the properties of *triangularity*, *wisdom*, and *redness*, respectively. Realists argue that only an ontology that includes properties has the resources to explain how sentences involving singular terms can be true. Anti-realist views, argue property-realists, have a hard time accounting for the truth of these kinds of statements. These two arguments in favor of property-realism represent a small sampling of the arguments put forward by metaphysicians for why we need properties in our overall account of the structure of reality.

THERE ARE NO PROPERTIES: PROPERTY-ANTI-REALISM

Let's turn now to those who answer in the negative, what we'll call "property-anti-realists." While property-anti-realism—also known as "extreme nominalism"—is a broad banner representing a host of different views, all such views maintain that talk of properties and characteristics over and above talk of particular charactered objects is metaphysical overkill.[9] Some of the most influential

---

[9]Why "extreme nominalism" here and not just "nominalism"? The reason is that nominalism has a wide range of meaning in these discussions and represents a spectrum of views from property-anti-realism to forms of property-realism that consider properties to be real but particular

metaphysicians in the twentieth century have advocated a brand of extreme nominalism about universals such as W. V. Quine and his student David Lewis.[10] Property-anti-realism is motivated primarily on the grounds of qualitative simplicity and the deep conceptual problems that lurk at the heart of the ontology of property-realism. While there are a host of different versions of property-anti-realism, space permits me to interact with three leading proposals, one rather ambitious and two more modest versions of extreme nominalism—and examine the arguments for and against each to see how they fare as an adequate metaphysical theory of properties for the Christian metaphysician.

SOME ARGUMENTS FOR PROPERTY-ANTI-REALISM: THEORETICAL SIMPLICITY, DIVINE ASEITY, AND BRADLEY'S REGRESS

All forms of property-anti-realism harbor the conviction that realism is not required in order to adequately account for the structure of created being; metaphysically, we can get by with a much leaner ontology. And if we can get by with being ontologically lean, property-anti-realists argue, we should. Even Peter van Inwagen, a leading property-realist, goes so far as to say that property-anti-realism is preferable at the outset, and we should try our best to be nominalists if we can get away with it.[11] Recall the guiding metaphysical maxim outlined at the beginning of the chapter: All else being equal, we should prefer metaphysical theories that are qualitatively simpler than their rivals. Property-anti-realists argue that their view is certainly qualitatively simpler than property-realism as it doesn't introduce an additional basic category of being, *Property*, over and above the basic category *Object* (recall our previous discussion of the color theories). But just how to get by, metaphysically speaking, without the existence of properties is what sets the various brands of property-anti-realism apart.

Apart from the claim that property-anti-realism is qualitatively leaner than property-realism, there are two other important motivations in favor of the

---

(trope nominalism). To think that "nominalism" consists in the blanket rejection of properties per se, as is often the case in more popular-level discussion of these matters, is mistaken.

[10]For a helpful overview of nominalism in contemporary metaphysics, see Gonzalo Rodriguez-Pereyra, "Nominalism in Metaphysics," Stanford Encyclopedia of Philosophy, April 2015, https://plato.stanford.edu/entries/nominalism-metaphysics/.

[11]See van Inwagen, "Theory of Properties," 107-38. As a property-realist, of course, van Inwagen doesn't think we can get away with it in the end.

view that we need to mention. The first reason is distinctively theological, that certain brands of property-realism (the Platonic sort as we will see in the final section) have problematic theological implications. More specifically, some Christian theists have argued that a robust view of divine aseity (see chap. 3) undercuts the entire metaphysical framework of property-realism, irrespective of the brand of property-realism one affirms.[12] If so, then the Christian metaphysician may well have strong theological motivations in favor of property-anti-realism.

A second, more widely influential argument for property-anti-realism stems from a perceived problem within the realist's own ontological camp, particularly as it pertains to the relation of exemplification and its role in explaining qualitative (Q1-Realism) and resemblance (R1-Realism) facts in general. Recall that for the property-realist, "The apple is red" is explained by the apple's exemplifying the property *redness*. According to the realist, exemplification serves to metaphysically link or relate the object (the apple) to the property (*redness*). But according to the realist, exemplification is also a relation, which is a certain kind of property that itself can be exemplified (more specifically, what philosophers call a "polyadic" or "many-place" property). But now a worry rears its head, a worry that is now famously known as Bradley's Regress, named after the British philosopher F. H. Bradley (1826–1924).[13] If unaddressed, Bradley's Regress threatens to unravel the entire framework of property-realism from the get-go.

To clearly grasp the worry, recall from chapter five that the job description of a relation is to metaphysically link or tie distinct entities together (like metaphysical glue). In this case the exemplification relation is said to link the following two entities: the apple and the property *redness* (apple—exemplification—*redness*). But now we might ask: What exactly makes it the case that the apple and the property *redness* are related by way of the exemplification relation? What links the linker to the apple and to the property *redness*? After all, if relations are themselves properties, they also must be

---

[12]See the cumulative work of William Lane Craig on God and abstract entities for a sustained defense of this claim. The reader should start with his "Nominalism and Divine Aseity," in *Oxford Studies in Philosophy of Religion*, vol. 4, ed. Jonathan L. Kvanvig (Oxford: Oxford University Press, 2012), and move to his *God over All: Divine Aseity and the Challenge of Platonism* (New York: Oxford University Press, 2016), and finally graduate up to his *God and Abstract Objects: The Coherence of Theism: Aseity* (Chaim, Switzerland: Springer, 2017).
[13]See F. H. Bradley, *Appearance and Reality* (Oxford: Oxford University Press, 1897).

exemplified in order to relate objects together. If so, we might ask: What's the additional relational glue that binds these three entities together—the apple, the relation of exemplification, and the property *redness*? We need another, overarching relation—call it "exemplification$_1$"—that serves to relate these three items together.

But the problem rears its ugly head yet again. Since exemplification$_1$ is itself a relation and needs to be exemplified in order to relate these three entities together, we might again ask: What's the further exemplification relation that relates the apple, exemplification, and *redness* by way of exemplification$_1$? You can see that this unrelenting demand for more and more exemplification relations will not let up and is deeply problematic.

In sum, the thorny problem for property-realism is that in order to explain simple qualitative facts like "The apple is red" (Q1) in terms of Q1-Realism, we need an endless series of exemplification relations that bind together previous instances of exemplification, that bind together previous instances of exemplification, and so on indefinitely. This is Bradley's vicious regress.

Property-realists have responded to Bradley's Regress in a variety of ways, from denying that the regress is problematic (though few take this route) to excluding the relation of exemplification from a realist analysis altogether and thereby taking it as ontologically bedrock and incapable of being further analyzed (i.e., primitive or unanalyzable). According to some property-realists, exemplification is "an unmediated linker" that is construed as a "nexus" or connecting link rather than a relation, strictly speaking.[14] As Moreland, a property-realist, helpfully puts it, "Just as one does not need superglue to connect two objects to normal glue in order to tie them together with normal glue, so relations are the sort of things that do not need to be related to their relata before they can relate those relata to each other."[15]

This move to take exemplification as primitive and unanalyzable is instructive since, as we will see shortly, *every* account of properties—whether realist or anti-realist—must introduce some rock-bottom and unanalyzable relation into the mix in order to deal with problematic regresses of this kind.

---

[14]See Michael Loux and Thomas Crisp, *Metaphysics: A Contemporary Introduction*, 4th ed. (New York: Routledge, 2017), 29-35. Also, see J. P. Moreland, *Universals* (Montreal: McGill-Queens University Press, 2001), 115-16.

[15]Moreland, *Universals*, 116.

PROPERTY-ANTI-REALISM: AUSTERE EXTREME NOMINALISM

With the above reasons on the table as to why someone might be drawn to property-anti-realism, let's move on to explore some versions of property-anti-realism. Let's start with a rather ambitious form of property-anti-realism, a version of extreme nominalism known as "austere" or "ostrich" nominalism. In comparison with property-realism, this view is ontologically lean indeed. According to austere nominalism, the only entities that exist are objects that are concrete and particular (see the definitions above); there are no properties or universals and no abstract objects of any kind.

How might the austere nominalist respond to the metaphysical argument from qualitative (Q1 and Q2) and resemblance facts (R1 and R2) above? Interestingly enough, the austere nominalist straightforwardly denies that any deeper metaphysical explanation is needed in order to explain qualitative and resemblance facts. The austere nominalist first claims that the qualitative fact that "the apple is red" (Q1) has no deeper metaphysical explanation; qualitative facts are what philosophers call brute, primitive, or fundamental facts about the world.[16] As our old friend from chapter one, W. V. Quine, put it, "That the house and roses and sunsets are all of them red may be taken as ultimate and irreducible."[17] After all, the austere nominalist argues, the demand for a deeper metaphysical explanation must hit bottom *somewhere* and thus cannot go on forever. So, if one must halt the demand for a deeper metaphysical explanation at some point, why not do so at the level of familiar concrete particular objects themselves (red apples and negatively charged electrons)?

Austere nominalists then draw on these primitive qualitative facts to explain resemblance facts (Declan and Hudson are both human). So, the austere nominalist construes both qualitative and resemblance facts as follows:

Q1-Austere Nominalism: "The apple is red" is true by virtue of the apple's being red.

R1-Austere Nominalism: "Declan and Hudson are both human" is true by virtue of Declan's being human and Hudson's being human.

---

[16]As austere nominalist Michael Devitt puts it, "We have nothing to say about what makes a F, it just is F; that is a basic and inexplicable fact about the universe." See Michael Devitt, "'Ostrich Nominalism' or 'Mirage Realism,'" *Pacific Philosophical Quarterly* 61, no. 4 (1980): 436.

[17]W. V. Quine, *From a Logical Point of View* (Cambridge, MA: Harvard University Press, 1953), 10. I owe this citation to Paul Gould, "There Are Universals."

The austere nominalist's denial that any deeper, metaphysical explanation is required for qualitative and resemblance facts is precisely why one philosopher has referred to the view, rather pejoratively, as "ostrich nominalism," since proponents appear to stick their heads in the sand when asked for a deeper metaphysical explanation of qualitative and resemblance facts.[18] The austere nominalist argues that since a property-realist explanation of Q1 and R1 (in terms of Q1-Realism and R1-Realism) has its own conceptual problems (as we will see below), there is little (if any) explanatory advantage on the side of property-realism. Even more, what explanatory advantage (if any) is enjoyed by the realist is counterbalanced by the high cost of an excessively "bloated ontology," one that is far less qualitatively simple than austere nominalism.[19]

Yet there are several charges that have been leveled against austere nominalism, only a few of which I can mention here. First, property-realists charge that the "ostrich" move to deny any deeper metaphysical explanation of qualitative and resemblance facts is deeply unsatisfying. Surely, the objection goes, there's a deeper ontological explanation for why the apple is red and why Hudson and Declan are both human. And, arguably, the austere nominalist's attempt to account for resemblance facts (R1-Austere Nominalism) in terms of qualitative facts (Q1-Austere Nominalism) leaves much to be desired. For those with realist leanings, the deeper explanatory itch remains, and this itch can only be adequately scratched by an ontological explanation of the realist variety outlined in Q1-Realism and R1-Realism.

A second worry for austere nominalism turns on its self-proclaimed superiority as being more qualitatively simple than property-realism. Recall that the austere nominalist advertises her view as more qualitatively simple than property-realism, since she includes fewer basic types of entities in her overall ontology (nothing more than primitively charactered concrete particular objects). On the surface, this claim to qualitative simplicity seems right, but the realist contends that at the end of the day such a claim amounts to false advertising. The realist counters that when you begin to peel back the layers of austere nominalism you quickly realize that the view is committed to an unwieldy number of basic types of concrete particulars. How so?

---

[18]See D. M. Armstrong, *Universals and Scientific Realism*, vol. 1, *Nominalism and Realism* (Cambridge: Cambridge University Press, 1978), 15-16.

[19]For a representative of both claims on behalf of the ostrich nominalist, see Devitt, "'Ostrich Nominalism' or 'Mirage Realism,'" 436.

In austere nominalism, *each* primitively charactered particular object—red-apple, sweet-tea, negatively-charged-electron, rusty-nail, etc.—is a basic type of particular, one that defies any deeper ontological analysis. Likewise, *each* dimension of resemblance among primitively charactered particulars—Hudson and Declan are both human, roses resemble tulips more than car tires, etc.—also amounts to a *basic* type of particular, one that defies any deeper ontological analysis.

Compare this with the realist ontology outlined in Q1-Realism and R1-Realism above. For the realist, there are two fundamental types of entities: concrete particular objects and properties (the latter includes the relation of exemplification since relations are widely considered to be a type of property). The realist wields these two basic types of entities to explain charactered objects and the dimensions of resemblance among them (in terms of Q1-Realism and R1-Realism). Thus, for the realist, red-things and sweet-things are not basic types of entities but are explained in terms of particulars standing in the exemplification relation to certain properties, *redness* and *sweetness* respectively. So, despite initial appearances, the shoe of qualitative simplicity here is on the other foot as austere nominalism is, in contrast to property-realism, committed to a dizzying array of basic types of concrete particulars and is less qualitatively simple on this front.

PROPERTY-ANTI-REALISM: CONCEPT EXTREME NOMINALISM

While there are several less austere versions of property-anti-realism (all forms of extreme nominalism), each of which differ from one another in important and technical ways, a full treatment of these views falls outside the scope of an introductory book like this. However, one form of extreme nominalism that we will need to consider at this point is known as "concept nominalism."[20] In contrast to austere nominalists, concept nominalists think there is indeed a deeper explanation for qualitative facts but that such an explanation need not appeal to a realist ontology of properties. Rather, a particular object is charactered along the lines of F (red, sweet, round, furry, human, etc.) by virtue of the fact that the object falls under the relevant human mental concept *Fness* (*redness, sweetness, roundness,* etc.). In this view,

---

[20]For a helpful overview and critique of concept nominalism, see M. Armstrong, *Universals and Scientific Realism,* as well as Moreland, *Universals,* 29-30.

human concepts are the products of human mental activity and thus dependent on human minds, that is, they exist only insofar as a human has them in mind.

More specifically, the concept nominalist aims to explain qualitative facts in the following manner:

> Q1-Concept Nominalism: "The apple is red" by virtue of the apple's falling under the (human) concept *redness*.

Again, note that the (human) concept nominalist does indeed attempt to explain the qualitative fact in question ("the apple is red") and thus refuses to bury their head in the sand like the austere nominalist.

Now, it may already be apparent to you why concept nominalism is nearly universally rejected in contemporary metaphysics. The reason is that the view has the disastrous consequence that all of reality is the way it is qualitatively *because* of human mental activity. Thus, had human mental activity been different—if, say, no one ever had the mental concept of *roundness* or *negative charge* in mind—the apple wouldn't have been round (Q1) or the electron wouldn't have been negatively charged (Q2). What a strange consequence! But this amounts to a radically human constructivist view of the shape of reality, one that is deeply problematic for the Christian metaphysician. Even more, are there not far more ways that reality is qualitatively structured than there are human concepts in existence? Might not reality far outpace what actual human concepts there are?

Another problem with concept nominalism is one that lies beyond the surface, in contrast with the previous objection. David Armstrong has noted that concept nominalism suffers from a problematic regress concerning the *falling under* relation.[21] What about the relation that relates the object (apple, electron) with the human mental concept (*redness, negative charge*)? Does the relation of *falling under* itself fall under a higher-order relation of *falling under₁*, and so on?

The careful reader will notice that this regress worry is a version of Bradley's regress, yet one that threatens to undermine the concept nominalist's attempt to explain qualitative facts along the lines of Q1-Concept Nominalism. In the same way that regress worries push the property-realist to construe the relation of exemplification as unanalyzable and rock bottom, so too the concept

---

[21]Armstrong, *Universals and Scientific Realism*, 18-21.

nominalist can make the same move here and take the relation of *falling under* as unanalyzable. Interestingly enough, Armstrong, himself a property-realist and thus no friend of concept nominalism, later noted his sympathy with this move on behalf of concept nominalism, insofar as "all solutions to the Problem of Universals, including realism about universals, require a fundamental relation" (although, Armstrong believes, concept nominalism has other grave difficulties).[22]

PROPERTY-ANTI-REALISM: RESEMBLANCE EXTREME NOMINALISM

Another less austere but more prominent version of property-anti-realism is known as "resemblance extreme nominalism" (REN for short). REN tries to explain qualitative facts (Q1: "The apple is red") in terms of resemblance facts (R1: "Hudson and Declan are both human"), yet without recourse to a realist ontology of properties. How do proponents of REN aim to do this? Well, first, they identify properties, like *redness* or *humanity*, with the set of charactered objects that resemble one another (and only one another) to some degree, in this case the set of red things or the set of humans.[23] Properties are nothing more than primitively resembling sets of charactered objects (red things, humans, etc.).

At this point, you should be asking yourself the following very natural question about REN: But what explains, in REN, why all red things or why all humans resemble one another (and only one another)? Isn't it true, after all, that all humans resemble each other because they are human? Not so, according to REN. Here, the proponent of REN takes resemblance between particulars to be primitive and unanalyzable (yet another appeal to a fundamental relation!). There is no deeper ontological account for why all members of the set of humans resemble one another; there's simply no deeper story to tell here in REN.

In fact, REN sets out to explain qualitative facts by means of these primitive resemblance sets. In other words, in REN, what makes humans human is that they resemble each other, not the other way around. More

---

[22]D. M. Armstrong, *Universals: An Opinionated Introduction* (Boulder, CO: Westview, 1989), 53–56.
[23]Recall that sets or classes are formal, theoretical entities. So, for example, the class of the three persons in the Holy Trinity consists of the Father, Son, and Holy Spirit and can be represented as {Father, Son, Holy Spirit}.

specifically, REN accounts for both qualitative and resemblance facts as follows (I put R1 prior to Q1 since this best reflects the order of explanation in REN):

R1-Resemblance EN: "Declan and Hudson are both human" is true but unanalyzable.

Q1-Resemblance EN: "The apple is red" by virtue of the apple's being a member of the set of resembling red things.

While there are a host of powerful arguments against REN, I'll just mention two.[24] First, REN seems to reverse the natural order of explanation here. As noted above, it seems more intuitive to think that all humans resemble each other because they are human, all red things resemble each other because they are red, and so on, *not the other way around*. The attempt to explain qualitative facts in terms of resemblance facts seems on the face of things to get the order of explanation just plain wrong.

A second well-known objection has to do with the nature of sets since, after all, REN identifies properties like humanity and redness with sets.[25] Individual sets have their members essentially; it is part of the nature of a set that it has the very members that it does (it could not exist without those very members). So, the set of all current NFL teams has thirty-two members (and only thirty-two members), no more and no less. If, say, the Raiders decided to bow out of the NFL (would anyone even care?), then the original set with thirty-two members would no longer exist. It is precisely because the nature of sets involves sole reference to their members ("same members, same set") that they are, we might say, ontologically fragile entities; lose or add even one member and the set no longer exists.

Now, if *humanity* is simply identical to the set of resembling humans, then it has its members essentially and can only exist with the very members it has (however many humans are in existence at present). This means that if there were one less (or more) human in existence, then the set of resembling humans would cease to be. But if the set of resembling humans ceases to be, then nothing would be human, since in REN humans are human solely *by virtue*

---

[24]For further objections to REN see Moreland, *Universals*. For the most robust yet very technical defense of REN, see Gonzalo Rodriguez-Pereyra, *Resemblance Nominalism: A Solution to the Problem of Universals* (Oxford: Clarendon Press, 2002).
[25]The objection has its origin in the work of Christian philosopher Nicholas Wolterstorff, *On Universals: An Essay in Ontology* (Chicago: University of Chicago Press, 1970), 175-76.

of being members of the set of resembling humans. This also implies that there strictly could not be one more or one less human in the world.[26] Yikes; a disastrous result!

THE PROPERTY NATURE QUESTION: ARE PROPERTIES UNIVERSAL OR PARTICULAR?

Suppose one leans toward property-realism of some kind and thinks that there are compelling reasons for thinking that characteristics in addition to charactered objects exist. How then are we to think about the nature of properties, what they are like essentially? Are they universal (sharable) or particular (nonsharable)? This brings us to our second guiding question, the Property Nature Question.

There are two overarching views that rival one another at this point, the view that properties are universals (sharable entities) and the view that properties are particular (nonsharable entities). Thus,

Properties Are Universals: Properties exist and are universals (sharable/repeatable).

Properties Are Particulars (a.k.a., "Trope Theory" or "Moderate Nominalism"): Properties exist but are particular (nonsharable/nonrepeatable).[27]

Let's first unpack the view that properties are best thought of as particulars, and then turn to explore the view that properties are best thought of as universals.

PROPERTIES ARE PARTICULARS: TROPE THEORY

The view that properties exist but are best thought of as particulars instead of universals is often referred to as "trope theory." A trope (sometimes and more aptly called a "mode") is simply a particular, nonsharable, and nonrepeatable property; a particular *way* or *mode* of an individual object.[28] So, the *redness* possessed by the red firetruck (*redness1*) and the *redness* possessed by the red

---

[26]This point is made well by Garcia, "Platonism and the Haunted Universe."

[27]Be careful: While trope theory is a version of nominalism (since all properties are particular), it is a version of property-realism in my classification of views and not a version of extreme nominalism.

[28]I leave aside more precise details about the nature of tropes or modes that are highly relevant to the adequacy of trope theory in general, including the difference between what Robert Garcia calls "modular" and "modifier" tropes. See Robert Garcia, "Two Ways to Particularize a Property," *Journal of the American Philosophical Association* 1, no. 4 (2015): 635-52.

CREATURELY CHARACTERISTICS

apple (*redness2*) are strictly not one and the same trope or mode. Although *redness1* and *redness2* highly resemble one another (they might even exactly resemble one another), they are not numerically one and the same property. Strictly speaking, since *redness2* is a particular mode of that very apple and not the firetruck, it essentially depends on the apple (that very apple) for its existence. Thus, no two objects share numerically one and the same property, in trope theory.

Yet, as with most brands of property-realism, trope theory holds that properties are real existing beings that serve to ground the qualitative character of the objects that have them (the fire truck and the apple are red *because* they exemplify their own, nonsharable *redness*). In this way, trope theory explains qualitative facts as follows:

> Q1-Trope Realism: "The apple is red" is true by virtue of the apple's exemplifying the particular property *redness1* (a trope).

An ontology of particular properties or tropes has a rich historical pedigree, with some claiming to find the notion in Aristotle, many medieval Aristotelians (including Thomas Aquinas depending on how you read him), John Locke, George Berkeley, David Hume, and contemporary philosophers like Keith Campbell, G. F. Stout, and D. C. Williams.[29]

To illustrate this historical pedigree, consider the following remark by medieval theologian and philosopher Thomas Aquinas,

> Even if *this* individual [say, Socrates] is a human being and *that* individual [say, Plato] is a human being, it is not necessary that both have numerically the same humanity—any more than it is necessary for two white things to have numerically the same whiteness. On the contrary, it is necessary [only] that the one resemble the other in having [an individual] humanity just as the other does. It is for this reason that the mind—when it considers [an individual] humanity, not as belonging to this [or that] individual, but as such— forms a concept that is common to them all.[30]

---

[29]For historical references on trope theory, see chap. 2 of Loux and Crisp, *Metaphysics,* as well as D. W. Mertz, *Moderate Realism and Its Logic* (New Haven, CT: Yale University Press, 1996).

[30]Quoted in Jeffrey Brower, "Aquinas on the Problem of Universals," *Philosophy and Phenomenological Research* 92, no. 2 (2016): 715-35. Emphasis original. See also Brian Leftow, "Aquinas on Attributes," *Medieval Philosophy and Theology* 11, no. 1 (2003): 1-41. For medieval views of accidents or attributes more broadly, see Robert Pasnau, *Metaphysical Themes: 1274-1671* (New York: Oxford University Press, 2011), part III.

While things are much more complicated than I can convey here, the point stands that Aquinas clearly denies that two resembling humans (Socrates and Plato) share numerically the same property (or kind), *humanity*. Socrates's *humanity* is not strictly identical to Plato's *humanity*, since Aquinas thinks that "no humanity that exists outside the mind is common to many."[31]

Why might one prefer trope theory over a view of properties as universals or sharable entities? There are several main motivating factors for thinking of properties as particulars, only a few of which I can mention here.

First, trope theorists claim the mantle of qualitative simplicity over and above postulating the existence of properties as universals. Since we already have concrete particulars (individual objects like trees and people, etc.) on the ontological books, we should aim to account for properties within this same category if we can; doing so is more qualitatively simple than adding the category of *Universal* into the ontological mix as well.

Second, on the surface, particular properties seem better suited to play the causal and explanatory role that properties are thought to play in one's ontology.[32] How so? When you visually perceive a rose, you appear to have a sensory experience of the *redness* of the rose, and the *redness* of the rose *causally* brings about certain conscious states in your mind (you're having the sensation of seeing red, for example). The *redness* of the rose and the *humanity* of Declan and Hudson appear to be spatially located where the objects exemplifying them are located. But if *redness* is the sort of entity that is a universal and abstract (that is, outside of space and time and causally inert, as Platonic accounts of universals maintain), then it is difficult to see how it could be an object of perception (or human knowledge for that matter!) and play a distinctive causal role in the world of space and time.

---

[31]Quoted in Brower, "Aquinas on the Problem of Universals," 9. Notice carefully that Aquinas's denial of sharable universals is not to deny the existence of objective essences or natures as such (*humanity* as such). Some quickly (too quickly in my estimation) move from the denial of sharable universals to the denial of essences full stop. See Scott Smith, "Craig's Nominalism and the High Cost of Preserving Divine Aseity," *European Journal for Philosophy of Religion* 9, no. 1 (2017): 63-85.

[32]See Lowe, *Four-Category Ontology*, 23-25; and John Heil, *The Universe as We Find It* (Oxford: Clarendon, 2012), chap. 5.

Getting Theological: Powerful Properties, Human Nature, and the Valuable Edges of Human Life

One historically prominent question about the nature of properties has to do with whether properties are themselves intrinsically powerful or, at the very least, confer powers on the objects that have them. What exactly do I mean here? We are naturally familiar with not only the ways objects are in their current state (*being white, being made of porcelain*, etc.), but also the various states objects have the power or potential to be in. For example, while the white porcelain vase is not currently broken into pieces, it nevertheless currently has the real power or tendency to break under certain conditions (say, when hit hard with a baseball bat). The porcelain vase has, to put it in much older philosophical language, the latent potentiality to break (and not, say, to turn into a bouquet of flowers or grow a root system), even if that latent potentiality is not currently *actualized*. And it is precisely *because* the vase has this disposition or power that it will break when struck, unless that power is blocked or prevented from being actualized (say, if you wrapped the vase in bubble wrap many times over). Remember: The vase has the real but latent tendency to break when struck by virtue of possessing this power or disposition, even if it forever remains untouched, safe inside grandma's hutch.

In contemporary metaphysics, some property-realists think that all properties are inert or powerless, that there are no real, fundamental potentialities or powers in the world. This view, known as "categoricalism," traces its intellectual genealogy back to early modern philosophers like Descartes and David Hume (who were generally suspicious of the notion of a power or disposition), and up through the influential work of contemporary philosopher David Lewis. Categoricalism is in stark contrast to what is known as "dispositionalism," which traces its intellectual lineage to Aristotle and up through the medieval Aristotelian tradition and has regained steam in contemporary metaphysics.

Dispositionalists hold that powers ("potentialities," "tendencies," or "capacities") like *fragility, solubility*, and *flammability* are real features of the world that cannot be explained away or reduced to nonpowerful properties. They argue that an adequate theory of properties that leaves out such powers is utterly inadequate to our natural world as intrinsically dynamic and primed with latent but real potentiality. Within the dispositionalist camp some think that merely *some* properties are powers ("dispositionalists"),[33] and others think that *all* properties are powers ("pandispositionalists").[34] Either way, powerful properties exist, and the substances that possess them have the latent power to do certain things and behave in certain ways, even if those powers remain temporarily latent or even forever unrealized (due to being hindered in some way from being exercised).

Consider carefully how this debate about the reality of powers applies to human nature, the image of God, and the value of human life. In a more classical view, human beings possess a certain range of powers or dispositions that are rooted in human nature and are partly what constitute the image of God in humans. If humans alone are rational animals, they thereby have certain powers that are unique to them, *rationality* (intellect and will) and *animality* (biological powers, e.g., sensation, assimilation, growth). The powers of *intellect* and *will* confer on human beings the capacity to contemplate and relate to God and others, to engage in deliberative judgment and high-level reflection, and to act in accordance with what they perceive to be genuinely good and worth pursuing. Part of what it means to be human (and not a tulip or an iPhone, say)—and thus an image-bearer of God—is at the very least to possess these latent powers and capacities that make it possible for humans to carry out their God-given task in creation (Genesis 1:27-28).

Yet, as we've seen regarding the nature of powers in general, these distinctively human powers of intellect and will can be possessed by a human being, even when these powers are not currently realized, or even when they are altogether hindered (think again of the porcelain vase possessing the real tendency to break even when hindered by being smothered in bubble wrap). By God's own design, the *exercise*

---

[33]For influential philosophers in the dispositionalist camp, see Brian Ellis, *Scientific Essentialism* (Cambridge: Cambridge University Press, 2001); and George Molnar, *Powers: A Study in Metaphysics* (New York: Oxford University Press, 2003).

[34]For influential philosophers in the pandispositionalist camp, see Alexander Bird, *Nature's Metaphysics* (2007); and Sydney Shoemaker, *Identity, Cause, and Mind: Philosophical Essays* (Cambridge: Cambridge University Press, 1984).

(though *not* the possession!) of these distinctively human powers of intellect and will requires the initial realization of certain *other* powers in order for them to be available for "in-hand" use, we might say. At least while embodied, human beings require the right sort of biological and neurological development in order to exercise (but *not* to possess!) these powers of intellect and will that are deeply rooted in human nature (just like a seed that is deeply rooted in the soil first requires the right physical conditions to develop its real but latent powers and capacities for a root system and to produce fruit).

Hopefully, you can already see the payout of a realist view of powers for moral issues related to the value of human life in all of its stages of development. A human embryo is a human being at its earliest stage of development. An embryo is *not* a potential human, as it is sometimes said. Rather, an embryo is a human that has real but latent potentiality to develop into a mature human organism. A human embryo possesses the very same essential powers of intellect and will that an adult human being possesses, the only difference being that such powers remain inoperative until the embryo first develops the necessary biological powers and capacities needed to exercise them (including a functioning brain and central nervous system). Precisely because of what a human embryo already is by nature (including its possession of real powers or potentialities), if given the right biological conditions (including the absence of hindered biological development), it will develop into a full-fledged mature human adult that will have the "in-hand" capacity to exercise the powers of intellect and will.

Tragically, through abnormal biological development, some human beings may never properly develop the biological capacities needed to exercise the powers of intellect and will. Likewise, some humans will sadly suffer severe injury and lose the biological and neurological capacities needed to exercise these essential human powers "in-hand" (such as those in a "persistent vegetative state"). But here's the rub: *All* are full-fledged human beings and divine image-bearers by virtue of simply possessing the essential powers of intellect and will that are deeply rooted within the soil of human nature. There is, then, no metaphysical difference in kind, nature, or essence between these groups of human beings. *All* equally possess the latent powers or dispositions that are rooted in human nature. If moral value and dignity are anchored in the possession (not exercise!) of these latent, human powers that constitute the image of God, then if any *one* human being has moral value and dignity, then they *all* do, even a tiny embryo.

PROPERTIES ARE UNIVERSALS

But there are problems with taking properties as nonsharable particulars instead of sharable universals. And it is these problems that defenders of universals latch onto in defense of their view.

On the one hand, property-realists who seek to analyze resemblance facts like R1 ("Hudson and Declan are both human") above will argue that viewing properties as nonsharable particulars yields a less than satisfying explanation of why things resemble each other to various degrees. According to trope property-realism, resemblance facts like R1 are explained in the following manner:

> R1-Trope Realism: "Declan and Hudson are both human" is true by virtue of Declan and Hudson exemplifying exactly resembling but nonidentical particular properties, *humanity1* and *humanity2* (two tropes).

Trope theorists explain resemblance facts by appealing to exactly resembling tropes. But the defender of sharable properties (i.e., universals) finds this less than satisfying as a deep, metaphysical explanation for why Declan and Hudson are both human. In fact, they argue, rather than explaining the phenomenon of resemblance, this move seems to push the question of resemblance back one step.

In addition, the resemblance relation *itself* seems to be functioning more like a universal than a particular in R1-Trope Realism above. How so? If Declan and Hudson resemble one another by way of exemplifying *humanity1* and *humanity2*, then the relation of resemblance links these two particular tropes together. But since Suzanne and Verity also resemble each other by way of their own respective humanity tropes—*humanity3* and *humanity4*—is it not the exact same relation of resemblance that links *humanity3* and *humanity4* together? If so, then resemblance is a universal as it is "sharable" and repeatable (multiply exemplifiable).

The trope theorist will insist, of course, that the relation of resemblance too is a particular and not a universal (a relational trope, to be exact). If so, then trope theory is saddled with a mind-boggling number of primitive relations of resemblance, one for *each and every* way that particulars resemble each other (e.g., for *every* two humans there is a primitive resemblance relation between them). If this is right, then trope theory is anything but qualitatively simple, as the trope theorist advertises.

THE PROPERTY LOCATION QUESTION: ARE PROPERTIES IMMANENT OR TRANSCENDENT?

For property-realists who favor an account of properties as universals, there remains the question of *where* exactly these universals are located, if anywhere at all. Are universals like *humanity*, *redness*, and *sweetness* within space and time (often called "Aristotelian" or "immanent realism"), or are they transcendent in the sense of being beyond space and time (often called "Platonic" or "transcendent realism")? More precisely, are universals *dependent* or *independent* of their instances (the things that have them)?

For the sake of simplicity, let's define the following two main views on this as follows:

> *Properties as Transcendent*: Properties are sharable universals that are not located in space and time and are independent of particulars.

> *Properties as Immanent*: Properties are sharable universals that are located within space and time and dependent on particulars.

Following Plato, defenders of transcendent universals hold that such entities are abstract, necessarily existent entities. Recall that an abstract entity is one that is both outside of space and time and causally inert in that it lacks causal power or oomph. In this Platonic realist version of property-realism, universals are necessary beings in that they couldn't have failed to exist (nor was there a time when they did not exist); as necessarily existing beings, universals must exist come what may (in every possible world, as some might put it). Influential nineteenth- and twentieth-century proponents of this Platonic realist ontology of universals include Gottlob Frege, Bertrand Russell, Alvin Plantinga, J. P. Moreland, Robert Adams, Peter van Inwagen, Roderick Chisholm, and others.

Along these lines, transcendent universals are independent of particulars in the specific sense that they would exist even if God freely chose to create a world completely devoid of creaturely particulars. So, abstract universals like *humanity, felinity, redness, sweetness,* and so on would exist regardless of whether any particular humans, felines, red things, or sweet things existed (hence why they are independent of particulars). Many Platonic realists affirm the existence of what philosophers call "uninstantiated universals," universals that are not had by any particular (*being a unicorn, being a square circle,* etc.). While some Platonic realists such as J. P. Moreland also believe that universals enter into the metaphysical makeup of particular substances (more on this idea in the next chapter), universals are not, strictly speaking, spatially present where the substance that exemplifies them is present.[35]

Contrast this Platonic view of universals with a more Aristotelian, immanent view of universals. D. M. Armstrong (1926–2014), whom we've met several times throughout this chapter and book as a whole, has been the most ardent defender of immanent universals on the contemporary metaphysical scene.[36] The view has also been ably defended by E. J. Lowe (1950–2014), one of my favorite contemporary metaphysicians.[37] For Armstrong, universals are spatially located where the objects that exemplify them are located; the universal *humanity* is located where Declan (a human) is located. Interestingly enough, since Armstrong thinks that *humanity* is a universal and thus sharable, the universal *humanity* is also located where Hudson (a human) and Verity (a human) are located. So, numerically one and the same universal—*humanity*—is simultaneously located at the place and time of every existing human being on the planet.[38]

One vitally important point of disagreement between transcendent realism and immanent realism is that the latter construes universals

---

[35]Moreland, *Universals,* 129-30.

[36]A good place to start with Armstrong's immanent realism is his "Universals as Attributes," which is chap. 5 of *Universals: An Opinionated Introduction.* For a technical study of an immanent realist view of mathematics, see James Franklin, *An Aristotelian Realist Philosophy of Mathematics* (New York: Palgrave Macmillan, 2014).

[37]In his work on properties and universals, Lowe defends a hybrid view that affirms the existence of both immanent universals as well as the existence of tropes (better: modes). Lowe thinks that particular tropes or modes, like *roundess1* and *redness1,* are instances of (and not to be identified with) the immanent universals *roundness* and *redness,* respectively.

[38]David Armstrong, *Universals: An Opinionated Introduction,* chap. 5.

(e.g., *humanity*) as requiring at least one instance (e.g., an individual human) in order to exist at all.[39] Following one natural way of interpreting Aristotle, immanent realists argue that universals broadly depend on particulars, not vice versa; if no human beings ever existed, then the universal *humanity* would not have existed.[40] Another way of putting this is that there are no "uninstantiated universals," that is, no universals that are not possessed by at least one particular. In immanent realism, universals, then, are contingent beings (they could have failed to exist) and not necessary beings as in Platonic realism.

Armstrong's own reasons for wanting to "bring universals down to earth" are many, but two reasons stick out for our purposes here. First, Armstrong points out that if universals are Platonic abstract entities and exist beyond space and time and lack causal oomph, then their explanatory relevance for causal explanation and the natural sciences seems questionable. How could a spaceless, timeless, necessarily existing being like *being negatively charged* play any role in explaining why electrons causally affect particles that are positively charged (e.g., protons)?

A second motivation for Armstrong in particular is his general suspicion of the idea that beings exist that do not exist somewhere in space and time (recall our discussion of "Naturalist-Friendly Theories of Existence" from chap. 4). Indeed, Armstrong's staunch commitment to metaphysical naturalism—the view that the totality of reality is exhausted by material reality—constrains him to look for universals within the realm of space and time. While this second motivation is not at all necessary to immanent realism (Lowe himself is no friend of naturalism), it is one that explicitly motivates Armstrong's own defense of the view.

The Platonic realist claims to have the upper hand here since only necessarily existing universals could account for modal truths like "necessarily, cats are mammals."[41] Since this truth is true in all possible worlds, we might ask: What makes it true in worlds where there are no cats or mammals? Platonic realists argue that the universals *being a cat* and *being a mammal* (and the necessary relation between the two) must exist in every possible world for

---

[39]See Lowe, *Four-Category Ontology*, chap. 6.

[40]This is not to say that humanity depends on *any one human in particular*, just at least *one particular human or other*.

[41]For this argument, see Roderick Chisholm, *On Metaphysics* (Minneapolis: University of Minnesota Press, 1989), 141-42.

such a modal truth to be true of necessity. After all, what else could make necessary truths like this true in worlds with neither cats nor mammals?[42]

Another notable argument in favor of transcendent or Platonic realism stems from some rather strange implications that follow from immanent realism. Recall that for Armstrong, an immanent universal like *humanity* is wholly located where each of its instances is located (where each existing human being is located). Transcendent realists have pointed out that if universals are located throughout space in this way, then the following problem arises.[43] Consider two brothers, Declan and Hudson, who both live in the same house in Wake Forest, North Carolina, located at place C. Suppose Declan is currently located at place A which is ten miles away from his house in place C. At the same time, Declan's brother Hudson is located at place B which is twenty miles away from his house in place C. If so, it follows that one and the same universal, *humanity*, can be both ten miles away *and* twenty miles away from the same place C at one and the same time. Even more strange is the fact that if Verity, their adorable little sister, was in the house at place C, it would follow that one and the same universal can be both ten and twenty miles away from *itself* at one and the same time. But this seems flat-out contradictory, doesn't it (like saying that one and the same book is both red all over and blue all over at the same time)? While the immanent realist is not without plausible responses to this worry, I leave it to the reader to explore these options.

THE PROPERTY-GOD QUESTION

We turn now to our final guiding question about properties, one that is vitally important for the Christian metaphysician: What role does God play, if any, regarding the existence of properties, what they are, where they are, and whether they are generally dependent or independent of the things that have them? In particular, what role does our metaphysical lodestar, divine aseity, play in influencing how we answer these questions?

---

[42]Depending on what you think about the relationship between God and modality (see chap. 6), one could argue that its being true that nothing has the causal power to bring about the truth of "possibly, it's not the case that cats are mammals" might serve to explain this necessary truth, without appealing to uninstantiated, Platonic universals. See also Brian Leftow, "God and the Problem of Universals," in *Oxford Studies in Metaphysics*, ed. Dean Zimmerman (Oxford: Oxford University Press, 2006), 2:326.

[43]This argument can be found in Moreland, *Universals*, 88-89.

In this final section I want to briefly introduce you to the contemporary lay of the land regarding the relationship between God and properties. But first, a few brief preliminary remarks on how I'm inclined to think a Christian metaphysician should approach this final question. In the spirit of my remarks in chapter three regarding the various habits of mind that should characterize the Christian metaphysician, I take a theo-centric and scriptural habit of mind to be central in properly navigating this area of debate in contemporary metaphysics. Regarding a theo-centric habit of mind, a Christian metaphysician should be constrained by the fact that God plays an indispensable explanatory role in anchoring the existence of all reality that is not strictly identical to God (Romans 11:36). Regarding a scriptural habit of mind, the Christian metaphysician should swim *with* (and not *against*) the strong current of biblical texts that attest to God's unique and absolute metaphysical ultimacy. With my own cards on the table, let's take a closer look at the Property-God Question.

Throughout the Christian tradition, there has been a strong inclination to reject a Platonic or transcendent view of properties as universals, at least in its absolute and unqualified sense. And for good reason. The doctrine of divine aseity (as introduced in chap. 3) is the view that God alone is metaphysically ultimate and the creative source of all that is not God. In the words of the second-century church father Irenaeus (ca. 120–ca. 200), "In all things God has the pre-eminence, who alone is uncreated, the first of all things, and the primary cause of the existence of all."[44] As we have seen in chapter three, this view of God's ultimacy has strong scriptural, creedal, and historical witness throughout the Christian tradition. And it is fairly easy to see how this strong view of divine aseity is on a crash-course collision with a full-strength Platonic realist view of universals as necessary, uncreated beings. Indeed, Thomas Aquinas had some sharp words for the compatibility of Plato's view of the Forms (necessarily existing universals) with the Christian doctrine of God when he said, "It seems contrary to the faith to hold, as the Platonists did, that the Forms of things exist in themselves."[45]

---

[44]Quoted in William Lane Craig, *God over All*, 33.
[45]Thomas Aquinas, *Summa Theologiae* I.84.5. See also Thomas Aquinas, Preface to Exposition of *On the Divine Names*, in *Thomas Aquinas: Selected Writings*, ed. Ralph McInerny (New York: Penguin Books, 1998), 505.

The tension between divine aseity and Platonic realism is even more apparent when it comes to explaining qualitative facts about God's *own* nature, such as God's *being all-loving, being all-wise*, and *being all-powerful*. Are these divine qualitative facts to be explained in the same way that creaturely qualitative facts are to be explained according to Platonic realism, that is, in terms of God's exemplifying a transcendent universal *being all-loving*? If so, does this Platonic metaphysical framework not undermine a strong version of divine aseity, since then God would be what he is by virtue of a necessarily existing, uncreated universal (*being all-loving*)?[46]

Following the exemplary work of Christian philosopher Paul Gould in this area, we can capture the core tension between a Platonic realist view of universals with divine aseity by the following three tenets that make up what Gould calls "The Inconsistent Triad":

(1) Platonic universals exist [Platonic/Transcendent Realism]

(2) If Platonic universals exist, then they are dependent on God [Divine Aseity]

(3) If Platonic universals exist, then they are independent of God [Platonist Assumption][47]

The problem is that (1)-(3) are formally inconsistent. They can't all be true at the same time; one of them must go. One must deny at least one of them to avoid inconsistency, but which one?

The denial of (1) amounts to an all-out rejection of Platonic realism in order to hold fast to divine aseity. As several have pointed out, this route is the traditional Christian response to the ontology of Platonic realism; there simply are no necessarily existent Platonic entities that are not identical to God.[48] The

---

[46]A classic treatment of this very issue is found in Alvin Plantinga, *Does God Have a Nature?* (Milwaukee: Marquette University Press, 1980).

[47]See Paul M. Gould, "The Problem of God and Abstract Objects: A Prolegomenon," *Philosophia Christi* 13, no. 2 (2011): 255-74. For a much fuller discussion, see his edited volume *Beyond the Control of God? Six Views on the Problem of God and Abstract Objects*, ed. Paul M. Gould (New York: Bloomsbury, 2014). I have slightly adapted Gould's Inconsistent Triad to reflect my limited discussion in this chapter to universals, not Platonic abstract objects more generally (including propositions, numbers, and other mathematical entities). Interested readers will also want to check out Matthew Davidson's excellent encyclopedia entry on this topic: Matthew Davidson, "God and Other Necessary Beings," Stanford Encyclopedia of Philosophy, August 2019, https://plato.stanford.edu/entries/god-necessary-being/.

[48]See in particular Lindsay K. Cleveland, "Divine Aseity and Abstract Objects," in *T&T Clark Handbook of Analytic Theology*, eds. James M. Arcadi and James T. Turner Jr. (New York: Bloomsbury, 2021); and Craig, *God over All*.

CREATURELY CHARACTERISTICS

denial of (2) amounts to abandoning (or weakening) divine aseity to hold on to full-strength Platonic realism. Finally, rejecting (3) amounts to modifying Platonic realism in order to preserve a form of divine aseity. In what follows, I'll lay out three different ways out of the Inconsistent Triad that have been defended by Christian metaphysicians, one for each tenet of the Triad.

Let's start by considering the denial of (1). By rejecting (1), the Christian theist bids farewell to Platonic realism and opts instead for an ontology—whether a version of property-realism or property-anti-realism—that denies the existence of transcendent universals. This would leave either property-anti-realism (which rejects the existence of properties altogether) or some version of property-realism like trope theory or immanent realism on the table. Is this a tenable way forward? Well, it depends. At bottom, it depends on how compelling you find the positive arguments for Platonic realism (together with the arguments against property-anti-realism). If, on balance, the scales are level or close to level between Platonic realism and property-anti-realism (or some other form of property-realism), then the deep tension with divine aseity may well tip the scales in favor of the rejection of Platonism.

Christian philosophers like William Lane Craig, Brian Leftow, and Thomas Ward have argued that the denial of (1) is the most plausible route for the Christian metaphysician.[49] They opt for either some version of property-anti-realism (William Lane Craig, Brian Leftow) or some version of property-realism in line with trope theory, immanent realism, or what some have called "divine exemplar nominalism" (which is, Thomas Ward argues, consistent with a variety of non-Platonic versions of property-realism regarding creaturely properties in particular).[50] In fact, some even suggest a hybrid view, a type of property-realist account to explain qualitative and resemblance facts among creatures (e.g., "Socrates is wise" and "Both Socrates and Plato are wise"), and a type of property-anti-realist account when it comes to qualitative facts about God's own nature (e.g., "God is wise").[51]

---

[49]See Craig, *God over All*; Leftow, "God and the Problem of Universals"; and Thomas Ward, *Divine Ideas* (New York: Cambridge University Press, 2020).

[50]In divine exemplar nominalism, God himself is the concrete pattern or exemplar for all creaturely properties understood as particulars (understood along the lines of property-realism), roughly like the artist's mental conception of a house and its various characteristics is the exemplar or mental blueprint for an actual house and its characteristics.

[51]This route involves rejecting the entire property-realist framework for accounting for divine qualitative facts in particular, but it need not entail this denial for creaturely qualitative facts.

Let me unpack one theistic defense of property-anti-realism that denies (1) of the Inconsistent Triad. Christian philosopher Brian Leftow has defended a theistic version of concept nominalism, what he calls "theistic-concept nominalism."[52] Leftow argues that since God is already on the ontological books, so to speak, we should strive to explain as much about creaturely reality as we can in terms of God.[53] Recall that in human concept nominalism in particular, qualitative facts like "The apple is red" are analyzed in terms of the apple's falling under the human concept *redness* (where the "falling under" relation was taken to be bedrock and unanalyzable). We noted that human concept nominalism is nearly universally rejected in contemporary metaphysics because of its problematic human constructivist implications.

In contrast to human concept nominalism, Leftow's theistic-concept nominalism aims to explain qualitative (Q1: "The apple is red") and resemblance (R1: "Declan and Hudson are both human") facts in terms of falling under a *divine* concept:

Q1-Theistic Concept Nominalism: "The apple is red" by virtue of the apple's falling under the divine concept *redness*.[54]

R1-Theistic Concept Nominalism: "Declan and Hudson are both human" is true by virtue of Declan and Hudson both falling under the divine concept *humanity*.

As you can see, Leftow's *falling under* relation takes the place of the property-realist's exemplification relation. Qualitative facts and resemblance facts are explained by divine mental activity, rather than human mental activity. Divine concepts like *redness* and *humanity* are particulars (and not universals) and

---

From what I can tell, this route has a historical pedigree in the Augustinian tradition. See Anselm, *Monologion* 16, in *Anselm: Basic Writings*, trans. Thomas Williams (Indianapolis: Hackett, 2007), 23; Cleveland, "Divine Aseity and Abstract Objects"; and Michelle Panchuck, "Created and Uncreated Things: A Neo-Augustinian Solution to the Bootstrapping Problem," *International Philosophical Quarterly* 56 (2016): 99-112.

[52]See his "God and the Problem of Universals."

[53]As Thomas Ward echoes, "As a matter of methodology, it seems clear to me that Christians should err on the side of having God explain too much rather than too little." *Divine Ideas*, 13.

[54]Of course, I am greatly simplifying Leftow's view here for the sake of exposition. Leftow has considerably more to say about the precise ontology underlying divine concept-possession in terms of divine mental activity, and how a creature's causally depending on divine mental activity helps explain creaturely qualitative facts like Q1 and R1. For an exhaustive treatment of Leftow's views, see Brian Leftow, *God and Necessity* (Oxford: Oxford University Press, 2012).

are the archetypes or blueprints according to which God creates individual red things and humans.

Leftow argues, quite plausibly in my opinion, that theistic-concept nominalism avoids most of the problems that plague human concept nominalism. Problem: In human concept nominalism, there are not enough human concepts to adequately account for the qualitative richness of reality. Solution: There are more than enough divine concepts on hand, indeed, infinitely many! Problem: Human concept nominalism wrongly entails that reality is the way it is because of human mental activity alone. Solution: Divine concept nominalism rightly entails that created reality is the way it is because of *divine* mental activity.[55]

Leftow acknowledges that his theistic-concept nominalism does not apply to God's own nature (what he calls "deity"), specifically, the qualitative facts about God's *being all-loving* and *being all-powerful*. That is, God doesn't make himself all-loving or all-powerful by virtue of falling under one of his own concepts. God's own essential character—God's own nature—simply is the way it is, end of story.[56] According to Leftow, when it comes to God's own essential nature, i.e., deity, we've hit rock bottom of the deepest explanatory well in reality.

Let's turn now to consider (2) of the Inconsistent Triad, the denial of which amounts to abandoning (or severely weakening) divine aseity in order to hold on to full-strength Platonic realism. Peter van Inwagen is perhaps the leading Christian metaphysician who holds tight to Platonic realism and rejects (2) of the Inconsistent Triad.[57] How might van Inwagen avoid the charge of running afoul of divine aseity? Van Inwagen responds by arguing that Platonic universals fail to depend on God precisely because they are abstract, necessarily existent entities; necessary beings just are not the right *sorts* of beings to depend on nor be created by God. Thus, for van Inwagen, it is metaphysically impossible for abstract objects to be created. As a result, the fact that such beings fall outside the creative activity of the triune God is not

---

[55]For an important objection and corrective to Leftow's view, in particular that in his view God's mental life alone orders and structures qualitative reality (leaving creaturely beings without a role to structure reality in any sense), see Cleveland, "Divine Aseity and Abstract Objects."

[56]He goes on to say regarding God's own nature, deity, "I suspect that no theory of attributes is adequate to it, and that the proper conclusion to draw from this is that it is not an attribute at all." See his "God and the Problem of Universals," 354.

[57]See Peter van Inwagen, "God and Other Uncreated Things," in *Metaphysics and God: Essays in Honor of Eleonore Stump*, ed. Kevin Timpe (London: Routledge, 2009), 3-20.

at all problematic, according to van Inwagen, and need not worry the Christian theist.[58]

If (and only if) one is keen to adopt the methodological constraints I've placed on the Christian metaphysician stated in chapter three, including the idea of taking a strong version of divine aseity as a metaphysical lodestar when doing metaphysics as a Christian, this way out of the Inconsistent Triad will be a nonstarter.

Finally, what about denying (3) and thus modifying or weakening full-strength Platonic realism to preserve a tenable version of divine aseity? Why not claim that necessarily existing abstract entities like Platonic universals are dependent on God in some sense or other? This is a venerable move, but one that raises a host of further questions. How, exactly, do Platonic abstract entities depend on God? Are they created by God? Do all abstract entities depend on God, or just some of them? Do God's *own* properties (*being all-loving, being all-powerful*, etc.) depend on God in this way?

At the risk of oversimplifying a very technical and important discussion among Christian metaphysicians (many of whom are dear friends), let me at least try to briefly summarize various ways theists have denied (3) in the contemporary literature. Theistic proposals that deny (3) of the Inconsistent Triad differ with respect to the kind of dependence Platonic entities have on God, as well as which Platonic entities depend on God in this way. Some theists—known as "Theistic Activists" or "Absolute Creationists"—deny (3) and maintain that necessarily existing Platonic entities are the products of God's mental activity and are eternally created by and thus causally dependent on God.[59]

Yet modifying Platonic realism in this way in order to preserve divine aseity suffers from a fatal flaw known as the "bootstrapping objection." The bootstrapping objection focuses in on the claim that God is the absolute Creator

---

[58]See also Nicholas Wolterstorff, *On Universals* (Chicago: University of Chicago Press, 1970), chap. 12. A similar but bit more restrained denial of (2) is Keith Yandell, "God and Propositions," in *Beyond the Control of God?*, 21-35.

[59]In his more recent work on this topic, *Where the Conflict Really Lies*, Plantinga hints at a version of Theistic Activism in that he thinks that Platonic entities are causally produced by God. See Alvin Plantinga, *Where the Conflict Really Lies* (New York: Oxford University Press, 2011), 291; *Does God Have a Nature?*; and "How to Be an Anti-Realist," *Proceedings and Addresses of the American Philosophical Association* 56, no. 1 (1982): 47-70. For an important defense of Theistic Activism, see Thomas V. Morris and Christopher Menzel, "Absolute Creation," *American Philosophical Quarterly* 23, no. 4 (1986): 353-62.

of all abstract entities, including God's own properties like *being all-powerful*. For God to create the property of *being all-powerful*, God arguably would already need to *be* powerful (after all, you need power to create something, don't you?). So, to create the property *being all-powerful* God would already need have the property in question; but if he already has the property, then God does not create the property. An unqualified Theistic Activism, then, entails a fatal circularity: that God must already possess the very properties God is said to create.

In order to avoid this fatal bootstrapping objection to Theistic Activism, some very fine philosophers have defended a "Modified Theistic Activism."[60] Defenders of this modified view maintain that some necessarily existing Platonic entities are "within" God's mind and are uncreated (propositions and God's own essential properties like *being all-powerful* and *being all-loving*), and others are "outside" God's mind and are created (all those properties and relations not exemplified by God like *dogness, redness, humanity*, etc.). Since this route excludes God's own essential properties (e.g., *being all-powerful*) from the realm of created reality, it thereby avoids the sting of the bootstrapping objection.

In the same spirit, other theistic philosophers who deny (3)—those who hold to what is known as "Theistic Conceptual Realism" or sometimes "Divine Conceptualism"—have argued that while Platonic entities are best thought of as God's ideas and are dependent on God (as thoughts are dependent on thinkers), they are nevertheless concrete and uncreated.[61] As God's ideas are concrete and not abstract, they have genuine causal power. As this particular way of modifying Platonic realism exempts God's own properties from being created, it also avoids the sting of the bootstrapping worry that plagued Theistic Activism.

Both Modified Theistic Activism and Theistic Conceptual Realism successfully avoid the bootstrapping objection and represent a promising way forward

---

[60]See Paul M. Gould and Richard Brian Davis, "Modified Theistic Activism," in *Beyond the Control of God? Six Views on the Problem of God and Abstract Objects*, ed. Paul M. Gould (New York: Bloomsbury, 2014).

[61]The leading contemporary defender of Theistic Conceptual Realism is Greg Welty. See his essay "Theistic Conceptual Realism," in *Beyond the Control of God? Six Views on the Problem of God and Abstract Objects*, ed. Paul M. Gould (New York: Bloomsbury, 2014), chap. 3. A quick clarification: Welty is emphatic that his published explication and defense of Theistic Conceptual Realism extends only to propositions and possible worlds, not properties. He is also clear that he thinks divine thoughts play the role of abstract objects.

for those who are independently motivated to hold fast to a version of Platonic realism alongside a version of divine aseity. However, in my humble estimation, both views do so at the expense of significantly weakening divine aseity.[62] In both Modified Theistic Activism and Theistic Conceptual Realism, God's own essential properties such as *being all-powerful* and *being all-knowing* are necessarily existing beings that are "in God" yet not numerically one and the same being as God.[63] So, we have entities that are not one and the same being as God—even though they remain "within" God's borders—that are both necessary and uncreated. In both views, God is not the sole uncreated, necessarily existing being, nor does God bring into existence all that is not God, strictly speaking.

Apart from maintaining that God and God's ideas are numerically one and the same being along the lines of divine simplicity, which is the standard historical move here to uphold a strong form of divine aseity, I take this to be a significant price to pay in exchange for a form of Platonic realism. Those who defend these modifications of Platonic realism will respond that the version of divine aseity their view preserves is theologically adequate and "aseity enough." This is a fair point, one that ultimately sheds light on the fact that these matters ultimately hinge on what version of the doctrine of divine aseity one believes is best attested scripturally and historically and how one weights the doctrine in one's metaphysical theorizing. As for this Christian metaphysician, and with respect to my friends and colleagues who come down in a different place than I do on this, my money's on the high-octane version of divine aseity.[64]

In conclusion, most Christian metaphysicians wholeheartedly agree that God makes a significant difference for one's ontology of properties. Yet not all agree as to *how* exactly God makes this significant difference. I leave it to the reader to wrestle with these challenging yet exciting questions in Christian theistic metaphysics.

---

[62]This worry is pressed by Craig, *God over All*, 80-84.

[63]If God's essential properties are neither one and the same being as God—as would be the case in divine simplicity—nor created by God (and thus not creatures), it is difficult to ontologically classify the properties that constitute God's nature.

[64]Stated as *divine aseity* in chap. 3.

GOING DEEPER: CREATURELY CHARACTERISTICS

Key Concepts

- properties
- universals
- abstract versus concrete
- nominalism
- trope theory
- austere nominalism
- Platonic heaven
- particulars and universals
- immanent realism about universals
- primary and secondary qualities
- types and tokens
- Ockham's razor

Historical

- Plato, *Republic* VI; *Timaeus* 27-39, 51-52
- Aristotle, *Categories* 2-5; *On Interpretation* 7; *Metaphysics* III.4, III.6, VII
- Thomas Aquinas, *On Being and Essence*, chap. 3
- Paul Spade, *Five Texts on the Mediaeval Problem of Universals: Porphyry, Boethius, Abelard, Duns Scotus, Ockham*
- Bertrand Russell, "The World of Universals," in *Problems of Philosophy*
- Peter Coffey, *Ontology or the Theory of Being: An Introduction to General Metaphysics*, chaps. 8, 10, 12

Contemporary

- Douglas Edwards, *Properties*
- J. P. Moreland, *Universals*
- Lindsay Cleveland, "Divine Aseity and Abstract Objects," in *T&T Clark Handbook of Analytic Theology*
- D. M. Armstrong, *Universals: An Opinionated Introduction*
- Robert K. Garcia, "Platonism and the Haunted Universe," in *Loving God with Your Mind*

- Paul M. Gould, *Beyond the Control of God? Six Views on the Problem of God and Abstract Objects*
- Peter van Inwagen, "God and Other Uncreated Things"
- Brian Leftow, "God and the Problem of Universals"
- William Lane Craig, *God over All: Divine Aseity and the Challenge of Platonism*
- Thomas Ward, *Divine Ideas*
- George Molnar, *Powers: A Study in Metaphysics*

8

CREATURELY OBJECTS

SUBSTANCES

THE WONDER OF UNITY AND STABILITY

We have been exploring together the contour of reality, the shape of being itself as well as the various kinds of beings that exist by God's creative design. We have seen that some metaphysicians remain convinced that we need to include properties (even universals!) like *humanity*, *redness*, and *sweetness* into an exhaustive inventory of reality, in addition to individual humans, red things, and sweet things. It is now time to turn to the general category of *Particular*, specifically the category of *Thing* or *Object*. Do particulars in the category of *Object* constitute a distinct ontological category in addition to *Property*? Are there different ontological types or categories of objects? If so, how should we understand the nature of objects themselves?

This may sound rather humdrum, but our ordinary experience of the world around us conveys to us that there are things or objects (e.g., apples, trees, and people), all of which are characterized in various ways (say, sweet, tall, and curious about metaphysics). I think our pre-philosophical sense that individual objects exist should be given significant epistemic weight and taken seriously when doing metaphysics.[1] We are also aware of the fact that some of the ordinary things of our experience are more or less stable in their existence than others. The surrounding trees change as their autumn leaves go from

---

[1]This in sharp contrast to those contemporary philosophers who argue in favor of "qualitativism," the view that the world is constituted by purely qualitative facts and that there are no individual things in our most basic inventory of reality. See Shamik Dasgupta, "Individuals: An Essay in Revisionary Metaphysics," *Philosophical Studies* 145, no. 1 (2009): 35-67.

green to red (at least in North Carolina!), and our children seem to continue
to grow like weeds.

Our ordinary experience also points toward the fact that some objects are
unified or whole, with some objects being more unified than others. Cars are
made of an assemblage of independent car parts (carburetors, pistons, doors,
etc.), fastened together in various ways, that often need to be replaced with
new parts that are always ridiculously expensive. Yet living organisms like
trees and animals seem, at least initially, to be more tightly unified things.
Living organisms are capable of taking in new bits of matter and losing other
bits, all while remaining deeply integrated and unified.

CATEGORIES OF OBJECT: SUBSTANCE AND AGGREGATE

Recall in our earlier discussion in chapter five about categorial ontology and
different kinds of objects, in particular, objects in the categories of *Substance*
and *Aggregate* (I'll use "aggregate" instead of "nonsubstance" going forward).
We noted in chapter five that ontological categories in general are carved out
by the natures of entities; different natures, different ontological categories, we
might say. So, in the case of entities in the category of *Object*, we might ask
what objects *are*, in the most basic ontological sense, in contrast to other kinds
of being such as properties (see chap. 7).

Most generally (and roughly), an object is an entity whose nature involves
being a property-bearer; objects have properties and are not themselves had
by any other kind of being.[2] Objects have or possess features or properties, not
vice versa. Yet, at least intuitively, not all objects are on equal ontological
footing, we might say. Traditional examples of *substances* include trees, humans,
dogs, water molecules, and the like, and examples of *aggregates* include artifacts like cars, pool tables, computers, beach chairs, and the like. We noted in
chapter five that differences among the ontological categories in general are
carved out by differences in the natures of entities, and in this case, a difference
in the natures of substances in contrast to the natures of aggregates.

How, exactly, do substances differ from aggregates within the category of
Object? Two traditional ways of distinguishing these two types of objects have
to do with *independence* and *unity*. Substances are the kinds of object that are
not metaphysically dependent on other kinds of beings and are unified in the

---

[2]This latter qualification is important, since if properties exist, they themselves have properties.
They are not objects in this sense since they are themselves had by other properties.

strongest sense. Substances are the most basic and rock-bottom units of being as they serve to ontologically anchor all other kinds of created being. Substances are deeply unified and ontologically stable objects and thus can remain constant as they undergo change through time. Aggregates, by contrast, are the kinds of object that are metaphysically dependent on other kinds of being, principally substantial being (in addition to properties and relations). Moreover, aggregates are unified in a much weaker sense than substances; aggregates like a ping-pong table are much less stable in their existence than, say, a substance like an oak tree or any other kind of living organism.

Getting Theological: Substance, Free Will, and Moral Responsibility

Briefly consider the stakes of the ontological distinction between substances and aggregates for human life and experience. If there are no substances and all objects are aggregates, then human beings are aggregates. If so, then you are the sort of object that is loosely unified, ontologically unstable, and radically dependent on the smallest substantial parts from which you are currently made (as is the case with aggregates like ping-pong tables and iPhones). As a result, it is difficult to make metaphysical sense of uniquely human activities and features such as conscious and deliberative thought, free agency, and maintaining strict personal identity and sameness through time and change (you plausibly are numerically the same person today as you were yesterday). For example, if you are an aggregate and thus a loosely unified collection of parts and strictly depend on those parts for your moment-to-moment existence, then every action you perform is determined by the collective action of your smallest parts working in concert. What *they* do determines what *you* do, and not vice versa. If so, then irreducible, personal agency disappears (since everything persons do is the result of the actions of their smallest, nonpersonal parts), and with it, the type of moral action necessary to ground human moral responsibility.[a]

---

[a]For a more in-depth treatment of this argument and the distinction between substances and aggregates, see my *Substance and the Fundamentality of the Familiar: A Neo-Aristotelian Mereology* (New York: Routledge, 2018), chap. 7.2 and chap. 3, respectively. For a fuller, clear-eyed discussion of the bearing of the ontology of substance on human agency and free will, see E. J. Lowe, *Personal Agency: The Metaphysics of Mind and Action* (New York: Oxford University Press, 2008).

WHAT ARE SUBSTANCES? RELATIONAL AND CONSTITUENT ACCOUNTS

With this preliminary distinction between different types of objects in hand, let's press on to explore how contemporary metaphysicians understand the metaphysical makeup of substances. What exactly *are* substances? How are they constructed and what are their basic ontological constituents or ingredients (if any), we might say? To help get a grip on the notion of an ontological ingredient, consider a cake. Cakes are made up or composed of different physical ingredients such as sugar, flour and, of course, frosting and sprinkles; each of these ingredients makes the cake the kind of thing it is (whether a chocolate cake, an ice-cream cake, etc.). In the same way, we might ask: What are the ultimate, metaphysical ingredients (if any) that make up objects in the category of *Substance* in particular (ingredients that make the object the *kind* of thing it is)? One way into this question is to ask the following guiding question about the metaphysical makeup of substances:

> *Constituent Question*: Do substances have metaphysical ingredients in the sense that properties somehow enter into their metaphysical makeup? Are properties somehow *in* their substances as more basic constituents (ingredients) that make them up?

RELATIONAL ACCOUNTS OF SUBSTANCE

Relational ontologies answer the Constituent Question in the negative: Properties in no way enter into the metaphysical makeup of substances as ontological ingredients. Thus:

> *A Relational Ontology of Substance*: Substances lack metaphysical ingredients and are not made up of more basic metaphysical constituents, including properties.

Many relational ontologies tend to view properties as transcendent universals along the lines of Platonic, transcendent realism (see chap. 7); properties, like *redness* and *sweetness*, exist necessarily and independently of whether there are ever any red or sweet things that have them.[3] If properties are transcendent

---

[3]A clear and helpful example of this ontology is explained and defended in Peter van Inwagen, "Relational vs. Constituent Ontologies," *Philosophical Perspectives* 25 (2011): 389-45; and his "Theory of Properties," in *Oxford Studies in Metaphysics*, vol. 1, ed. Dean Zimmerman (Oxford: Oxford University Press, 2004).

universals in this sense, then one might indeed wonder how such universals could enter into the very being of a substance like an apple.

How, then, do properties relate to substances according to a relational ontology? Properties are related to substances by way of the relation of exemplification. Fido the dog, a substance, exemplifies or has properties like *brownness* and *furriness* by being linked or tied to them in a basic way. However, Fido is not brown by having *brownness* and *furriness* as ontological constituents or ingredients (in roughly the same way that the cake is chocolaty by having chocolate as one of its ingredients). Another way of saying this is that substances are entirely devoid of any ontological complexity; they do not have any ontological components, whether properties or anything else (like substrata, as we'll see below). While substances can be made up of ordinary, material objects like hearts, cells, atoms, and so on, they are not constructed out of more basic, metaphysical constituents of any kind. On a relational ontology, substances are what David Armstrong calls ontological "blobs" in that they are devoid of any internal ontological complexity.[4]

One chief virtue of relational ontologies is that by denying that substances have any underlying ontological complexity, they avoid the deep conceptual difficulties that accompany constituent ontologies, whether bundle theories or substratum theories (more on this below). Second, many metaphysicians like Peter van Inwagen and E. J. Lowe have argued that it is misguided to think that properties can be constituents or parts of substances. Properties are not parts of any kind, they argue.[5]

However, one notable objection to relational ontologies of substance has to do with the exclusively relational nature of the way in which substances have properties. If substances are the way they are, say an apple's being red or sweet, solely by virtue of standing in a relation (exemplification) to a realm of independently existing transcendent universals (*redness*, *sweetness*), then all facts about what substances are like are purely relational. Yet we might ask: Is there no way that substances are in themselves, without their standing in a relation to some other existing thing that is not

---

[4]David Armstrong, *Universals: An Opinionated Introduction* (Boulder, CO: Westview, 1989), 76-77.

[5]See van Inwagen, "Relational vs. Constituent Ontologies"; and E. J. Lowe, "A Neo-Aristotelian Substance Ontology: Neither Relational nor Constituent," in *Contemporary Aristotelian Metaphysics*, ed. Tuomas Tahko (New York: Cambridge University Press, 2012).

a constituent of them? Do substances have any intrinsic character in their own right, or is their character entirely borrowed, we might say, from things outside their boundaries?

CONSTITUENT ACCOUNTS OF SUBSTANCE

Metaphysicians who reject a relational account of substance answer yes to the Constituent Question. They think that properties do enter into the very being of substances as ingredients and hold to what is called a "constituent ontology of substance," which we can state as follows:

> A *Constituent Ontology of Substance*: Substances have metaphysical ingredients and are made up of more basic metaphysical constituents, including properties.

Philosophers who defend a constituent ontology of substance maintain that substances are built up out of more fundamental, ontological constituents, ingredients that serve to explain what the substance is and how it is characterized. In this view, substances have internal metaphysical complexity beyond the ordinary, run-of-the-mill part-whole complexity that comes with being composed of atoms, molecules, cells, hands, a heart, and so on (see chap. 9). It is for this reason that David Armstrong has famously dubbed constituent ontologies "layer-cake" ontologies of substance (in contrast to relational ontologies as "blob" ontologies of substance as noted before).[6] So, the properties *brownness* and *furriness* enter into the very being of Fido the dog. Properties like *brownness* and *furriness* are ontological ingredients of Fido that characterize how Fido *is* in particular ways (namely, brown and furry).

BUNDLE THEORIES OF SUBSTANCE

Broadly speaking, there are two main types of constituent views about the nature of substance. Let me try to unpack the first variety of constituent ontology, which is known as the "Bundle Theory of Substance," which says:

> *Bundle Theory of Substance*: Substances have properties as their sole metaphysical constituents (i.e., substances are nothing but bundles of properties).

Informally, if you were to build a substance, the only type of construction materials you would need, metaphysically speaking, would be properties

---

[6]Armstrong, *Universals: An Opinionated Introduction*, 76-77.

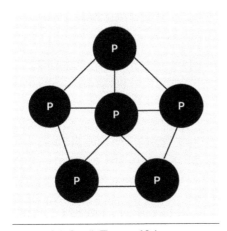

Figure 8.1. Bundle Theory of Substance

(including relations), nothing more. Properties are the *sole* ontological building blocks of substances. Actually, saying that substances are "built up" of properties is a bit misleading, since it suggests that substances are something over and above what they are constructed out of. The reality is that according to Bundle Theory, substances are *one and the same* as bundles of properties (and the relations that link those properties together), as a bundle of sticks is one and the same as the various sticks that are tied together by a strand of twine. Thus, Fido the dog is nothing over and above a bundle or cluster of properties like *being canine, furriness, four-legged, mammalian, brownness*, all of which are related together in various ways. We can depict Bundle Theory as figure 8.1, where "P" stands for properties and the solid lines stand for the relations that link them together.

Versions of Bundle Theory have been defended by a number of important and influential philosophers in the history of Western philosophy, including David Hume, George Berkeley, Bertrand Russell (in his later thought), A. J. Ayer, D. C. Williams, Herbert Hochberg, Hector-Neri Castañeda, Keith Campbell, Peter Simons, Laurie Paul, John O'Leary-Hawthorne, and J. A. Cover, among others. Different versions of Bundle Theory can be divided on the basis of how they answer the following two questions:

(a) What is the nature of the properties that enter into the makeup of substances? Are they universals or particulars?

(b) What is the specific type of relation that binds the various properties into a single bundle?

Let's focus on the former question first, question (a), concerning the nature of the properties that enter into the makeup of substances on Bundle Theory.

Let's consider our first version of Bundle Theory, call it "Universal Bundle Theory":

Universal Bundle Theory: Substances have universals as their sole metaphysical constituents (substances are nothing but bundles of universals).

Where "U" stands for universals, we can represent this view as figure 8.2.

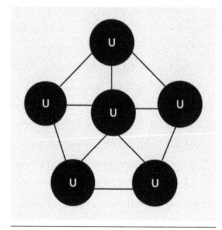

Recall from the previous chapter that universals are sharable entities; one and the same universal can be had by two, distinct substances. So, the *brownness* that makes up the bundle that is Fido is one and the same *brownness* that makes up the bundle that is Rover, another dog. Substances just are bundles of sharable universals, nothing more.[7]

Figure 8.2. Universal Bundle Theory

A second version of Bundle Theory, call it "Trope Bundle Theory," takes substances to be nothing but bundles of particular (nonsharable) properties, that is, tropes:

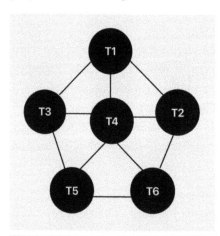

Trope Bundle Theory: Substances have particular tropes as their sole metaphysical constituents (substances are nothing more than bundles of particular tropes).[8]

We can illustrate this version of Bundle Theory as figure 8.3, where the various numbered "T's" stand for individual tropes.

Unlike universals, tropes are nonsharable; thus, no two bundles can include one and the same trope. The *redness*₁ trope that is included

Figure 8.3. Trope Bundle Theory

---

[7]Universal Bundle Theory has been defended by the likes of Bertrand Russell, A. J. Ayer, Herbert Hochberg, Hector-Neri Castañeda, John O'Leary-Hawthorne, and J. A. Cover. For a contemporary defense, see John O'Leary-Hawthorne and J. A. Cover, "A World of Universals," *Philosophical Studies* 91, no. 3 (1998): 205-19.

[8]Proponents of Trope Bundle Theory include D. C. Williams, Keith Campbell, and Peter Simons.

in the firetruck is numerically different from the *redness*$_2$ trope included in the apple.

How might either version of Bundle Theory answer question (b) regarding how properties—whether universal or particular—can be unified into a *single* bundle? At this point, you, the reader, should immediately be asking yourself the following two questions: What exactly unifies universals to make them a single thing, one property-bundle rather than a mere plurality of properties? What is the bundling relation, exactly, and is it strong enough to capture our intuitive notion that substances are deeply unified and stable units of being? And if you thought of these two questions on your own at this point, kudos are in order, well done!

Some bundle theorists—including proponents of Universal Bundle Theory as well as Trope Bundle Theory—appeal to an unanalyzable relation called "compresence," which means that the properties are all included in the same property-bundle only because they are in the same place at the same time, nothing more.[9] Compresence, it is argued, is entirely sufficient to ontologically "glue" the various properties together into a single bundle.[10] But this seems unlikely, since compresence seems to *presuppose* (and thus not explain) what needs to be explained: Why, exactly, are all and only those very properties (pointing to that particular bundle) in the same place at the same time; why do they always show up together in the first place?

Other bundle theorists—proponents of Mereological Bundle Theory— claim that the bundling relation that unifies properties is the ordinary part-whole relation (which we will explore in more depth in the next chapter).[11] So, two properties, *brownness* and *furriness*, are included in the same property-bundle, Fido, if (and only if) they are parts of Fido. We can illustrate a trope-theory version of Mereological Bundle Theory as

[9]See Bertrand Russell, *An Inquiry into Meaning and Truth* (New York: Routledge, 1992), 104ff.

[10]For a helpful discussion of the problems with appealing to a relation of compresence in this way, see D. M. Armstrong, *Nominalism & Realism—Universals & Scientific Realism*, vol. 1 (Cambridge: Cambridge University Press, 1978).

[11]For a next step on Mereological Bundle Theory, see Laurie Paul, "Mereological Bundle Theory," in *The Handbook of Mereology*, eds. Hans Burkhardt, Johanna Seibt, and Guido Imaguire (Munich: Philosophia Verlag, 2010). For a defense of a Mereological Bundle Theory that takes substances to be mereological fusions of tropes, see D. C. Williams, "Universals and Existents," *Australasian Journal of Philosophy* 64 (1986): 1-14; and his "Elements of Being I," *Review of Metaphysics* 7, no. 1 (1953): 3-18. For a more technical explication and defense of a version of Mereological Bundle Theory, see Laurie Paul's essay "Logical Parts," *Noûs* 36, no. 4 (2002): 578-96.

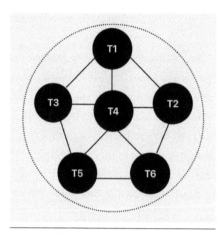

Figure 8.4. Mereological Bundle Theory

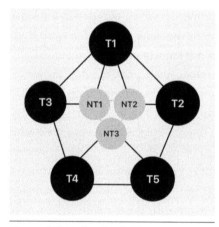

Figure 8.5. Nuclear Bundle Theory

figure 8.4, where the dotted line around the individual tropes signifies that the tropes in the bundle are parts of the bundle as a whole.

Another interesting version of Trope Bundle Theory defended by contemporary philosopher Peter Simons—called "Nuclear Bundle Theory"—holds that the essential natures of substances are constituted by a core group of tropes—what he calls the "essential nucleus" of the substance—that are bundled together by way of being mutually, ontologically dependent on each other (and only each other).[12] So, creatively imagine the small grouping of tropes that make up the essential bundle of the substance as little puzzle pieces that interlock with one another (and only one another) such that they couldn't possibly exist without one another.

We can represent Nuclear Bundle Theory as figure 8.5, where the gray bundle at the core represents the essential nucleus of codependent, individual tropes ("NTs"), the gray lines represent relations of mutual ontological dependence, and the black bundle represents the accidental tropes that are linked to the nucleus.

---

[12]Peter Simons, "Particulars in Particular Clothing," *Philosophy and Phenomenological Research* 54 (1994): 553-76. Simons appeals to the idea of a "founding relation" (light gray lines in figure 8.5) to unite the tropes that make up the "nucleus" or the essence of the substance. He says, "the result is that Husserl's idea of using foundation as the cement of groups of tropes into more substantial wholes will only work for tropes which are individually founded on one another. Between contingent or accidental tropes (even though they be of kinds, of each of which an instance is required) there is no foundation relation" (560).

But let's ask the million-dollar question here: Why hold to the Bundle Theory in the first place? One driving factor, perhaps *the* primary factor, in favor of a bundle theory of any stripe has to do with qualitative simplicity; Bundle Theory promises to offer a lean and streamlined ontology. If we can get away with reducing the category of *Substance* to the category of *Property*, they say, we should. Bundle theorists hold out hope for a one-category ontology and argue that we can adequately map the contour of reality by appealing to a single ontological category, *Property*. A second, historically influential argument in favor of Bundle Theory, one that we will discuss below, is the general suspicion toward alternative Constituent Ontologies of substance. If Bundle Theory can avoid a strange and bloated ontology, the more power to it.

It should be pointed out that the overwhelming majority of contemporary metaphysicians who endorse Bundle Theory defend a version of Trope Bundle Theory, that substances are nothing more than bundles of particular tropes (rather than universals). Fido the dog is nothing more than a bundle of particular properties, properties that he does not share with any other canine. There are some very good reasons why this brand of Bundle Theory is the version of choice among contemporary bundle theorists. Let me mention just two.

One very influential worry for Universal Bundle Theory stems from the idea that universals are fully sharable entities. Here's the particular worry. It seems to follow from Universal Bundle Theory that if two bundles, A and B, are made up of exactly the same universals, U1 and U2, then A and B are exactly the same bundle. Why think that? Well, with Bundle Theory, it's very hard to see what else could distinguish A and B from one another if not properties, especially since properties are the *only* metaphysical ingredients that make up substances in this view (and the assumption here is that A and B share all their properties and relations, since relations are universals, in common). But here's the rub. Universal Bundle Theory seems to commit us to accepting a principle about identity that most metaphysicians think is false, what is known as "the Identity of Indiscernibles."

Recall from chapter five that the Identity of Indiscernibles states that necessarily, if two things share all of their properties in common, then they are numerically identical and one and the same thing. Further, recall that while the related principle of the Indiscernibility of Identicals is widely affirmed in contemporary metaphysics, its cousin the Identity of Indiscernibles is widely rejected (the wording of the two principles is flipped, did you catch that?). Very roughly, the reason many philosophers think the Identity of Indiscernibles is false is that there appear to be some very strong philosophical arguments that favor the possibility of there being two numerically distinct things with exactly the same properties.[13] If there's good reason to reject the Identity of Indiscernibles—and most metaphysicians think there is—and Universal Bundle Theory requires that it be true, then this is a significant mark against Universal Bundle Theory. Since in Trope Bundle Theory, substances are not made up of universals but particular tropes, which are themselves nonsharable, no two bundles can share exactly the same trope and the worry is avoided.

A second worry here for Universal Bundle Theory is if universals like *brownness* and *furriness* are understood along Platonic realist lines, they are necessarily existing abstract entities. Recall from the previous chapter that in a Platonic view of universals, *brownness* is an abstract entity that exists of necessity, is causally inert (powerless), and is transcendent (beyond space and time). If so, and if Fido is nothing more than a bundle of such entities, then it seems that Fido too will be identical to a bundle (or composed of a bundle) of abstract entities. It seems plausible to think that something that is wholly made up of abstract objects is itself an abstract object. So, Fido turns out to be a rather strange sort of necessarily existing, causally inert, and transcendent object, in Universal Bundle Theory. This, of course, is a really bad result. Fido, the beloved house pet, seems to be a living, breathing animal that brings about a great deal of joy in his owner; but not so if Fido is an abstract entity. This is one reason most metaphysicians who defend Universal Bundle Theory reject a Platonic view of properties and adopt in its place an immanent, Aristotelian view of universals, where universals are not transcendent, abstract entities but are located in space and time. However, as we noted in the previous chapter, many philosophers think there are deep conceptual problems with an immanent view of universals. If so, then many will find even the most defensible version of Universal Bundle Theory problematic.

There are some powerful arguments against Bundle Theory in general. Let me quickly outline several of the most influential objections. First, is it really

---

[13]See Max Black, "The Identity of Indiscernibles," *Mind* 61, no. 242 (1952): 153-64.

all that plausible to think that substances—traditionally understood as stable, enduring, and highly unified kinds of being—are nothing more than swarms or bundles of properties? Our ordinary, commonplace intuition is that properties are the sort of things that are *had* by something; they are not ontologically free-standing in the way that Bundle Theories suggest. Rather, things or subjects *have* properties and are thus *more* than properties, or so it seems. For many, myself included, Bundle Theories seem to get the nature of substance flat-out wrong.

Let me see if I can bring this first worry a bit closer to home. Certainly, if anything is a substance, *you* are. Are *you* a mere swarm or bundle of properties? Well, David Hume supposedly thought so.[14] But here's the thing: Hume was wrong. Hume's thought was that when you introspect, all you are aware of is a series of mental qualities buzzing by your conscious awareness (e.g., sensing pain, hearing the clock tick, desiring ice cream, etc.); you are not aware of anything like an enduring or unified bearer of properties. But think about it: The very idea of being aware of *these* and *only these* mental qualities presupposes a deeper unity to them than Hume recognized; after all, I'm not aware of *your* mental qualities and you are not aware of *mine*, precisely because they are possessed by distinct unified subjects. So, Hume just assumes what he's trying to reject, that you are a unified bearer of properties.

Even more, there's a lot about you and your experience that is very difficult to metaphysically explain if you are a mere bundle of properties, however construed. For one, if you are identical to a bundle or properties—even a sum or fusion of properties—it is difficult to see how you are the sort of being that is deeply unified. How are you any more unified than a heap of sand or a pile of trash?

According to this view, if you are unified at all, you are unified in a very weak sense. This is a problem for several reasons. First, everything you, a swarm of properties, do can be explained in terms of the actions of the properties that make you up. You also are a thinking being; you are currently engaged in careful and sustained reflection about the nature of reality, substances in particular. But thinking is a highly unified activity, not something that can arguably be done by a plurality of things that happen to be in the same place at the same time. Since a bundle theory of substance doesn't fit or

---

[14]David Hume, *A Treatise of Human Nature*, eds. Lewis Amherst Selby-Bigge and P. H. Nidditch (Oxford: Clarendon, 1992), book 1, part IV, section VI, on "Personal Identity."

match the way things intuitively seem to us, let's call this first worry the "Mismatch Objection."

A second influential worry for most versions of bundle theory has been called the "ultraessentialist" worry.[15] The worry is that since a substance, Fido, is strictly identical to a particular bundle of properties—*brownness, furriness, four-leggedness,* and so on—then every one of Fido's properties is essential to him. In the same way that a bundle of three sticks is what it is by virtue of those very sticks (remove one and you no longer have numerically the same bundle), so too Fido is what he is by virtue of those very properties (remove one and you no longer have the same bundle of properties). The deeply disastrous result here is that every truth about Fido, say "Fido is four-legged" and "Fido is furry," is an essential truth of Fido; a truth about Fido that is definitive of what he is and must be true of him in order for him to exist. Fido could not exist without being four-legged and without being furry. But it seems flat-out wrong to say that there are no accidental truths about Fido, and that Fido could not exist without being four-legged or furry; surely Fido could be an unfortunate accident that leaves him with only three legs or the victim of a bad haircut (or, heaven forbid, both!).[16]

SUBSTRATUM THEORIES OF SUBSTANCE

So, we've seen both the prospects and the perils that accompany an account of substance along the lines of Bundle Theory, however construed. The above worries have led many philosophers to think that properties simply cannot be the sole constituents of substances, that substances must be more than just bundles of properties. Besides properties, what other sort of ontological ingredients might there be within the metaphysical makeup of a substance? One well-known and historically influential version of a Constituent Ontology of Substance holds that the ingredients that make up a substance must include the notion of a "substratum" (plural: substrata), an underlying bearer and subject in which properties inhere. So:

---

[15]Michael Loux and Thomas Crisp, *Metaphysics: A Contemporary Introduction*, 4th ed. (New York: Routledge, 2017), chap. 3.

[16]The careful reader will note that I said that the ultraessentialist worry applies to *most* versions of bundle theory. I think Peter Simons's Nuclear Bundle Theory has the resources to avoid this worry, and indeed this provides one of the main motivating reasons Simons offers in favor of his view. I think Simons's view is the best version of Bundle Theory on offer. I do, however, think his view suffers from other powerful objections.

Substratum Theory of Substance: Substances have substrata as metaphysical ingredients, in addition to properties.

According to this view, substances are built up not just of properties but also of an underlying support, substrate, or bearer of those properties, what philosophers have called a substratum. Thus, in some versions of Substratum Theory, a substance such as Fido the dog is an object that is made up of a substratum and the various properties that inhere in that substratum.

Let's slow down and ask the obvious question: What exactly *is* a substratum, and why think there is such a thing in addition to the properties that make up a substance? Well, for many substratum theorists past and present, substrata are defined chiefly by the particular metaphysical role they play in one's view of the world. Traditionally, the metaphysical job description of substrata includes serving as the underlying bearer and support of the properties a thing has, that which remains the same through various kinds of changes in properties, and that which individuates or metaphysically distinguishes one substance from another. Let's take these three roles or job descriptions in turn, with the hope of gaining some clarity about the nature of substrata.

As for the metaphysical role of property-bearer, think of how the fundamental job of a pincushion is to underlie, support, and hold together the various sewing pins that are stuck in it; the pincushion *has* the pins, and the pins are *in* and supported by the pincushion. In (very!) roughly the same way, the substratum theorist argues that the properties that enter into the metaphysical makeup of substances are had by an underlying substratum that unifies, stabilizes, and holds the properties together. For many, a substance, Fido, is canine insofar as Fido has as ontological ingredients both the property of *being canine* as well as the underlying substratum in which that property inheres.

Second, substrata have been thought to be what remain stable and constant through certain kinds of change. Historically, metaphysicians have traditionally distinguished between "substantial change" and "accidental change." Take Socrates, the famous philosophical martyr for truth. When Socrates changes from *being pale skinned* to *being tan skinned* after a nice, long holiday at the Aegean Sea perhaps, he loses one accidental property and gains another at a later time. By contrast, a substantial change is when something, Socrates, comes into existence from previously existing material or stuff, or ceases to exist altogether. The matter from which Socrates comes into existence is organized and structured in a way that it once previously was not, namely *human-wise*.

Following the monumental influence of Aristotle, many philosophers have thought that *all* change, whether accidental or substantial change, requires the existence of something (but not necessarily some *thing*) that remains the same through the change. Otherwise, there would be no change at all, just the successive replacement of one thing after another.[17] In the case of accidental change, Socrates himself is the underlying subject of change that remains the same; in the case of substantial change, the underlying substratum is the subject of change that gains and loses properties at various times. The thought is that if there were no underlying, enduring substratum that remained the same through substantial change, then there would be no genuine coming to be or ceasing to be.

A final influential reason to believe in substrata has to do with the substratum's role as that which individuates or metaphysically distinguishes one substance from another. Consider the following, using Fido and Rover, two dogs of exactly the same species that share all of the same sharable properties (universals) in common like *brownness, furriness, four-leggedness, caninity, playfulness,* and so on. If Fido and Rover are two distinct dogs yet share all of their universals in common, what could possibly serve to metaphysically distinguish them as two and not just one dog? After all, they possess numerically the same universals. The substratum theorist argues that we have reason, then, to introduce a further metaphysical ingredient of both Fido and Rover at this point, one that is unique to each dog yet itself not a property (universal), and that serves to metaphysically individuate the two, exactly similar dogs. Without a substratum to play the role of individuator, it is argued, facts about numerical diversity are difficult to explain at a deep, metaphysical level.[18]

---

[17]Aristotle, *Physics* 1.7 (189b30-191a22), in *The Complete Works of Aristotle*, ed. Jonathan Barnes (Princeton, NJ: Princeton University Press, 1991), 1:12-15. See also Aquinas's commentary on Aristotle's *Metaphysics*; Thomas Aquinas, *In Meta* 8.1.1688.

[18]Historically, the question of what metaphysically individuates has been a central topic in metaphysics. For a historical overview, centered on medieval thinkers such as Thomas Aquinas, Duns Scotus, and Francisco Suarez, see Edward Feser, *Scholastic Metaphysics: A Contemporary Introduction* (Neunkirchen-Seelscheid: Editiones Scholasticae, 2014), 198-201. For a contemporary and more challenging introduction, see E. J. Lowe, "Individuation," in *Oxford Handbook*

It is very important to note that these three metaphysical job descriptions require substrata to be both something other than a property (since they serve as the "extra ingredient" in addition to properties which individuates and unifies substances) and themselves "bare" or property-less (since they themselves are the underlying bearers and unifiers of properties). If the substratum is what all the properties inhere in (like pins in the pincushion) and remains the same through substantial change, then the nature of the substratum—*what* it is in itself—must not include properties. If the substratum itself consisted of properties—even essential properties it couldn't fail to lose and still exist—then it seems that we would naturally want to know what additional, underlying substratum supports or unifies *its* properties. Thus, we would be off on a problematic regress of underlying substrata.

Some version or other of the Substratum Theory has been very influential in the history of metaphysics, and for good reason. Thinkers such as John Locke, Gustav Bergmann, D. M. Armstrong, J. P. Moreland, and (according to many) much of the medieval Aristotelian tradition have defended a version of the view.[19]

As with Bundle Theory, there are different versions of Substratum Theory, and each can be distinguished by how they answer the following questions:

(a) What is the nature of the substratum?

(b) What is the relationship between a substance, its underlying substratum, and its properties?

Regarding question (a), space prevents a fuller discussion of the various ways Substratum Theories differ as to what substrata are like in themselves. Suffice it to say that the primary nub of the issue is whether substrata are individual objects in themselves, or more like nonindividual, undifferentiated material stuff (what Aristotelians refer to as "prime matter").

of Metaphysics, eds. Michael J. Loux and Dean W. Zimmerman (New York: Oxford University Press, 2005).

[19]For a helpful discussion of medieval hylomorphism as a kind of substratum theory, see chap. 6 of Robert Pasnau, *Metaphysical Themes: 1274-1671* (New York: Oxford University Press, 2011).

VARIETIES OF SUBSTRATUM THEORY:
THIN, THICK, AND MIXED PARTICULARISM

Let's move on now to question (b), which may shed a bit more light on question (a) as well. To help get clear on the precise relationship between a substance, its substratum, and its properties, consider the following ordinary statements about Fido the dog:

(i) Fido is brown.

(ii) Fido is playful.

(iii) Fido is canine.

Statements (i) and (ii) are both accidental truths about Fido (Fido might acquire gray hair, and perhaps no longer be playful with old age). Statement (iii), by contrast, is a nonaccidental, essential truth about Fido, one that gets to the metaphysical heart (or bullseye, see fig. 6.1) of his very identity or essence. What might the subject of these ordinary statements about Fido be? Naturally, you might think that Fido himself is the subject of such claims. However, proponents of the substratum theory themselves disagree here, and this in-house disagreement helps us get clear on the varieties of Substratum Theory on offer.

To see why, let's look at an influential distinction from substratum theorist David Armstrong between what he calls a "thin particular" and a "thick particular."[20] For Armstrong, a thin particular is just the substratum itself, considered apart from the properties that are tied to it (the pincushion on its own apart from the pins, we might say). So, this would be Fido's unique substratum that distinguishes him from other dogs of the same species, say Rover. The thick particular, by contrast, is the entire complex or whole that is made up of Fido's substratum as a constituent along with all of Fido's properties, both accidental and essential, such as *brownness, playfulness, being canine*, etc. The thick particular in this sense is Fido himself along with all of his accompanying properties, the substance that has the substratum and properties as constituents.

To illustrate the difference between a thin and a thick particular, let's lean into our working illustration of the pin cushion (substratum) and the various

---

[20]Armstrong, *Universals*, 95. See also his *A World of States of Affairs* (New York: Cambridge University Press, 1997), 123-26.

sewing pins within it (round pins: accidental properties; starred pins: essential properties). We can illustrate the two views as figure 8.6:

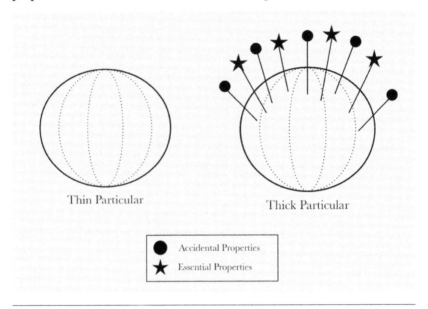

Thin Particular

Thick Particular

● Accidental Properties
★ Essential Properties

Figure 8.6. Thick versus thin particular

So, let's go back to the rather mundane statements (i)-(iii) above. Some Substratum Theories hold that Fido, the substance, just *is* (numerically identical to) the thin particular itself. As the thin particular, Fido is a substratum whose being is defined independently of properties (as is the case for substrata in general) but is the bearer of all of his essential and accidental properties such as *brownness, playfulness,* and *being canine.* As Fido is identical to the thin particular itself (substratum alone), the thin particular is the subject of statements (i)-(iii) about Fido. For this reason, let's refer to this version of Substratum Theory as "Thin Particularism."[21]

Other versions of Substratum Theory maintain that the substance Fido, the living and breathing animal organism, is instead identical to the thick particular, the entire complex or whole that has the substratum and each of his properties, both accidental and essential, as ingredients (so Fido is *not* identical to the substratum alone). While Fido is brown, playful, and canine by virtue of

---

[21]Here I borrow these labels for these two brands of Substratum Theory from Jeffrey Brower, *Aquinas's Ontology of the Material World* (New York: Oxford University Press, 2015), 135-36.

his having the properties *brownness*, *playfulness*, and *being canine* as metaphysical ingredients, the entire complex—Fido—is the subject of these ordinary statements (i)-(iii), and not the thin particular or substratum. For this reason, let's refer to this version of Substratum Theory as "Thick Particularism."

So, we have the following two versions of Substratum Theory, each differing as to how they answer question (b) above:

> *Thin Particularism*: The substance (Fido) is identical to a substratum only and is the bearer of all of its properties.

> *Thick Particularism*: The substance (Fido) is identical to the entire complex that has a substratum and all of its properties (both essential and accidental) as constituents.

We can draw on our pincushion example from figure 8.6 to illustrate these two versions of Substratum Theory. If the pincushion represents the substratum and the different types of pins represent different types of properties (both accidental and essential), we can illustrate these two versions of Substratum Theory as figure 8.7:

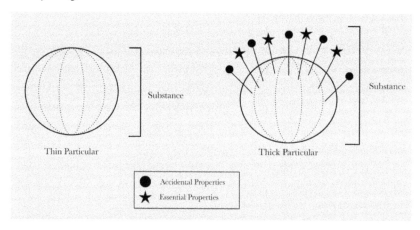

Figure 8.7. Thick versus Thin Particularism

There are worries with each of these versions of Substratum Theory. Let me first say a few words about the most important objections to Thin Particularism that you should be aware of.

An important dilemma lingers for Thin Particularism. First, if substances are identical to substrata, and substrata are strictly speaking property-less or "bare" (as philosophers put it) as many believe, then substances are just that, property-less or bare. This, of course, is unacceptable for any view of substance, since substances are the premier property-bearers; in fact, it's what partly sets them apart from other kinds of beings, most notably beings within the category of *Property*. But more than that, if substances are property-less substrata as they are in Thin Particularism, then it would seem to follow that substances lack essential properties or natures and thus, contrary to what seems obvious to us, there are no essential truths about them. This is known as the "anti-essentialist" worry for Thin Particularism.[22]

But, on the other hand, if substances are property-bearers, and substances are identical to substrata, then substrata really *do* have properties, both essential and accidental (and thus are not "bare"). But recall that one of the chief reasons substrata were introduced in the first place (in response to Bundle Theory) was to provide an underlying support for properties (a pincushion to support the pins), a substrate that is what it is without reference to properties. But if substrata themselves possess properties, as they do in Thin Particularism, then we'll need a further substratum to support the properties of the substratum, and so on, and so on.

In short, the dilemma is this: If Thin Particularism is true, then either substances are bare, or they are not. If substances are bare, then they neither are property-bearers nor do they have natures, which is a big problem. If substrata are not bare and thus do have properties, then we introduce a regress of substrata so that substrata no longer can play the metaphysical role they were introduced to fulfill.

What about Thick Particularism? Does it fare any better? Yes, in many ways, it does. Thick Particularism allows Fido to be a genuine property-bearer insofar as substances are not identical to completely bare substrata. Fido also has an essence in this view, since Fido can be the genuine bearer of essential properties and he is thought to have all of his constituent properties essentially, including the property of *being canine* (thereby avoiding the anti-essentialist worry). However, if *all* of Fido's constituents are essential to him, including all of his properties, then none is accidental. This is a significant problem indeed, as it is abundantly clear that statements like (i) and (ii) from the beginning of this section are accidental truths about Fido, truths that

---

[22]Loux and Crisp, *Metaphysics*, chap. 6.

could be false and Fido still exist (say, if he were spray-painted pink and then became grumpy about it). This is known as the "ultra-essentialist" worry for Thick Particularism.[23]

Last, some historically influential versions of Substratum Theory, namely views that trace their lineage to Aristotle in his work *Metaphysics* and that fall within the camp known as "hylemorphism" (Gk. *hylē*, "matter," and *morphē*, "form"), take a mixed approach to answering question (b) and thus the relationship between a substance, its substratum, and its various properties. You might think that some of Fido's properties, his essential properties like *being canine*, are possessed by his substratum (the pincushion), while other properties, his accidental properties *brownness* and *playfulness*, are possessed by the entire complex (substratum plus essential properties, i.e., the pincushion plus the starred pins). Fido, the substance, is identical to the entire complex that has the substratum and essential properties (*being canine*) as metaphysical ingredients. All of Fido's constituents are essential to him, his substratum and his essential properties. But—and this is key—the properties that Fido has as constituents do not exhaust *all* of Fido's properties. Rather, Fido *himself* can also serve as the underlying substratum or property-bearer for all his accidental properties.

For this reason, let's refer to this third version of Substratum Theory as "Mixed Particularism." It is important to note that in Mixed Particularism there are two distinct things that play the role of property-bearer, one as the bearer of essential properties (the substratum itself as a constituent of the substance) and the other as the bearer of accidental properties (the substance itself, Fido). In contrast to both Thin Particularism and Thick Particularism, this view holds that substances do not possess all of their properties in precisely the same way.

Mixed Particularism has a slightly different take on the thin versus thick particular distinction mentioned above. On the one hand, the thin particular just *is* the entire complex substance itself, which is built up from the more basic constituents of a substratum and essential properties (the pincushion and the starred pins); so, Fido is identical to a thin particular with the following metaphysical ingredients: a substratum that possesses the property *being canine*. The thick particular, on the other hand, is the substance, Fido, together with

---

[23]Loux and Crisp, *Metaphysics*, chap. 6.

all of Fido's accidental properties like *brownness, playfulness, furriness*, and so on (the pincushion and starred pins in conjunction with round pins).

One interesting thing to note about Mixed Particularism is that it seems to require two distinct ways of having or possessing a property, what we might simply refer to as "firsthand" and "secondhand" property possession. Something's having a property F "firsthand" is for it to have F in its own right or plain and simple, without inheriting it from something else. By contrast, to have a property F "secondhand" is to have F by virtue of one of your metaphysical ingredients having F firsthand (in its own right). This distinction, albeit with different terminology, is recognized by J. P. Moreland, one of the chief contemporary proponents of what I'm calling Mixed Particularism. Moreland, in reference to the way in which bare particulars have properties, puts it this way: "A bare particular is called 'bare,' not because it comes without properties, but in order to distinguish it from other particulars like substances and to distinguish the way it has a property (F is tied to x) from the way, say, a substance has a property (F is rooted within x)."[24] Let me spell out these two different ways of having a property, once again using our beloved house pet, Fido. Fido's substratum has the property of *being canine* firsthand, since it exemplifies the property *being canine* in its own right. Fido, the substance, does not have this property firsthand, but secondhand, by virtue of having a substratum as an ontological ingredient that itself has this property firsthand. According to Mixed Particularism, Fido has all of his accidental properties firsthand, like *brownness* and *playfulness*, since he himself exemplifies these properties, yet he has all of his essential properties secondhand, like *being canine*, by virtue of the fact that his substratum exemplifies this property firsthand.

With this distinction in hand, we can state Mixed Particularism as follows:

Mixed Particularism: The substance is identical to the complex that has the substratum and essential properties as metaphysical ingredients. The substance possesses all of its essential properties secondhand and all of its accidental properties firsthand.

Again, using our pincushion and pins, we can depict Mixed Particularism along with the two different types of property possession, as figure 8.8:

[24]J. P. Moreland, "Theories of Individuation: A Reconsideration of Bare Particulars," *Pacific Philosophical Quarterly* 79 (1998): 257.

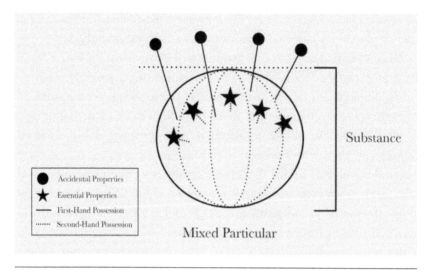

Figure 8.8. Mixed Particularism

Historically there have been different versions of Mixed Particularism, depending on the precise nature of the substratum, question (a) above (e.g., whether the substratum is itself simple and without parts and whether it is an individual or nonindividual and more like an undifferentiated portion of physical stuff). However, a detailed discussion of these versions lies well beyond the scope of the present chapter.

To my mind, Mixed Particularism fares the best when it comes to handling some of the thorniest objections to Substratum Theory. First, it avoids the worry of a substance's lacking an essence as in Thin Particularism (the "anti-essentialist worry," that all of its properties come out accidental). Moreover, it avoids the worry that a substance lacks accidental properties, as in Thick Particularism (the "ultra-essentialist worry," that all of a substance's properties come out essential).

Yet, there are some interesting consequences of Mixed Particularism that should be noted. First, it strikes some as odd that Fido (and substances in general) has his essential, kind-defining properties secondhand and not firsthand or in his own right (Fido has them by virtue of his substratum exemplifying them firsthand). Remember: in Mixed Particularism, substances are not identical to their substratum as the latter is one of the substance's more basic ontological ingredients (and of course no ingredient is identical to what it makes up). So, Fido is what he is by virtue of the fact that some thing that is *not* Fido, his substratum, exemplifies the kind-defining property *being canine*. But if substances are fundamental and independent beings in a robust sense, can they really have *any* of their properties secondhand in this sense, let alone their essential, kind-defining properties? This strikes some as in tension with a view of substances as truly fundamental, bedrock kinds of beings.

Another interesting worry with Mixed Particularism is what some have called the "Overcrowding Objection."[25] If Fido's substratum genuinely has the property of *being canine* (albeit firsthand), and Fido also genuinely has the property of *being canine* (albeit secondhand), then it would seem that either both are canine or neither is canine. If both Fido and Fido's substratum are canine, then of course we have an overcrowding of canines; there are two canines where Fido is, Fido and his substratum canine-constituent. Bad result. If neither is canine, then Fido isn't a canine. Again, a bad result.

Of course, a proponent of Mixed Particularism could say that only one of these forms of property-having, secondhand property possession, actually makes a thing characterized by the property in question (*being canine*), in this case Fido and not Fido's substratum. But it's hard to see what principled reason there is for this claim. Even more, in this line of thinking it's difficult to see how having a property firsthand is really a genuine form of property possession at all. If having a property firsthand or in its own right (Fido's substratum having the property *being canine* firsthand) doesn't confer on its bearer any qualitative character, then in what sense is it a form of property possession at all? And, if firsthand property possession is not a genuine form of property possession, then it is hard to see how a substratum is not entirely bare and property-less in the problematic sense discussed above.[26]

But what of Substratum Theory on the whole? Is it defensible? Many have thought so, and for good reason; it avoids some of the most challenging objections to both a relational ontology as well as other constituent ontologies on the market. Yet, as you might guess, many philosophers in the Western tradition have harbored deep suspicions about Substratum Theory, and the very notion of a substratum has been at the heart of this uneasiness.

---

[25] Andrew Bailey, "No Bare Particulars," *Philosophical Studies* 158 (2012): 31-41.
[26] If a bare substratum can exemplify the property of *being canine* and yet not be an individual canine (or even *canine* at all), in what sense does it "have" or "possess" the property in question? If firsthand property possession doesn't confer any qualitative character on the thing that has the property in its own right, then it's hard to see how bare substrata can be anything *but* bare.

First, a historically well-known objection to the very notion of a substratum stems from a theory of knowledge known as "empiricism." We've already explored the nature and merits (or demerits!) of empiricism as a theory of knowledge in chapter two in regard to various critiques of traditional metaphysical reflection based on rational insight alone. Yet, many metaphysicians who have rejected substrata have done so on the basis that substrata are not empirically detectable—you can't see them, touch them, taste them, and so on—since they are bare and supposedly lack properties altogether.

This worry, however, is massively underwhelming. For one, it assumes the truth of empiricism, an epistemological position that the Christian metaphysician has ample reason to reject (again, see chap. 2). Second, it assumes that bare substrata are not empirically detectable because they don't have properties in themselves. But can't the substratum theorist reply that while bare particulars are property-less in themselves, they always have properties linked to them, and we can know them by way of their empirically detectable properties? We can have knowledge of Fido's substratum by way of being aware of the essential properties tied to it (*being canine, being a mammal, being alive*, etc.).

Perhaps the most serious philosophical worry with a Substratum Theory of Substance has to do with the charge of straightforward incoherence: How in the world is it even possible for something to have a nature that excludes properties altogether? Isn't it the case that bare substrata, at the very least, have the following properties: *being bare, being a particular, being a thing*, and *being self-identical*?

But we've already seen how the defender of Substratum Theory, specifically the defender of Mixed Particularism, can deflect this charge of incoherence. Recall the distinction between the two different ways of having a property in Mixed Particularism, whether firsthand by having a property in its own right (without inheriting or borrowing that property from a metaphysical ingredient), or secondhand (by having a property by virtue of one of your metaphysical ingredients having that property firsthand). In response to the charge of incoherence, J. P. Moreland has argued that such a charge misunderstands what the substratum theorist means (or should mean) when they say that substrata are "bare." Moreland argues that bare substrata *do* have properties in the firsthand sense; when it comes to having a property in the firsthand sense, substrata are not bare since they have essential properties linked to them in their own right (*being bare, being particular, being canine, being human*, etc.). Nevertheless, substrata are indeed "bare" in the secondhand sense in that they do not have properties as further metaphysical ingredients.[27] While this move does raise further questions (already noted above)—namely, the Overcrowding Objection and the fact that substances do not have their essential, kind-defining properties firsthand in this view—it offers a way for the defender of Mixed Particularism to successfully and definitively put the incoherence charge to rest.

SUBSTANCES AS FUNDAMENTAL: A NEO-ARISTOTELIAN PROPOSAL

In conclusion, let me raise one final point that applies to all Constituent Ontologies in general, that is, to both Bundle Theory and Substratum Theory of any variety. According to some contemporary philosophers who identify as "neo-Aristotelians"—those influenced by the broad contour of Aristotle's metaphysics to some degree or other—the fundamental mistake at the heart of a Constituent Ontology in general has to do with the underlying claim that substances are built or made up of more fundamental or basic metaphysical ingredients. But why think that substances are built up at all in this way? Why not think instead that substances are truly metaphysically rock bottom and fundamental *in their own right*, not constructed from any prior metaphysical ingredients, whether properties or substrata?

This Aristotelian-inspired ontology of substance has been ably defended by contemporary philosophers such as Michael Loux and E. J. Lowe.[28] Lowe is a

---

[27]In Moreland's language, a property's (*being canine*) being "tied to" a bare particular (Fido's substratum) is what I'm calling "firsthand property possession," and a property's being "rooted within a substance" (Fido) is what I'm calling "secondhand property possession." For Moreland, only secondhand property possession confers on a thing a qualitative character and kind. For more on this view, see Moreland's article "Theories of Individuation: A Reconsideration of Bare Particulars."

[28]If you've read this far in the book, you will have no doubt noticed that the title "Aristotelian" in contemporary metaphysics is a rather broad label. Regarding the nature of substance, metaphysicians who line up under the banner of "neo-Aristotelianism" differ on the nature of substance precisely because Aristotle himself offers variations of his account of substance throughout his writings. Some neo-Aristotelian accounts of substance, like that of Loux and Lowe, are more influenced by Aristotle's early work *Categories* (particularly *Categories* 5), which emphasizes the basic and fundamental nature of substances. Others are more influenced by Aristotle's later work *Metaphysics*, where he unpacks substances as complexes of matter and form ("hylemorphism," a version of what I am calling Substratum Theory here generally, and Mixed Particularism specifically). Loux and Crisp, in their outstanding introductory book *Metaphysics: A Contemporary*

prominent contemporary proponent of this neo-Aristotelian view of substance and is openly critical of hylemorphism, a version of what I'm calling Mixed Particularism. Lowe puts the worry as follows in the context of critiquing constituent ontologies in general:

> The underlying error is to think that an individual substance is any kind
> of *complex* at all, at least insofar as it is propertied in various ways. Indi-
> vidual substances may be complex in the sense of being composite, that is,
> in the sense of being composed of lesser substantial parts, as for example,
> a living organism is composed of individual cells. . . . However, it is the
> individual substance itself which provides their "support" in this entirely
> legitimate sense, and this it can do without the spurious aid of some
> mysterious "substratum."[29]

If one thinks of substances along these particular neo-Aristotelian lines, then substances are metaphysically fundamental and irreducible in the strongest sense and thus are not built up out of prior or more basic metaphysical building blocks, whether properties or substrata. This, of course, puts this particular neo-Aristotelian view of substance at odds with all forms of constituent ontologies that construe substances as complexes of more basic ontological ingredients (all "layer-cake" ontologies of substance, to use our previous terminology). While Aristotelian substances have ontological structure in the sense that they are various *kinds* of beings (humans, trees, tulips, etc.) characterized by various properties (*rational, living,* and *fragrant*), they ought to be understood as holding ultimate ontological pride of place in the grand categorial scheme of created being.

As with the previous accounts of the nature of substance, this neo-Aristotelian view is not without its problems, one of which is how to account for the individuation of distinct substances (if there is no bare substratum to play this role).[30] Yet a treatment of the prospects and perils of

---

Introduction, also defend a version of a neo-Aristotelian view of substance I hint toward here (see their chap. 3, pp. 104-14). For a full-scale defense of this neo-Aristotelian view of substance, see Michael J. Loux, *Substance and Attribute: A Study in Ontology* (Dordrecht, Holland: D. Reidel, 1978). For adventurous and undaunted readers, E. J. Lowe's article "A Neo-Aristotelian Substance Ontology: Neither Relational Nor Constituent" is a must-read.

[29]E. J. Lowe, *Four-Category Ontology* (Oxford: Oxford University Press, 2006), 27.

[30]Another worry stems from whether this view is "Aristotelian" at all. For those who argue that such a view best captures Aristotle's own view of substance, see the work of Theodore Scaltsas, *Substances and Universals in Aristotle's Metaphysics* (Ithaca, NY: Cornell University Press, 1994);

this neo-Aristotelian view falls outside of the scope of this chapter. My aim here is only to kick up some philosophical dust and point you to a defensible, Aristotelian alternative that is worthy of further consideration.[31]

GOING DEEPER: SUBSTANCES

Key Concepts

- substance
- particular
- Bundle Theory versus Substance-Attribute Theory
- substratum
- form and matter

Historical

- Aristotle, *Categories* 5
- Thomas Aquinas, *On the Principles of Nature*
- Medieval Philosophers on Substance: Robert Pasnau, *Metaphysical Themes: 1274–1671*, part II
- René Descartes, *Principles of Philosophy* I.51-52
- John Locke, "Substance," chap. 23, "Of the Complex Ideas of Substances," *An Essay Concerning Human Understanding*
- David Hume, 1.1.6 "Of Modes and Substances," 1.4.5 "Of the Immortality of the Soul," 1.4.6 "Personal Identity," in *Treatise of Human Nature*
- Gottfried Wilhelm Leibniz, *The Monadology*; *Discourse on Metaphysics*
- Peter Coffey, *Ontology or the Theory of Being: An Introduction to General Metaphysics*, chaps. 8-9, 13

Contemporary

- Howard Robinson, "Substance," Stanford Encyclopedia of Philosophy (Fall 2021 Edition), ed. Edward N. Zalta, https://plato.stanford.edu/archives/fall2021/entries/substance/

---

and Anna Marmodoro, "Aristotle's Hylomorphism without Reconditioning," *Philosophical Inquiry* 37 (2013): 5-22.

[31]For a book-length account of a neo-Aristotelian view of substance as metaphysically fundamental and the work such a view can do regarding puzzles in contemporary metaphysics of material objects, see my *Substance and the Fundamentality of the Familiar: A Neo-Aristotelian Mereology*.

- Thomas Crisp and Michael Loux, *Metaphysics: A Contemporary Introduction*, 4th ed.
- Peter van Inwagen, "Relation vs. Constituent Ontologies," in *Philosophical Perspectives*
- D. C. Williams, "Elements of Being"
- Peter Simons, "Particulars in Particular Clothing: Three Trope Theories of Substance"
- Edwin Allaire, "Bare Particulars"
- J. P. Moreland, *Universals*, chap. 7
- David Oderberg, *Real Essentialism*, chap. 4
- Ross D. Inman, *Substance and the Fundamentality of the Familiar: A Neo-Aristotelian Mereology*, chap. 3
- Jeffrey Brower, *Aquinas's Ontology of the Material World*
- Michael Loux, *Substance and Attribute: A Study in Ontology*
- E. J. Lowe, "A Neo-Aristotelian Substance Ontology: Neither Relational nor Constituent," in *Contemporary Aristotelian Metaphysics*
- Edward Feser, *Scholastic Metaphysics: A Contemporary Introduction*, chap. 3
- Donnchadh O'Conaill, *Substance* (Cambridge Elements in Metaphysics)

9

CREATURELY OBJECTS

PARTS AND WHOLES

THE WONDER OF UNITY AND PLURALITY

The world is an astounding place, really. When we ponder the manifold works of God on display in material creation, we are immediately struck by both plurality and unity. Let's start with plurality. Look around you right now, wherever you are. You will immediately notice that you are surrounded by both a vast number and a wide variety of material beings (perhaps immaterial beings too, 2 Kings 6:15-17). At this very moment you are hemmed in by a countless host of ordinary and not-so-ordinary material objects. Some of these material objects are visible with the unaided human eye (the sun, but don't look directly at it!), and some are not (electrons); some are alive (your dog or favorite succulent), and some are not (notebook, lamp); some are rather materially complex (computer), and some are not (a piece of paper). All in all, there is an astonishing variety to the contour of created material reality.

At the same time, we are also keenly aware of unity amid such dizzying plurality. Some of the ordinary material beings that we are aware of in our everyday experience—wood desks, Lego cars, coffee mugs, and trees, just to name a few—are themselves unified or one. Material beings of our everyday experience exhibit what I'll call "part-whole unity." So, a wood desk strikes us as one, unified whole, even though it is made up of or composed of many parts (pieces of wood, screws, glue, etc.), parts that are themselves composed of distinct material beings (that are themselves composed of even further parts, e.g., chemical compounds, atoms, electrons, etc.). Ordinarily, if you were asked to count the number of material objects around you at present, you would likely count the desk as a *one thing*, not a *plurality of things* fastened together. Similarly, a Lego car is built or constructed out of pre-arranged Lego pieces—Lego wheels, Lego windshield, Lego chassis, etc.—each of which fit together in a pre-determined pattern that is methodically articulated in a Lego instruction manual. Yet, we naturally consider the Lego car itself to be a unified material being—*one* thing—that is made up out of many different things; there is an intuitive difference between a messy heap of Lego pieces (many things) and a completed Lego car (one thing). This much is obvious to us (or at least those of us with young kids!)

We could say the same thing about more natural, organic material beings like palm trees. A palm tree is a type of plant that belongs to the *Arecaceae* family and is widely known for its large leaves or fronds that sit atop a bare, branchless stem; they are unique-looking trees, no doubt. We ordinarily think that both the palm fronds and the stem of the palm tree are different component *parts* of the whole tree; yet we can also easily think of both the fronds and the stem as each serving to partly compose the *one* tree. When we think or talk about the palm tree, we naturally take ourselves to be thinking and talking about a single, material being that is itself made up of many other material beings. Again, there is an intuitive difference between a random pile consisting of a stem, fronds, coconuts, etc. and a mature, flourishing palm tree.

If you've journeyed with me this far in the book, it will not surprise you in the least that metaphysicians, both past and present, have long pondered the precise nature of this unity and plurality in the material world. In fact, the question of how the material world is structured by way of unity and plurality has been a topic at the heart of metaphysical reflection since the time of the pre-Socratic philosophers. Metaphysicians have been keen to explore whether material reality exhibits deep part-whole unity at all, or whether all material beings are nothing more than pluralities or collections of other material beings (like heaps of sand or bundles of sticks). Is there part-whole unity at all in material reality, or are there only pluralities?

PARTS, WHOLES, AND THE SPECIAL COMPOSITION QUESTION

As we have been keen to do up to this point in the book, let's take our first appearances of material unity amid plurality seriously when doing metaphysics, at least initially. In this spirit, consider the following principle:

Unified Objects (UO): There seem to be unified, material objects (wholes), objects that are one, yet made up of many distinct material objects (parts).

UO is the rather straightforward report that our ordinary, everyday experience of the world seems to be of part-whole unity amid plurality; that there seem to be unified wholes that are composed of distinct parts.

Historically, the philosophical study of parts and wholes has been called "mereology" (Gk. *meros*, "part"), a word that is not to be confused with "Mariology" (trust me, I know this from experience). As a subarea of metaphysics, the area of mereology aims to explore the following types of questions:

- Are there unified, composite wholes in the first place? Or are there just pluralities of noncomposed (simple) bits of matter?
- What kinds or categories of composite objects are there? What are the deep metaphysical differences between the natures of these different composite objects (substances and aggregates)?
- What is the precise relationship between wholes and their parts? What *is* the composition relation, and what are its characteristics?
- Under what conditions does a plurality of material beings (say, a pile of automobile parts) bring about a unified, composite whole (an automobile)? That is, when do some things become parts of something else?

We've already explored some of these questions in previous chapters, in particular, the different categories of object in terms of substance and aggregate (see chap. 8). In this chapter, I want to focus in on that last question in particular, a question that Peter van Inwagen—a leading thinker responsible for reinvigorating the study of mereology in contemporary metaphysics—has dubbed "The Special Composition Question," or SCQ for short.

Before doing so, let me briefly define a few terms. Let's call a "mereological whole" or "composite object" or "complex object" (I use all of these synonymously) a material object that is itself composed of further objects. So, very simply, composite objects are objects (e.g., tables) that have parts (e.g., a tabletop, legs, etc.), and the various parts are said to compose or make up the one whole. Also, let's call a "material simple" or a "noncomposite material object" (I use these interchangeably) an object that itself lacks parts; material simples are material objects that are not composed of parts at all.

With these definitions in hand, we can, following van Inwagen, informally state the SCQ as follows:

Informal SCQ: Suppose one had certain objects at one's disposal. What would one have to do—what could one do—to get those objects to compose something?[1]

The key question here is this: When does a plurality of material objects ever compose a single, composite whole?

This rather informal statement of SCQ brings to light the deep underlying aim of our inquiry here: Can genuine part-whole unity ever arise out of a plurality of material beings? Again, this fundamental metaphysical query taps into a deep source of human wonder, namely, how the material world is built up and compositionally structured in various ways.

With this informal statement of SCQ in hand, it will be helpful to have a more formal explication of SCQ going forward (where "*xs*" is simply a formal, logical way of referring to either a plurality of things or a single thing):

Formal SCQ: For any plurality *xs*, the *xs* compose one thing *y* if and only if the *xs* _____.

That is, for any plurality of material things whatsoever (*xs*), that plurality gives rise to a unified whole (*y*) when (and only when) some specific conditions are in place. Providing an intuitive yet philosophically adequate answer to SCQ involves filling in the above blank, that is, providing a precise and informative set of conditions that can withstand scrutiny and preserve our deeply held ordinary beliefs about the structure of material reality.

There are three general answers to SCQ that have been widely discussed and debated in contemporary metaphysics. But before we examine each of these views in detail, including reasons to endorse or reject each of them, let's first get an initial handle on how each of them answers the following informal version of SCQ: "When do some objects compose a single, composite whole?"

Never: Pluralities *never* compose a unified, composite whole.[2]

Sometimes: Pluralities *sometimes* compose a unified, composite whole.[3]

Always: Pluralities *always* compose a unified, composite whole.[4]

---

[1]Peter van Inwagen, *Material Beings* (Ithaca, NY: Cornell University Press, 1990), 31.
[2]Also known as "Mereological Nihilism" or "Eliminativism."
[3]Also known as "Moderatism" or "Restricted Composition."
[4]Also known as "Universalism" or "Unrestricted Composition."

At its deepest level, then, SCQ aims to explore whether material beings ever stand in part-whole relations to one another, whether there are any composite wholes in the first place.

Let me try to illustrate these three general answers to SCQ. Suppose we consider a plurality of material objects a, b, and c and ask whether these objects together compose a further object, O. Our three initial, broad answers to SCQ can be visually illustrated by figure 9.1:

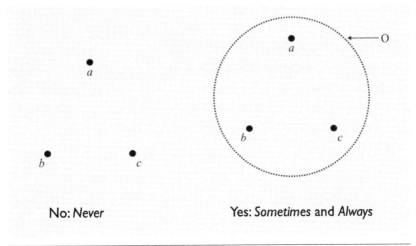

No: *Never*   Yes: *Sometimes and Always*

Figure 9.1. Special Composition Question

As is evident, the *Never* answer to SCQ—also known as "Mereological Nihilism" because it holds that absolutely no material being stands in part-whole relations to any other material being—sees the material world as completely devoid of part-whole unity. There truly are no composite or complex material beings in this sense. The only material beings that exist are mereological simples or noncomposite objects, normally very small bits of matter at the lowest physical level as described by fundamental physics.

The *Sometimes* answer to SCQ—also known as "Moderatism" or "Restricted Composition"—states that a, b, and c do indeed compose a unified whole, namely, O, and that a, b, and c are all distinct parts of O. As such, those who espouse a version of the *Sometimes* answer to SCQ hold that there is at least some part-whole unity in the world. The difficult task of those who defend a version of the *Sometimes* answer to SCQ is to specify what conditions need to be in place for such part-whole unity to arise, that is, how a, b, and c need to be arranged or structured in order to bring about O.

Finally, the *Always* answer to SCQ—also known as "Mereological Univer-salism" or "Unrestricted Composition"—says that *a*, *b*, and *c* do indeed compose a further composite whole O, but they do so precisely because any and all pluralities of objects automatically compose a composite whole. So, for any two things whatsoever—no matter how spatially distant or unrelated they are to each other—say your left big toenail and the painting *Mona Lisa* in the Louvre in Paris—there is a composite whole that has your left big toenail and the *Mona Lisa* as parts. Pretty wild, no?

NEVER: MEREOLOGICAL NIHILISM

Recall that the mereological nihilist rejects that the material world includes part-whole unity; the only material beings that exist are those that lack parts entirely, that are mereologically simple. With Formal SCQ as our guide, we can state mereological nihilism more precisely as follows:

> *Mereological Nihilism*: For any *xs*, the *xs* compose *y* if and only if <u>there is only one of the *xs*</u>.

While I don't have the space to fully unpack the view here, the core idea is that the mereological nihilist believes that the only time composition occurs is when a single, material simple exists and composes itself.[5] But when there are two or more material simples, there are no conditions under which those two objects compose a further object.

Why would anyone affirm Mereological Nihilism, especially in the face of the seemingly obvious part-whole unity on display in the material world (as captured previously in UO)? Are not tables and trees single, unified wholes that are composed of parts? As there are several prominent contemporary metaphysicians who endorse mereological nihilism such as Ted Sider and Cian Dorr, the view deserves careful attention.

There are at least three standard reasons contemporary metaphysicians are attracted to Mereological Nihilism. First, many nihilists contend that the view has the advantage of providing a simple and elegant answer to SCQ. The view is simple precisely because it answers the question "When are some objects parts of other objects?" with a resounding "Never!" All things being equal, if

---

[5]There's a standard difference between what philosophers call proper and improper parthood. We can think of a proper part as a part of an object that is not identical to that object. An improper part, by contrast, is a part of an object that is numerically identical to that object. In this sense, everything has itself as an improper part.

we can get by with a leaner ontology, we should. As we will see shortly, the nihilist is not saddled with the tricky business of trying to locate the precise point at which (and under what conditions) some objects are parts of other objects, as the *Sometimes* view is.

Second, the view claims the added virtue of providing an elegant solution to many of the thorniest puzzles concerning material objects. Suffice it to say here that if there strictly are no bronze statues that are composed of many different parts, then the difficult conundrums that come in the wake of believing in such objects disappear entirely.[6] Without a doubt, mereological nihilism's potential power to explain away these difficult metaphysical conundrums is the strongest argument in favor of the view.

Last, and this point is a bit trickier to state, it is a virtue of Mereological Nihilism that it can avoid being committed to the odd view that some aspects of reality are genuinely vague and blurry. Let me try to unpack this in more detail. We are familiar with the fact that some linguistic terms, such as the English words *bald* or *rich* can be vague in the sense that it is not always clear-cut when the word applies to someone and when it doesn't, what philosophers call "semantic vagueness." Is your uncle Rob *really* "bald" or "rich"? What is the minimal amount of money Uncle Rob needs in his bank account in order to rightly be considered rich, or the maximum number of hairs he needs to have on his head to rightly be considered bald? Linguistic terms are often vague in just this way.

Moreover, we are also familiar with the fact that our knowledge of reality can often be vague due to cognitive gaps and sheer ignorance. So, while you may well think the term "bald" or "rich" aptly apply to Uncle Rob, you will likely be wildly ignorant of the precise amount of money and number of hairs it takes to count as "rich" and "bald" (assuming there is a precise number at all!). This kind of vagueness is a feature not of our language but of our knowledge, what philosophers call "epistemic vagueness."

---

[6]Or at least some think. See Bradley Rettler, "Mereological Nihilism and Puzzles about Material Objects," *Pacific Philosophical Quarterly* 99, no. 4 (2018): 842-68, for an interesting argument that many of such puzzles remain in Mereological Nihilism. For an accessible introduction to the various puzzles concerning material objects in general, see Earl Conee and Ted Sider, *Riddles of Existence: A Guided Tour of Metaphysics*, 2nd ed. (Oxford: Oxford University Press, 2014), chap. 7. For a more demanding treatment of these puzzles and the bearing of a classical Aristotelian ontology of substance on these puzzles, see my *Substance and the Fundamentality of the Familiar* (New York: Routledge, 2018), chaps. 5-6.

But some philosophers think that not only can our language and knowledge be blurry or fuzzy in these senses, but reality itself (apart from the way we think about it or talk about it) can be genuinely vague, lacking clear-cut and precise ontological boundaries. Philosophers call this variety of vagueness "ontological" or "metaphysical vagueness." Metaphysical vagueness is very odd indeed.[7] As we will see in our discussion of the various versions of the *Sometimes* answer to SCQ, some defenders of Moderatism or Restricted Composition feel compelled to believe in metaphysical vagueness concerning the number of objects that exist in reality. To be clear, the idea here is not that *exists* is a vague linguistic term, or that we simply are blissfully ignorant as to how many things exist in reality. Rather, the idea here is that this blurriness is a genuine feature of reality in itself. If an answer to SCQ can avoid the oddity of metaphysical vagueness, then this is a mark in its favor, or so says the nihilist.

There are, however, several powerful objections to Mereological Nihilism in the contemporary literature. I will mention one theological inkling and three quick philosophical arguments against Mereological Nihilism as a *Never* answer to SCQ.

First, a theological inkling. The Scriptures portray aspects of material reality, at the very least, *as if* they display part-whole unity. In particular, the Scriptures speak of the human body as a "whole" in contrast to its many parts like a foot, an ear, an eye, a head, etc. (Psalm 139:13; Proverbs 26:22; 1 Corinthians 12:12-26).[8] Of course, while the human and divine authors of Scripture in no way have the technical, metaphysical issue of answering the SCQ in mind when attributing such part-whole structure to the human body, it is at least metaphysically suggestive that the very theological analogy made by the apostle Paul about the holistic unity of the church, the body of Christ, seems to hinge on the fact that human bodies are *wholes* that have many distinct objects as *parts*, all of which work together for the integral functioning of the whole body (1 Corinthians 12:12-26).

Second, Mereological Nihilism cuts against our ordinary, commonsense beliefs that there are objects composed of other objects as captured in

---

[7]Even David Lewis, perhaps the most influential metaphysician of the latter half of the twentieth century, was quite uneasy with metaphysical vagueness. See his *On the Plurality of Worlds* (Malden, MA: Wiley-Blackwell, 1986), 212.
[8]The Scriptures attribute part-whole unity to animals as well (Exodus 12:9).

UO above. It strongly seems that there are tables and trees and the like, all understood as composite objects that have objects as parts. If Mereological Nihilism requires us to abandon these deeply held pre-philosophical beliefs about how the world seems to us—like the fact that tables and trees have parts—then so much the worse for Mereological Nihilism.

Third, consider the following philosophical argument offered by Peter van Inwagen against Mereological Nihilism—call it the "Close to Home Argument":[9]

1. I exist.

2. I am not mereologically simple (that is, I am composed of parts).

3. Therefore, at least one object exists that is not mereologically simple.

4. Therefore, Mereological Nihilism is false.

The argument is deceptively simple, is it not? The driving force of the Close to Home Argument is this: You exist and are, at least intuitively, not mereologically simple. At the very least, you *seem* to have hands, a head, a heart, and each of these seem to be part of your body. Should we not render these epistemic appearances concerning your parts innocent until proven guilty?

However, there is a slight tangle here, at least for those who think they are *not* identical to their bodies, which clearly seem to have distinct parts (head, heart, hands, etc.). In fact, some proponents of a nonmaterialist view of human persons known as "substance-dualism" reason *from* the mereological simplicity of the self *to* the further claim that the self is therefore (by Leibniz's Law) *not* identical to the human body. So, it would be nice to have a version of the Close to Home Argument that is friendly to versions of materialism as well as nonmaterialism, like substance dualism.

Now, van Inwagen is a type of materialist about human persons. He thinks that human persons are identical to wholly material human bodies. If human bodies do indeed have parts, and you just *are* a wholly material human body (that is what you are numerically identical to), then it, of course, follows that you have parts. But how might those who emphatically reject this particular materialist view of human persons (such as substance dualists and materialists of a different variety) press this argument against Mereological Nihilism?

---

[9]Van Inwagen, *Material Beings*, 73.

Consider the following slight revision of the Close to Home Argument:

1. Human bodies exist and I have one.[10]

2. Human bodies are not mereologically simple (that is, human bodies are composed of parts).

3. Therefore, at least one object exists that is not mereologically simple.

4. Therefore, Mereological Nihilism is false.

Since nonmaterialists think they have but are not identical to a human body, and human bodies are in fact composite—human bodies have parts—the argument still hits fairly close to home. As Mereological Nihilism entails a grand, sweeping denial of any and all part-whole unity in the world, if it can reasonably be established that there is just one instance of such unity, then one has solid reason to reject Mereological Nihilism.

A fourth and final argument against Mereological Nihilism focuses on the notion of a material simple, a material object that lacks parts entirely. What if it turns out that our best science reveals that every material object is further composed of other material objects, all the way down without end, so to speak? That is, what if there are no material simples? If so, and if Mereological Nihilism is true, then there are no material objects. This, of course, is a bad result.

But the worry with material simples doesn't stop there. Most metaphysicians think that whatever answer to SCQ is true, it is true of *necessity*; that is, as the answer to the question "When are some objects parts of other objects?" seems to be a law or principle of reality itself, it doesn't just happen to be true (and thus could have been false). If this is right, as most philosophers think it is,[11] then Mereological Nihilism faces a challenge from the mere *possibility* of

---

[10]For both non-standard materialists and those who reject materialism about the human being outright, there are many different ways of "having a material body" without being numerically identical to it. One version of materialism known as "constitutionalism" states that one can be *constituted* by one's body, but not identical to it, where constitution is a type of unity relation close to but strictly not identity. In one version of substance dualism, one can be integrally, causally related to a body, but not identical to it (Cartesian dualism). In another version of substance dualism, one can have a body as a part (Compound dualism) or even as a mode of oneself, where a mode is a way that the person (the soul) exists (a *bodily* mode of existence, we might say). For explications and critiques of each of these accounts of the nature of human beings, see Jonathan J. Loose, Angus J. L. Menuge, and J. P. Moreland, eds., *The Blackwell Companion to Substance Dualism* (Hoboken, NJ: Wiley-Blackwell, 2018).
[11]Though some argue that matters related to when composition occurs are contingent and not necessary (and thus could have been different). See Ross P. Cameron, "The Contingency of Composition," *Philosophical Studies* 136, no. 1 (2007): 99-121.

a world devoid of material simples. The challenge is this: Even if material simples do indeed exist in our world, they certainly could have failed to exist (try to conceive of a material world where there is no rock-bottom physical level, rather, every object has further parts and so on). If it is possible that simples fail to exist, then it is possible that Mereological Nihilism is false (since it *requires* the existence of simples). But to say that it's possible for Mereological Nihilism to be false is just to say that it is *not* necessarily true. But Mereological Nihilism will be true of necessity, if true at all. Therefore, Mereological Nihilism is not true.

ALWAYS: MEREOLOGICAL UNIVERSALISM (A.K.A. UNRESTRICTED COMPOSITION)

This brings us to the other extreme answer to the SCQ, the view that answers the question "When are some objects parts of other objects?" with a re-sounding "Always!" Here is a statement of Mereological Universalism from David Lewis, perhaps the most influential defender of the view in contem-porary metaphysics: "I claim that mereological composition is unrestricted: any old class of things has a mereological sum. Whenever there are some things, no matter how disparate and unrelated, there is something composed of just those things."[12] The takeaway is this: Just any old class of things com-poses a mereological whole. Yes, you heard that right: *any* plurality of things, no matter how those things are arranged with respect to one another. In sharp contrast to Mereological Nihilism that says under no scenario are ob-jects parts of other objects, Mereological Universalism swings to the other extreme and says that under (just about) every scenario objects are parts of other objects.

Let's state mereological universalism more formally as follows:

Mereological Universalism: For any *xs*, the *xs* compose y if and only if <u>the *xs* exist and do not share parts</u>.

So, for any two existing objects that do not share any parts in common (they do not mereologically "overlap" as philosophers put it), no matter how unre-lated or spatially separated from each other, those objects together compose a common whole (recall my example of your left big toenail and the painting *Mona Lisa*).

---

[12]Lewis, *On the Plurality of Worlds*, 211.

Note how radically counterintuitive this view is. When we think about wholes and their parts, we normally think that objects need to be related or structured in a particular way in order to make up a whole (think again of the intuitive difference between a pile of unassembled car parts and a working car). But in Mereological Universalism, the conditions under which composition occurs make absolutely no mention of seemingly important notions like structure, or the ways objects are related to one another to make up a further object.

Yet some of the most prominent contemporary metaphysicians, both Christian and non-Christian, are proponents of Mereological Universalism.[13] In fact, Hud Hudson, a Christian metaphysician who ardently defends mereological universalism, says this about the enshrined status of the view in contemporary metaphysics:

> Among many of our most distinguished analytic metaphysicians UMC ["unrestricted mereological composition," i.e. mereological universalism] has an honorary status approaching that of a logical truth; it is the sort of thing you just do not mess with. . . . Come what may . . . thou shall not restrict composition.[14]

But again, why might someone be attracted to this second extreme answer to SCQ, especially since it flies in the face of many of our pre-philosophical beliefs about the shape and structure of material reality? Let me unpack several of the most prominent reasons proponents of Mereological Universalism have offered in defense of the view.

First, as with Mereological Nihilism, Mereological Universalism offers a simple and elegant response to SCQ. When asked "When are some objects parts of other objects?" the universalist can offer an unequivocal reply, "Always." As a completely unrestricted view of composition, universalism avoids the need to identify precise conditions under which some objects are and are not parts of other objects.

A second virtue of Mereological Universalism is that, in stark contrast to Mereological Nihilism, the view does not eliminate ordinary composite objects from an ontological account of reality. Tables and trees exist and are genuine composite wholes made up of parts. Insofar as this preserves our

---

[13]Including Michael Rea, Hud Hudson, and David Lewis.
[14]Hud Hudson, "Confining Composition," *The Journal of Philosophy* 103, no. 12 (2006): 636.

pre-philosophical belief in the existence of ordinary, run-of-the-mill material objects, this is a mark in favor of universalism.

Third, as it was the case with proponents of Mereological Nihilism, many philosophers are drawn to universalism precisely because of the perceived problems with a moderate or restricted view of composition. In particular, many metaphysicians worry that any version of a moderate or restricted view of composition—a *Sometimes* answer to SCQ—brings with it a host of untoward commitments, including a commitment to metaphysical vagueness. While we have already introduced this worry in our discussion of Mereological Nihilism above, it is time to put a finer point on the objection as this argument—call it the "Vagueness Argument"—is perhaps the primary motivation for an extreme answer to SCQ in general and Mereological Universalism in particular.

Consider the following illustration that aims to get to the nub of the very technical worry underlying the Vagueness Argument for Mereological Universalism. Suppose you had a bag of beach sand at your disposal, and you wanted to create a new heap of sand. And supposing you had the ability to isolate a single grain of sand at a time, you begin constructing your heap of sand, grain by grain. As you've enjoyed playing in the sand since childhood, you are generally aware of what a heap of sand is, namely what generally constitutes a heap and what does not (a few grains in the palm of your hand, say, does not make the cut). So, off you go. You start with grain1, then grain2, then grain3. If you were to stop at grain3, then you would clearly not have a heap of sand. So, you keep at it, adding one grain of sand at a time to the others. Let's fast forward a long while and imagine that you clearly have a large heap of sand in front of you, one that you've painstakingly constructed, grain by grain. There is, then, a series (grain1, grain2, grain3 . . . Heap) that connects clear instances of a nonheap of sand (grain1, grain2, grain3) with a clear instance of a heap of sand (Heap).

Now, when it comes to a series of this sort (what philosophers call a "Sorites series"), there is, at some point or other, a transition that takes place from having a nonheap to having a heap of sand. But at what exact point did this crucial transition take place? Note our only two options in response to this question are the following: Either there is a clear-cut point in the series when a heap comes into existence (perhaps grain1000!), call this first route "Clear," or there is not a clear-cut point when a heap comes into existence, call this second route "Not-Clear."

Interestingly enough, both Clear and Not-Clear have problematic consequences. According to Not-Clear, the point at which grains of sand make up a heap is genuinely blurry or vague (i.e., there is no well-defined point at which the heap comes to be, whether grain50 or grain51), which of course commits one to the view that reality itself (and not just our language or knowledge about reality) can be blurry or vague, that is, metaphysical vagueness.

According to Clear, by contrast, there is, in fact, a clear-cut point in the series that marks the difference between mere grains of sand and a heap of sand. That is, there is a definite point—perhaps the transition from grain999 to grain1000—at which you go from a nonheap to a heap. But notice a rather strange consequence of Clear: One tiny, insignificant grain of sand can make the difference between a nonheap and a heap. After all, you constructed the heap a single grain of sand at a time. But isn't it wildly implausible to think that one tiny, insignificant grain of sand can make this kind of metaphysical difference?

There are problems, then, with both Clear and Not-Clear as answers to the question, "At what precise point did the crucial transition from a nonheap to a heap take place in the series?" The one—Not-Clear—entails metaphysical vagueness. The other—Clear—entails that extremely minute differences can account for the coming into existence of some things. In light of these problems, you might conclude that the best way forward is to think that either *no* grains of sand make up a heap (there are no heaps), or that just *any* plurality of grains of sand make a heap. We should, then, reject the underlying idea that sometimes there are heaps and sometimes there are not.

Let me transpose this illustration onto our discussion of the Vagueness Argument for Mereological Universalism. Assume the general truth of a *Sometimes* answer to SCQ, the view that composition sometimes does and sometimes does not occur. If so, then there is a continuous series of cases that begins with a clear instance where composition does not occur (a mere plurality) and ends with a clear instance where composition does occur (a single, unified object). As with the illustration of the grains and the heap of sand, there is, at some point or other in the series, a transition that takes place from noncomposition to composition. But at what precise point did this crucial transition take place? Either there is (Clear) or there is not (Not-Clear) a clear-cut point at which this transition occurs. Saying that there is not a clear-cut point at which composition occurs commits one to the view that it is genuinely metaphysically vague whether certain objects compose other objects (and, by consequence, it's truly vague how many composite objects exist). But saying that there is a clear-cut point at which composition occurs commits one to the wild implausibility that minute insignificant differences can indeed make a significant metaphysical difference.

Since both of these routes are problematic, the defender of the Vagueness Argument contends, the best way forward is to think that either *no* objects are parts of other objects (there are no composite objects—Mereological Nihilism), or that *any* objects whatsoever compose an object (Mereological Universalism). We should, then, embrace either *Never* or *Always* and reject *Sometimes* and the underlying idea that sometimes objects compose and sometimes they do not. As you can see, the Vagueness Argument is strictly an argument against the *Sometimes* answer and in favor of an extreme answer to SCQ, whether Mereological Nihilism or Mereological Universalism.

Let's turn now to some philosophical and theological reasons that count against mereological universalism. First, many have pointed to the downright craziness of the view itself, call this the "Craziness Objection."[15] In universalism, there truly are more—astronomically and innumerably more—material objects in existence than meets the eye. While you might naturally think that your left big toenail and the *Mona Lisa* both exist, it is a stretch too far for many to think that these two radically distant and causally unrelated objects together compose a single object, call it *toenail-Lisa*. How could it be *this* easy for some plurality of objects to compose a single, composite object? For many, the view gives rise to the famous "incredulous stare" noted by David Lewis in another context, a stare of sheer disbelief.[16]

A common universalist reply to the Craziness Objection can be captured in something like the following speech:

> I completely agree that our ordinary way of speaking about reality does not involve talk about such exotic objects like *toenail-Lisa*. Our ordinary discourse about reality includes talk of toenails and paintings, of course, but not the mereological whole that has these two existing objects as parts. But

---

[15]See Ned Markosian, "Restricted Composition," in *Contemporary Debates in Metaphysics*, eds. Theodore Sider, John Hawthorne, and Dean Zimmerman (Oxford: Blackwell, 2008), 341-65.
[16]Lewis, *On the Plurality of Worlds*, 133-35.

the fact that our ordinary ways of speaking about reality fail to mention *toenail-Lisa* is no good reason to think that such a composite object does not exist.[17]

What might be said in response to this counter-reply to the Craziness Objection?

It is important to point out that many who reject Mereological Universalism do so on the deeper grounds that it fundamentally misconstrues material objects along formal, mathematical lines akin to sets in set-theory. The formal set {Al Plantinga, my iPhone, and the lint in Joe Biden's pockets} exists when and only when Al Plantinga, my iPhone, and the lint in Joe Biden's pockets exist, nothing more. In general, sets are ontologically cheap; the members of a set need not stand in any tight structural relation or causal connection to one another. As such, sets are the sort of entities whose coming into existence are blind to any notion like that of structure.

Mereological Universalists tend to model all ordinary material objects like trees and tables akin to formal sets.[18] And if the analogy between sets and ordinary composite objects rings true, then the universalist would be correct indeed in saying that composite objects are very easy to come by. However, many contemporary metaphysicians are leery of viewing ordinary composite objects akin to sets in this way, precisely because it neglects the crucial aspect of *structure* to the question of composition. Objects are parts of other objects when the former are structured in a particular way.[19] And the fact that Mereological Universalism is blind to any robust notion of structure when it comes to answering SCQ is a genuine metaphysical deficiency—a failure to adequately capture the *nature* of material objects—and not merely a deficiency in the way we talk about or formally-logically represent reality.

---

[17]This little speech is inspired by the one given by Lewis, *On the Plurality of Worlds*, 213.

[18]There are notable historical and philosophical reasons for this similarity. In its earliest development, mereology—the formal study of parts and wholes—was offered as an extreme nominalist substitute for set-theory. Stronger forms of what is known as "classical extensional mereology"—which construes material objects in similar terms as sets—include Mereological Universalism as a foundational axiom. See Kathrin Koslicki, *The Structure of Objects* (New York: Oxford University Press, 2008), chap. 1.

[19]For an excellent (though intermediate) analysis of classical extensional mereology (which views ordinary objects as akin to sets in this way) from an Aristotelian perspective, see Koslicki, *Structure of Objects*.

Getting Theological: God, Creation, and Mereological Composition

The great medieval theologian and philosopher Thomas Aquinas once said (quoting Pseudo-Dionysius), "'There can be no touching Him [God] nor any other union with Him by mingling part with part.'"[a] This rather enigmatic statement is meant to convey a deep insight about the way in which God can and cannot be related to creatures that are themselves mereologically composite. For Aquinas, "it is not possible for God to enter into the composition of anything," that is, become a proper part of any composite creature. Why not, we might ask? For Aquinas and most classical Christian theists, God is the first efficient cause of creaturely being, as well as the sole ultimate reality and metaphysical bedrock on which all creaturely beings depend. First, as the first efficient cause, God acts and does what he does in his own right and not by virtue of another; but no proper part of a composite acts in its own right but, rather, by virtue of the whole of which it is a part. As Aquinas illustrates, "for the hand does not act, but the man by his hand; and, fire warms by its heat."[b] Consequently, God cannot be a part of a creaturely composite. Second, as the sole, ultimate, and fundamental reality, God is prior to all beings that are not God. But, Aquinas argues, the proper parts of a composite (whether matter or form) are either in potentiality (matter) or dependent on another for their existence (form). As God can be neither of these things, God cannot be a part of a creaturely composite. Thus, Aquinas's understanding of divine aseity precludes God standing in certain relations to creatures, in this case, composition or part-whole relations.

Herein lies an important theological worry for Mereological Universalism.[c] Recall my recommended metaphysical lodestar for Christian metaphysicians, divine aseity. According to divine aseity, God is the sole, ultimate reality, and absolutely all non-God reality is derived from and brought into existence by God. The guiding force of divine aseity for metaphysics is striking: Everything that is not God—whether concrete or abstract (see chap. 7)—finds its creative, ontological source in God.

Now, recall that Mereological Universalism is the truly unrestricted view that for absolutely any two objects (that do not share parts), there is a further object that those two objects compose. Let's assume this view is true to see what tensions might arise with it and divine aseity. If Mereological Universalism is truly universal in this sense, then the view entails that there are innumerable composite (concrete) objects of which even the triune God is a part. Let's focus on just one composite (concrete) object among the myriad of composite objects of which God is a part: *God-moon*, the existing object that is composed of God and the moon (remember: only on the assumption of universalism does such an object exist). In Mereological Universalism, *God-moon* is a real, existing composite object that is not numerically one and the same as its parts—God and the moon—and is as real as you or me. The very important part here is that *God-moon* is *not* identical to God. Thus, on the assumption of divine aseity, *God-moon* is derivative on, created by, and sustained by God.

But let's now ask: What exactly would it take for God to be the Creator of *God-moon*, to be causally responsible for bringing this composite (concrete) object into existence? Well, one natural thought here is that for God to be the Creator of something, say water as H_2O, then God would need to be the Creator of each and every essential chemical element of H_2O, namely hydrogen and oxygen. If God were only responsible for creating hydrogen but not oxygen, say, then it seems that God would only be the partial Creator of H_2O and not its absolute Creator (especially since hydrogen and oxygen are water's only essential chemical parts).

Go back to our strange object, *God-moon*, the composite with the triune God and the moon as its sole parts. God and the moon are the only two essential parts of *God-moon*; the nature of *God-moon* is determined solely by God and the moon, nothing more. So, in order for God to be the absolute Creator of *God-moon*—that very composite object—it seems as though God would need to be causally responsible for bringing *both* of these parts into existence. But, of course, this is impossible, as God cannot be the absolute Creator of God (as self-creation is impossible). As a result, our original assumption of the truth of Mereological Universalism has generated a tension here. We seem to be left with the untoward option of choosing between the possibility of self-creation and the view that there are a countless number of composite (concrete) objects that are not identical to God, but that are not created by God, which is clearly in tension with divine aseity. One might conclude from this that Mereological Universalism, together with Christian theism, generates a deep tension with divine aseity. For Christian metaphysicians who take a strong form of divine aseity as a metaphysical guiding light, this is reason to push back against Mereological Universalism.

[a]*Summa Theologiae* Ia, q.3, a.8.

[b]*Summa Theologiae* Ia, q.3, a.8.

[c]For a full treatment of this worry and others, see Ross D. Inman and Alexander Pruss, "On Christian Theism and Unrestricted Composition," *American Philosophical Quarterly* 56, no. 4 (2019): 345-60.

SOMETIMES: MODERATISM OR RESTRICTED COMPOSITION

We have thus far explored reasons for and against two extreme answers to SCQ, Mereological Nihilism and Mereological Universalism. This brings us to the *Sometimes* answer to SCQ, that sometimes composition occurs and sometimes it does not. There are a host of versions of Restricted Composition, some more defensible than others.[20] Consider the following two, initially plausible versions of Restricted Composition:

Contact: For any xs, the xs compose y if and only if the xs are in contact.

Fastening: For any xs, the xs compose y if and only if the xs are fastened together.

Both Contact and Fastening appeal to what strikes many as natural and intuitive when it comes to the question "When are objects parts of other objects?," namely *structure* (whether close spatial proximity or being physically related to one another in some way or other).

But on immediate inspection, a host of questions and problems arise for our first two versions of Restricted Composition, Contact and Fastening. First, what exactly does it mean for two objects to be in contact or fastened together in such a way? For starters, if by "contact" one means that two objects are "not spatially separated from one another," then Contact as an answer to

---

[20]For a fuller treatment of different versions of Moderatism (as well as the accompanying problems with each), see the now classic work by Peter van Inwagen, *Material Beings* (Ithaca, NY: Cornell University Press, 1990).

SCQ faces some immediate counterexamples. I rest my hand on your shoulder in order to console you in a difficult time; my hand is now not spatially separated from your shoulder. According to Contact, my placing my hand on your shoulder in this way brings into existence a new composite object, the object composed of you and me. A simple act of consolation yields the existence of a new composite object in reality; this is bad news, indeed, as surely composition can't be *that* easy to come by! Contact, then, is much too permissive of an answer to SCQ.[21]

But a similar fate awaits Fastening. First, what exactly are we to make of the notion of two objects being fastened together in such a way? Do we mean that they are incapable of being separated from one another, do we mean that they always move around together, or what? If we mean incapable of being separated from one another, then, as van Inwagen points out, a similar worry arises as in Contact.[22] Suppose, again, I rest my hand on your shoulder to console you in your trouble. But suppose my hand and your shoulder become stuck together in such a way that they are no longer capable of being removed or separated from one another. According to Fastening, you and I now together compose a new composite object. Again, this seems much too permissive an answer to SCQ.

SOMETIMES: ORGANICISM

The shortcomings of various moderate answers to the SCQ (like Contact and Fastening and others like it) have led van Inwagen to defend a version of Restricted Composition called "Organicism," which appeals to more robust, biological connections between objects as an answer to SCQ.[23] Very roughly, Organicism says that several objects become parts of another object when (and only when) the activity of the two objects constitutes a biological life. Let me state the view more formally as follows:

> *Organicism*: For any *xs*, the *xs* compose *y* if and only if the activity of the *xs* constitutes a life.

But what exactly does it mean for the activity of some things to "constitute a life"? According to van Inwagen, composition occurs when some

---

[21]See van Inwagen, *Material Beings*, chap. 3.
[22]See van Inwagen, *Material Beings*, 57-58.
[23]See van Inwagen, *Material Beings*, chap. 9.

things are arranged in a specific manner, namely living organism–wise. Granted, while the notion of being arranged living organism–wise is still quite vague, van Inwagen roughly articulates the notion as follows: "What I am observing is an unimaginably complex self-maintaining storm of atoms. This storm moves across the surface of the world, drawing swirls and clots of atoms into it and expelling others, always maintaining its overall structure."[24] So, being arranged living organism–wise is, at the very least, the type of relational structure that allows for organic biological functioning and self-maintenance. So, as the idea of "constituting a life" is strictly a biological and thus an empirical notion, it belongs to the discipline of biology to tell us what precise biological structures allow for organic, biological functioning and self-maintenance.

One important implication of Organicism—one that you may have no doubt spotted already—is that the view entails that the only composite objects that exist are living, biological organisms. So, pool tables, coffee mugs, and automobiles (and the rest) strictly do not exist, since they are not biologically alive in the above sense, according to van Inwagen. Yet, according to Organicism, while there are not tables in the sense that they are composite objects, there are things—mereological simples to be precise—that are arranged table-wise. While there are no composite objects that are tables, there are various table-wise arrangements of simple material beings (pluralities that are arranged in table-wise fashion).

So, we've seen that Organicism has some similarities with Mereological Nihilism, in particular the denial of a large class of composite objects recognized by common sense such as tables, chairs, and coffee mugs. Yet, on the other hand, Organicism recognizes *some* composite objects, namely living, biological organisms. While the view shares certain virtues with Mereological Nihilism, it also inherits some of the same vices. For one, the view is extremely restrictive in its elimination of *all* nonliving, composite objects, including scientifically respectable ones like carbon atoms and H_2O. For many, this is a serious strike against Organicism. Second, as van Inwagen himself recognizes, the view entails a variety of metaphysical vagueness insofar as it is genuinely blurry when some object "constitutes a life" and thereby becomes a part of a living organism.

---

[24]Van Inwagen, *Material Beings*, 87.

SOMETIMES: BRUTALISM

One final version of Restricted Composition is what is often called "Brutal Composition" and has been defended by philosopher Ned Markosian.[25] Roughly, the view, call it "Brutalism," questions whether there can be any informative and uniform conditions under which some things are parts of other things. Brutalism is largely a response to the difficulty of formulating an adequate moderate answer to SCQ. Just because we are not able to identify general and informative conditions under which composition occurs, this should not undermine our sense that composition is, in fact, restricted.

According to Brutalism, while composition sometimes does and sometimes does not occur, it is simply a brute fact when composition occurs. Recall from chapter seven the idea that brute or primitive facts are the sorts of facts that themselves are true but are not explained in terms of some other fact. So, facts about when composition occurs are not explained in terms of spatial contact, fastening, or the activity of some objects jointly constituting a biological life. In other words, then, there is no general, one-size-fits-all answer to SCQ. While there are specific composition conditions for each composite object (trees, tables, atoms, etc.), making a list of such conditions for each composite object would be incredibly complex and very long indeed.

NEO-ARISTOTELIAN OBJECTS AND THE
VAGUENESS ARGUMENT REVISITED

But what might the proponent of Restricted Composition say in response to the thorny Vagueness Argument outlined above? Recall that the Vagueness Argument takes aim at *all* moderate answers to SCQ that aim to restrict the conditions under which composition occurs (those that fall under *Sometimes*). We have so far examined four versions of Restricted Composition—Contact, Fastening, Organicism, and Brutalism.

So, how might a firm believer in mereological modesty respond to the Vagueness Argument? There have been a host of responses to the Vagueness Argument on behalf of Restricted Composition, some very technical and nuanced that fall outside our scope in this book. Here I will focus on two

---

[25]Ned Markosian, "Brutal Composition," *Philosophical Studies* 92, no. 3 (1998): 211-49.

responses. The first response provides the initial building blocks for the second, what I consider to be a more promising neo-Aristotelian solution to the Vagueness Argument in defense of Moderatism.

Recall the driving question behind the Vagueness Argument: At what exact point did the crucial transition from noncomposition to composition take place? This question gave rise to two exhaustive responses (both problematic to the defender of the Vagueness Argument), Clear (there is a clear-cut point at which this transition occurs) and Not-Clear (there is no clear-cut point at which this transition occurs). One response to the Vagueness Argument is to challenge the alleged implausibility of Clear. Why think that minute differences cannot make a significant metaphysical difference for when composition occurs? What's the argument for this claim?

Trenton Merricks, a Christian metaphysician and staunch proponent of a restricted view of composition, has argued that there is indeed a clear-cut, nonarbitrary point at which composition definitively occurs.[26] The sharp cutoff for when composition occurs is the existence of new, fundamental (irreducible) causal powers, causal capacities of the whole that cannot be explained in terms of the causal powers of each of the parts individually or even collectively (which is why they are fundamental or irreducible). Merricks creatively illustrates–by way of the idea of "whistling composites"—the notion of a clear-cut point at which new, fundamental causal powers of the whole come to be:

> Moreover, pretend the following story is true. Necessarily, simples are silent but composite objects emit a loud whistling noise. (That's right, they whistle.) Their whistling, according to this story, is not reduced to the collective activity of their parts. For example, it is not reduced to the spatial interrelations among the composite's parts, as it would be if the wind's blowing through the composite caused the whistling. Instead, whistling is a necessary result of composition itself. The whistling of composites, according to this story, is in some sense "emergent." And, finally, let us add that it cannot possibly be vague whether the whistling occurs.[27]

---

[26]See the stellar book *Objects and Persons* (New York: Oxford University Press, 2001) for Merricks's own book-length defense of his *Sometimes* view of the composition of material objects.

[27]Trenton Merricks, "Composition and Vagueness," *Mind* 114 (2005): 628. For critical discussion, see Elizabeth Barnes, "Vagueness and Arbitrariness: Merricks on Composition," *Mind* 116 (2007): 105-13.

In this example, whistling is meant to pick out an irreducible activity of the whole that cannot be accounted for by way of the activity of the parts individually or collectively. So, if we were to move along our continuous series that includes clear cases of noncomposition and clear cases of composition, it is clear, for Merricks, when composition occurs—just listen! Merricks's general move aims to challenge the assumed implausibility of Clear and, more broadly, the inference that if Restricted Composition is true, then composition is sometimes metaphysically vague.

Merricks's response to the Vagueness Argument against Restricted Composition is an interesting one that deserves to be taken seriously. However, at the end of the day, Merricks is less than optimistic that very many of our ordinary composite objects have fundamental causal powers in this strong sense. For him, the causal activities of ordinary objects like baseballs, computers, pool tables, and automobiles can be entirely explained or reduced to the causal activities of their parts working together, nothing more.

According to Merricks, the only composite objects that have fundamental causal powers in this sense are beings that have conscious mental properties; strictly speaking, only the actions undertaken by conscious beings defy deeper explanation in terms of the action of the individual atoms that compose them (or even the joint activity of such atoms). It follows, then, that only conscious beings—human beings like us and perhaps other higher-order animals (dolphins, dogs, etc.)—survive elimination in this view. To put it bluntly: There simply are no composite beings that are not conscious.

While this route yields a response to the Vagueness Argument in general—thereby allowing the defender of Restricted Composition to avoid extreme answers to SCQ—it is not without its problems. One of the most notable problems is that it eliminates all nonconscious ordinary and scientifically respectable objects from our ontological inventory of created reality. In this view, nonconscious living organisms (cells, bacteria, plants, etc.) as well as nonliving composite objects (gold, H_2O, DNA, electrons, etc.)—objects that play an important role in some of our best scientific theories about the natural world—do not exist. If we can identify a way to block the Vagueness Argument that doesn't deny the existence of ordinary and scientifically respectable objects, we would be on much firmer philosophical ground.

While I don't have the space to fully unpack the view here, I'll gesture toward what I think is a more promising way forward in defense of Restricted

Composition.[28] Recall that what the defender of a *Sometimes* answer to SCQ is looking for in response to the Vagueness Argument is a nonarbitrary cutoff point at which a plurality composes a single, unified composite object; that is, a way to challenge the perceived implausibility of Clear and, more broadly, the inference that if Restricted Composition is true, then composition is sometimes metaphysically vague. Suppose, then, we adopt a neo-Aristotelian view of objects, one that distinguishes between objects in the category of *Substance* and those in the category of *Aggregate*. As we noted at the beginning of chapter eight, the natures of substances and aggregates differ with respect to whether they are independent/dependent and the degree to which they are unified. For the neo-Aristotelian, substances are metaphysically independent and unified in the strongest sense and are metaphysically fundamental (ontologically rock bottom). They are strongly unified in that they are not built up or dependent on any more fundamental metaphysical ingredients. This isn't to deny that familiar substances like living organisms, H_2O, and human beings lack ordinary, material parts and are not composite objects; indeed, they are! Rather, in this neo-Aristotelian view, substances are metaphysically fundamental in their own right and unified to such a high degree that they are metaphysically prior to (and more fundamental than) the many parts that compose them. The parts of substances are metaphysically dependent on the wholes of which they are parts; they *exist* and *are what they are* (their essence) by virtue of the substance as a whole.

The same is true for objects in the category of *Aggregate*, but just the reverse. Aggregates are metaphysically derivative (nonfundamental) and dependent kinds of objects. Moreover, they are weakly unified in the sense that they are composed of objects that are more fundamental than they are, namely substances. Aggregates like pool tables, cars, and computers are metaphysically dependent on the substantial parts that compose them; they *exist* and *are what they are* (their essence) by virtue of their substantial parts and the relations among them.

Let's now apply this Aristotelian machinery to the Vagueness Argument against Restricted Composition. *If* it's metaphysically clear-cut (i.e., not ontologically fuzzy or blurry) when the relation of metaphysical dependence

---

[28]For a more technical and in-depth explanation of this response, see my *Substance and the Fundamentality of the Familiar: Towards a Neo-Aristotelian Mereology* (New York: Routledge, 2017), 183-88.

holds—*if* there is an objective fact of the matter as to when one thing metaphysically depends on another for its existence and nature, irrespective of whether or not we are cognitively aware of when this occurs—then the neo-Aristotelian can tell the following story regarding a sharp cutoff for composition and thereby avoid metaphysical vagueness.

When it comes to substances like living organisms and human beings, the sharp cutoff for composition occurs when a plurality of objects (xs) together come to metaphysically depend on a common object (y), a substance. Likewise, when it comes to aggregates like pool tables, cars, and computers, the sharp cutoff for composition occurs when a plurality of objects (xs) together ontologically ground the existence of a common object (y), an aggregate. With the composition of every composite substance, you have a plurality of objects that together metaphysically depend on a common object; likewise, with the composition of every composite aggregate, you have a plurality of objects that together metaphysically ground a common object (aggregate). These clear-cut (nonvague) metaphysical dependence relations are a "necessary result" (as Merricks would put it) of composition for each respective category of object. Consequently, neo-Aristotelian proponents of Restricted Composition have the ontological resources to challenge the Vagueness Argument and to keep metaphysical vagueness at bay.

One virtue of this neo-Aristotelian response to the Vagueness Argument is that it allows the proponent of Restricted Composition to continue to affirm the existence of nonconscious composite objects (both living and nonliving), in contrast to Merricks's own route. At bottom, both responses to the Vagueness Argument on behalf of the *Sometimes* answer to SCQ—Merricks's and my own neo-Aristotelian alternative—affirm that the implausibility of Clear is overstated and that minuscule differences can indeed yield significant metaphysical differences when it comes to part-whole unity, especially with respect to the composition of ordinary, composite objects.

GOING DEEPER: PARTS AND WHOLES

Key Concepts

- mereology
- part
- proper part

- sum
- fusion, mereological
- gunk
- unrestricted mereological composition
- Special Composition Question
- set
- ship of Theseus

Historical

- Verity Harte, *Plato on Parts and Wholes*
- Kathrin Koslicki, "Ancient Structure-Based Mereologies," part III of *The Structure of Objects*
- Aristotle, *Metaphysics*, book 5 (Delta)
- Medieval Views on Parts and Wholes: Robert Pasnau, *Metaphysical Themes: 1274–1671*, chap. 26
- Thomas Aquinas, *On the Mixture of the Elements*; *Commentary on Aristotle's Metaphysics*, book V, lecture 21, and book VII, lectures 13, 16 (see also John Wippel, *The Metaphysical Thought of Thomas Aquinas: From Finite Being to Uncreated Being*, 295-375)
- Robert Boyle, "The Excellency and Grounds of the Corpuscular or Mechanical Philosophy"
- Gottfried Wilhelm Leibniz, *The Monadology*

Contemporary

- Roderick Chisholm, *Person and Object*
- Trenton Merricks, *Objects and Persons*
- E. J. Lowe, "Substance and Dependence," chap. 6 in *The Possibility of Metaphysics*
- Peter van Inwagen, *Material Beings*
- J. P. Moreland, "Parts and Wholes," in *Body & Soul: Human Nature and the Crisis in Ethics*, 68-85
- Peter Simons, *Parts: A Study in Ontology*
- Kathrin Koslicki, *The Structure of Objects*
- Daniel Z. Korman, *Objects: Nothing Out of the Ordinary*

- *James van Cleve*, "The Moon and Sixpence: A Defense of Mereological Universalism"
- Theodore Sider, "The Argument from Vagueness," in *Four-Dimensionalism: An Ontology of Persistence and Time*, chap. 4, section 9 (chap. 50 in *Metaphysics: An Anthology*)
- Ross D. Inman, *Substance and the Fundamentality of the Familiar: A Neo-Aristotelian Mereology*, chaps. 3-6

ON METAPHYSICS AND MAPMAKING

For those who have traveled with me thus far, the journey has been steep and challenging. You have explored some perennial metaphysical paths as old as Western philosophy itself, paths that have been blazed and traversed by others who have come before you. Though the path has been steep at times, my hope is that the views have been illuminating and rewarding! To recap where we've been together, the following questions have guided us on our journey:

- What, exactly, *is* metaphysics? (chap. 1)
- Are metaphysical discoveries possible? Is pure (*a priori*) rational insight an intelligible mode of human inquiry that yields genuine knowledge of reality? If so, how? (chap. 2)
- How should one go about doing metaphysics in a distinctively Christian key? What habits of mind should a Christian metaphysician strive to cultivate? (chap. 3)
- What is it to *be* or *exist*, and are there different ways and degrees of being? (chap. 4)
- What is identity and how does it account for sameness and difference in the world? Is reality classifiable into mind-independent, ontological categories? (chap. 5)
- What accounts for modal truths, truths about what *must* be (necessary) and what *could* be (possible)? What are creaturely natures or essences,

and do possible worlds help shed light on this question? How might God play a role in grounding modal truths? (chap. 6)

- Do characteristics or properties exist? If so, are properties particular (nonsharable) or universal (sharable)? What might God have to do with the age-old debate about properties? (chap. 7)
- What are substances as unified property-bearers? Is there an ontological distinction between the categories of *Substance* and *Aggregate*? Do substances have metaphysical ingredients such as properties and/or substrata that enter into their makeup? (chap. 8)
- Is there deep unity in the material world in the midst of widespread plurality? Are material objects ever composed of other material objects? (chap. 9)

Let me leave you with a brief reflection on the importance of metaphysical inquiry for successfully navigating human life and living well in Christ. If God has created the world with a deep, natural grain to it—an objective (mind-independent) metaphysical order that specifies what is real, what we *are* as humans, and what we humans are *for*—then wisely discerning and living with (and not against) this deep natural grain is vital to a human life well-lived (Proverbs 8:22-36). Biblically speaking, "wisdom is the power to see, and the inclination to choose, the best and highest goal, together with the surest means of attaining it."[1] This multifaceted conception of wisdom, of course, assumes that the shape of reality exhibits deep metaphysical structure (not just shallow structure), namely that some realities exist that are more existentially weighty and worthy of our reverence, care, and attention than others, and that human beings are divinely endowed with the power to discern and lay hold of such realities if they so choose. If we fail to attend to this deep, natural grain to reality, we will fail to align ourselves with reality to our peril (Proverbs 8:36).

Traditional metaphysical inquiry is a bit like mapmaking, that is, cartography (the study and practice of making and using maps). A mapmaker sets out to chart the scope and extent of an existing geographical region, whether local (a city, country, metro system, mountain range, etc.) or global (the entire world), ultimately for the sake of helping others successfully navigate the region in question. The map, of course, is not identical to the complex reality depicted; it's only a more or less accurate human representation of it.

---

[1] J. I. Packer, *Knowing God* (Downers Grove, IL: InterVarsity Press, 1973), 80.

Constructing certain types of maps—topographic maps in particular (look up "topographic map" online for a visual)—involves accurately depicting not only realities such as city streets, rivers, mountains, valleys, oceans, and forests, but also the geographical contour and elevation levels of the landscape in question. Some coordinates in a geographic region (mountain peaks) will naturally be higher and more elevated than others (valleys). And successfully tracking the changes in elevation of the landscape is vital to not only accurately depicting the landscape for its own sake, but also to successfully navigating it. Imagine trying to successfully hike Yosemite National Park without a topographic map rightly indicating the increased elevation levels at key regions such as Half Dome, El Capitan, or Sentinel Dome. It would be near impossible to rightly orient yourself to Yosemite National Park if you were fundamentally mistaken about the existence and location of these elevated regions. An accurate topographic map of Yosemite National Park enables successful navigation of the park *as it truly is*, ultimately for the purpose of rightly beholding and truly enjoying the jaw-dropping beauty of the Eastern Sierras.

Metaphysics shares some similarities with topographic mapmaking. Like topographic mapmaking, metaphysics involves charting not only the scope and extent of existing reality, but also its contour or shape, ultimately for the sake of successful navigation. Unlike mapmaking, however, metaphysics aims at charting (as much as is humanly possible) the general scope, extent, and fundamental contour of *reality as a whole*—whether physical or nonphysical reality—ultimately for the sake of successfully navigating *human life as a whole*; metaphysical inquiry aims at existential mapmaking for human wayfarers on the journey of life.

Like topographic maps of specific geographical regions, existential maps of reality have specific metaphysical coordinates, contours, and changes in "existential elevation," we might say. While our existential maps constructed by way of metaphysical inquiry are not identical to the complex realities they represent, they are indispensable aids to properly orienting us to these realities. Some coordinates on an existential map will be existentially "higher" in the sense that they will be more fundamental and worthy of our loving care, reverence, and attention than others; the knowledge and pursuit of these elevated coordinates are of paramount importance to living well. According to an existential map shaped by the Christian story, the most elevated metaphysical coordinate that we ought to be aware of and rightly orient ourselves to is first and foremost the triune God, as well as his good and restorative purposes for all of creation in Jesus Christ, the one from whom and in whom created being finds its deepest meaning. If one's existential map fails to recognize or attend to metaphysically elevated coordinates such as these, then one will be unable to orient themselves to reality as it truly *is* and thereby navigate human life well (Proverbs 1:7; 9:10).[2]

Christian metaphysical reflection can help direct our attention to which coordinates are metaphysically "higher" than others, clarify and defend the various coordinates of a Christian existential map, and challenge excessively thin, one-dimensional existential maps that omit coordinates that are indispensable to a flourishing human life under God (2 Corinthians 10:3-6).[3] But, at the end of the day, an existential map is good and fitting only insofar as it adequately depicts how things really are and can reliably guide us to our God-appointed destination on the journey of life. As wayfarers on life's way, if we are to steadily walk in the "good way" (Jeremiah 6:16) for which we were made, then having an adequate existential map—one with metaphysical coordinates and proper elevation levels that are true to the way things actually are—is indispensable to living well at present and in reaching our God-appointed destination in the life to come.[4]

---

[2]Recall from chap. 4 that Augustine's one-dimensional, materialist metaphysic made it impossible for him to conceive of God as he truly is (nonphysical).

[3]These metaphysical coordinates include (but are not limited to) the existence of God, the intelligibility/classifiability/knowability of mind-independent reality, and deep metaphysical classifications, including the reality of objective essences or natures, human nature, and the immaterial soul.

[4]For a fuller treatment of the general role of Christian philosophy (including metaphysics) in the Christian life, see my *Christian Philosophy as a Way of Life: An Invitation to Wonder* (Grand Rapids, MI: Baker Academic, 2023).

NEXT STEPS

There are many outstanding introductory textbooks on metaphysics out there. So, if you've made it to the end of this book and you still want more metaphysics (one can only hope!), here are my personal recommendations for next steps by way of notable textbooks in the field (in ascending order of difficulty and marked with a * for those I find most helpful). If you are looking for readings that are subject specific and beyond a survey of key issues in contemporary metaphysics, see the "Going Further" sections at the end of each chapter.

ESSENTIAL REFERENCE WORKS

- *Helen Beebee, Nikk Effingham, and Philip Goff, *Metaphysics: The Key Concepts* (New York: Routledge, 2011)
- Robin Le Poidevin, Peter Simons, Andrew McGonigal, and Ross P. Cameron, *The Routledge Companion to Metaphysics* (New York: Routledge, 2012)
- Jaegwon Kim, Daniel Z. Korman, and Ernest Sosa, *Metaphysics: An Anthology*, 2nd ed. (Malden, MA: Wiley-Blackwell, 2012)

NEXT STEPS FOR BEGINNERS

- *Anna Marmodoro and Erasmus Mayr, *Metaphysics: An Introduction to Contemporary Debates and Their History* (New York: Oxford University Press, 2019)
- Kris McDaniel, *This Is Metaphysics* (Chichester, UK: Wiley & Sons, 2020)
- Edward Feser, *Scholastic Metaphysics: A Contemporary Introduction* (Editiones Scholasticae, 2014)

- Michael Rea, *Metaphysics: The Basics*, 2nd ed. (New York: Routledge, 2021)

NEXT STEPS FOR INTERMEDIATES

- *Robert C. Koons and Tim H. Pickavance, *Metaphysics: The Fundamentals* (Chichester, UK: Wiley & Sons, 2015)
- Jonathan Tallant, *Metaphysics: An Introduction*, 2nd ed. (New York: Bloomsbury Academic, 2017)
- Alyssa Ney, *Metaphysics: An Introduction*, 2nd ed. (New York: Routledge, 2023)
- *Thomas Crisp and Michael Loux, *Metaphysics: A Contemporary Introduction*, 4th ed. (New York: Routledge, 2017)
- E. J. Lowe, *A Survey of Metaphysics* (New York: Oxford University Press, 2002)

NEXT STEPS FOR THE ADVANCED

- Roderick Chisholm, *On Metaphysics* (Minneapolis: University of Minnesota Press, 1989)
- Michael J. Loux and Dean W. Zimmerman, *The Oxford Handbook of Metaphysics* (New York: Oxford University Press, 2005)
- *E. J. Lowe, *The Possibility of Metaphysics* (New York: Oxford University Press, 1998)
- Robert C. Koons and Tim H. Pickavance, *The Atlas of Reality: A Comprehensive Guide to Metaphysics* (Chichester, UK: Wiley & Sons, 2017)

GENERAL INDEX

SCRIPTURE INDEX

QUESTIONS

IN CHRISTIAN

PHILOSOPHY

How do we know? What should we do? What is real? What is art?

Philosophy, which means "the love of wisdom," asks such questions in its pursuit of the knowledge and understanding of all facets of life: existence, knowledge, ethics, art, and more. But what does it mean for Christians to pursue wisdom when Scripture affirms that the crucified and risen Christ is "the wisdom of God" (1 Corinthians 1:24)?

IVP Academic's Questions in Christian Philosophy (QCP) series seeks to help readers in their pursuit of wisdom from a Christian perspective by offering introductory textbooks on the various branches of philosophy. Designed for students with little or no background in the discipline, this series draws on experts in the field and lays a solid foundation for further philosophical reflection in pursuit of divine wisdom.

SERIES EDITORS

- James K. Dew Jr., president and professor of Christian philosophy, New Orleans Baptist Theological Seminary

- W. Paul Franks, associate professor of philosophy, Tyndale University, Toronto

CURRENT AND FORTHCOMING QCP VOLUMES

- James K. Dew Jr. and Mark W. Foreman, *How Do We Know? An Introduction to Epistemology*, 2nd ed.

- Forrest Baird, *How Do We Reason? An Introduction to Logic*

- Dennis P. Bray and David W. McNutt, *What Is Art? An Introduction to Aesthetics*